INVESTOR'S RESOURCE MANUAL

to accompany

Gitman/Joehnk

Fundamentals of Investing

Sixth Edition

 HarperCollins*CollegePublishers*

Acknowledgments: Grateful acknowledgment is made to Moody's Investors Services; Morningstar, Inc.; Standard & Poor's Corporation; and Value Line Publishing, Inc., for granting permission to reprint their materials in this supplement. We also thank Tootsie Roll Industries, Inc., for permission to reproduce their 1994 annual report in its entirety.

Reports on pages 3, 25, 28, 31, 51, and 83:
Copyright © 1995 by Value Line Publishings, Inc.; used by permission. For subscription information to the Value Line Investment Survey, please call (800) 634-3583.

Reports on pages 6-24, 26-27, 29-30, 55-80, and 81-82: Standard & Poor's Reports, © 1995, reprinted by permission of Standard & Poor's, a Division of The McGraw-Hill Companies.

INVESTOR'S RESOURCE MANUAL to accompany Gitman/Joehnk, Fundamentals of Investing, Sixth Edition.

ISBN: 0-673-99823-1

 4 5 6 7 8 9 -DOC- 01 00 99 98

Contents

Part One
Materials for Analyzing Tootsie Roll Industries *1*

INDUSTRY REPORTS *3*
Value Line Report: Food Processing *3*
Moody's Industry Review: Candy and Gum *4*
S&P's Industry Survey: Food, Beverages, and Tobacco 6

COMPANY REPORTS
S&P's Stock Report: Tootsie Roll Industries *23*
Value Line Report: Tootsie Roll Industries *25*

S&P's Stock Report: Hershey Foods Corp. *26*
Value Line Report: Hershey Foods Corp. *28*

S&P's Stock Report: Wm. Wrigley Jr. Co. *29*
Value Line Report: Wm. Wrigley Jr. Co. *31*

TOOTSIE ROLL 1994 ANNUAL REPORT *33*

Part Two
Materials for Analyzing Liz Claiborne Corporation *49*

INDUSTRY REPORTS
Value Line Industry Report: Apparel *51*
Moody's Industry Report: Apparel--Women's *52*
S&P's Industry Survey: Textiles, Apparel and Home
        Furnishings *55*

COMPANY REPORTS
S&P's Stock Report: Liz Claiborne *81*
Value Line Report: Liz Claiborne *83*

Part Three
Morningstar Mutual Funds Reports   *85*

AIM Aggressive Growth Fund   *87*
Fidelity Equity-Income II Fund   *88*
Vanguard Index 500 Fund   *89*
Vista Tax-Free Income A Fund   *90*
Fidelity Convertible Securities Fund   *91*
GAM International Fund   *92*

Part Four
Sources of Financial Information   *93*

Financial Publications, Journals, and Newspapers   *95*
Investment Advisories and Newsletters   *98*
Academic Journals   *103*
Professional Journals and Publications   *104*
Commercial Bank Letters and Reports   *107*
Institutional Publications   *108*
Investors' Subscription Services   *111*
Books for Investors   *115*
Mutual Fund Directories   *117*

Part Five
Guide to Professional Certification Programs   *119*

PART ONE

●∙∙∙●

Materials for Analyzing
Tootsie Roll Industries

INDUSTRY REPORTS
Value Line Industry Report: Food Processing *3*
Moody's Industry Review: Candy and Gum *4*
S&P's Industry Survey: Food, Beverages, and Tobacco *6*

COMPANY REPORTS
S&P's Stock Report: Tootsie Roll Industries *23*
Value Line Report: Tootsie Roll Industries *25*

S&P's Stock Report: Hershey Foods Corp. *26*
Value Line Report: Hershey Foods Corp. *28*

S&P's Stock Report: Wm. Wrigley Jr. Co. *29*
Value Line Report: Wm. Wrigley Jr. Co. *31*

TOOTSIE ROLL 1994 ANNUAL REPORT *33*

Private labels remain the bane of companies in the Food Processing Industry, especially as store brands have limited the shelf space for, and prevented more-than-modest price increases of, nationally branded items. Nevertheless, the industry still has many avenues of growth. Investors may find a few stocks here that are interesting selections.

Private Labels: Tough Competitors

Private label foods have been around for many years. And they've always enjoyed periods of expansion when economic conditions were tough and the consumer wanted more for his or her money. In fact, the most recent recession brought about renewed growth in private label shipments and, sensing improved profitability from this trend, many supermarket chains have not slowed the pace of introducing their store-brand products, even during the current period of economic growth.

Moreover, something new has been added in the past couple of years. Whereas store-brand goods used to connote "low price/low quality", we've seen the development of a premium class of private-label products, with names to match—for example, President's Choice and Master Choice—which are now found in many supermarket chains. Though priced above the standard store brands, they still carry lower prices than most near-parity national-brand products.

The variety of private-label product categories is also expanding. Indeed, almost no food item, except perhaps baby food, has been safe from private-label incursion. The number of store-brand categories continues to grow beyond the traditional array of goods, such as milk, bread, soft drinks, fruit spreads, cereals, canned fruit, pasta, and frozen vegetables. Recent entries in the private-label arena include frozen dinners, cookie dough, egg substitutes, and naturally flavored ice teas. Moreover, the number of choices within each category is also rising, including, sometimes, varieties (e.g., new types of cereals) that have no equivalent selection in the "branded world".

Perhaps the biggest influence of private label products is that, even if they have taken little market share, they help keep branded food prices in check. On the positive side, this has helped keep inflation, as a whole, low. But most food processors, and potential buyers of food processor stocks, are very aware of the negative side. Even the branded products that enjoy the

---

strongest loyalty, and likely still hold a dominant market share, have had to reduce prices and/or increase promotional spending in order to compete. Even so, . . .

Growth Opportunities Remain

Most of the bigger food processors are pushing overseas, especially into the emerging economies in the Asia/Pacific region, Latin America, and Eastern Europe, to increase revenues. Indeed, many companies with foreign operations have been exhibiting faster sales and earnings growth overseas than at home. Much of the growth has been due to outright acquisitions, joint ventures, or establishing wholly owned factories on foreign soil.

Then, too, expansion possibilities in the U.S., already a mature market, still exist. Acquisitions to obtain new product categories with little R&D investment are widespread. In addition, when conditions allow, the food processors will purchase smaller rivals, including divisions of other foodmakers that make like products, in order to build revenues and market share. Such acquisitions also help increase operating efficiency, given synergies derived from consolidation.

New product development, one of the pillars for internal growth, appears to have become even more active with the pressure private label products have put on many traditional items. Most frequently, new products are merely older products with new flavors. Another method has been the application of specific technologies to more than one food category. An example would be wrap-around pie shells, once exclusively filled with fruit for desserts and snacks, now also being filled with meats, cheeses, and vegetables (known as "pocket" sandwiches). Other new products are aimed at rapidly growing markets. Prime examples are foods of the low-fat, non-fat, low-cholesterol, and/or sugar-free variety.

Investment Advice

We recommend, as always, that investors hold stocks ranked either 1 or 2 for Timeliness in their portfolios, but note that certain issues may not be all that desirable for long-term holding, as they may carry such high prices that their 3- to 5-year total annual return prospects are limited. Even so, conservative investors may find a number of issues, especially those of the larger companies, of interest, primarily because their long-term prospects are relatively well defined.

Phillip M. Seligman

Composite Statistics: FOOD PROCESSING INDUSTRY*

1991	1992	1993	1994	1995	1996		98-00
159.6	161.8	171.5	197.6	210	225	Sales ($bill)	250
10.6%	10.8%	10.8%	11.5%	11.5%	12.0%	Operating Margin	12.5%
4.1	4.4	4.9	5.9	6.5	7.0	Depreciation ($bill)	9.0
6.9	7.2	7.8	9.1	10.0	11.5	Net Profit ($bill)	15.0
36.6%	36.7%	35.2%	36.8%	37.0%	37.0%	Income Tax Rate	37.0%
4.3%	4.5%	4.6%	4.6%	4.8%	5.1%	Net Profit Margin	6.0%
11.0	11.6	10.8	10.5	11.0	11.0	Working Cap'l ($bill)	15.0
15.5	17.0	18.0	26.9	27.5	27.5	Long-Term Debt ($bill)	27.5
41.0	43.3	43.7	51.4	58.0	66.0	Net Worth ($bill)	80.0
13.5%	13.2%	13.8%	13.0%	14.0%	14.0%	% Earned Total Cap'l	16.0%
16.9%	16.7%	17.9%	17.7%	17.0%	17.0%	% Earned Net Worth	19.0%
11.0%	10.7%	11.4%	11.7%	10.0%	10.0%	% Retained to Comm Eq	12.0%
38%	38%	39%	36%	37%	37%	% All Div'ds to Net Prof	38%
16.1	18.4	17.0	14.4	*Bold figures are*		Avg Ann'l P/E Ratio	17.5
1.03	1.12	1.07	1.10	*Value Line*		Relative P/E Ratio	1.30
2.3%	2.1%	2.3%	2.3%	*estimates*		Avg Ann'l Div'd Yield	2.3%

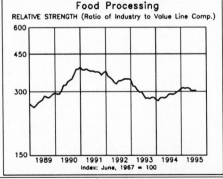

Food Processing
RELATIVE STRENGTH (Ratio of Industry to Value Line Comp.)

Index: June, 1967 = 100

MOODY'S INDUSTRY REVIEW
October 6, 1995
Volume: 14 No: 17

CANDY & GUM

COMPARATIVE STATISTICS

COMPANY	FISCAL DATE	EXCH	SYMBOL	PRICE RANGE (12 MOS.) HIGH	PRICE RANGE (12 MOS.) LOW	RECENT PRICE	EARNINGS PER SHARE LATEST 12 MOS.	EPS 1994	EPS 1993	EPS 1992	IND. CASH DIV.	1994 BOOK VALUE PER SH.	1994 STKHLDRS' EQUITY ($ MILL)	1994 LONG-TERM DEBT (%)
GRIST MILL CO.	5/31	NMS	GRST	13⅜	7¾	9⅝	0.66	0.66	0.16	0.54	Nil	4.73	31.52	8.79
HERSHEY FOODS CORP.	12/31	NYS	HSY	64⅞	44½	64⅜	2.30	2.12	3.31	2.69	1.440	11.39	1441.10	8.78
TOOTSIE ROLL INDUSTRIES, INC.	12/31	NYS	TR	41	26⅛	39⅝	1.74	1.69	1.58	1.43	0.250	6.35	240.46	2.93
TOPPS COMPANY, INC. (THE)	2/25	NMS	TOPP	7⅛	4⅛	6½	0.17	0.33	0.57	0.40	Nil	1.08	73.87	...
WRIGLEY (WILLIAM) JR. CO.	12/31	NYS	WWY	51¼	39½	50½	1.86	1.98	1.50	1.27	0.560	5.92	688.47	...

† Indicates previous year's data. • Indicates subsequent year's data.
Ind. cash div. excludes stk. splits & stk. divs.

FINANCIAL DATA–LATEST ANNUAL RANKINGS

REVENUES ($ MILL.)

RANK	COMPANY	'94 AMT
1	Hershey Foods Corp.	3606.27
2	Wrigley (William) Jr. Co.	1661.25
3	Tootsie Roll Industries, Inc.	296.93
4	Topps Co. Inc. (The)	268.34
5	Grist Mill Co.	78.92

NET INCOME ($ MILL.)

RANK	COMPANY	'94 AMT
1	Wrigley (William) Jr. Co.	230.53
2	Hershey Foods Corp.	184.22
3	Tootsie Roll Industries, Inc.	37.93
4	Topps Co. Inc. (The)	15.75
5	Grist Mill Co.	4.56

OPERATING PROFIT MARGIN (%)

RANK	COMPANY	'94 AMT
1	Wrigley (William) Jr. Co.	21.36
2	Tootsie Roll Industries, Inc.	20.20
3	Hershey Foods Corp.	10.22
4	Topps Co. Inc. (The)	10.03
5	Grist Mill Co.	9.57

RETURN ON CAPITAL (%)

RANK	COMPANY	'94 AMT
1	Wrigley (William) Jr. Co.	32.74
2	Topps Co. Inc. (The)	18.86
3	Tootsie Roll Industries, Inc.	14.38
4	Grist Mill Co.	12.65
5	Hershey Foods Corp.	9.26

CASH & MARKETABLE SECURITIES ($ MILL.)

RANK	COMPANY	'94 AMT
1	Wrigley (William) Jr. Co.	230.25
2	Tootsie Roll Industries, Inc.	62.37
3	Hershey Foods Corp.	26.74
4	Topps Co. Inc. (The)	17.79
5	Grist Mill Co.	6.81

WORKING CAPITAL ($ MILL.)

RANK	COMPANY	'94 AMT
1	Wrigley (William) Jr. Co.	413.41
2	Hershey Foods Corp.	152.45
3	Tootsie Roll Industries, Inc.	92.63
4	Topps Co. Inc. (The)	30.92
5	Grist Mill Co.	9.99

CURRENT RATIO

RANK	COMPANY	'94 AMT
1	Tootsie Roll Industries, Inc.	4.53
2	Wrigley (William) Jr. Co.	2.97
3	Grist Mill Co.	1.98
4	Topps Co. Inc. (The)	1.63
5	Hershey Foods Corp.	1.19

INVENTORY TURNOVER

RANK	COMPANY	'94 AMT
1	Grist Mill Co.	9.38
2	Topps Co. Inc. (The)	6.92
3	Tootsie Roll Industries, Inc.	5.32
4	Hershey Foods Corp.	4.67
5	Wrigley (William) Jr. Co.	3.51

PRICE-EARNINGS RATIO

RANK	COMPANY	'94 AMT
1	Grist Mill Co.	13.99
2	Tootsie Roll Industries, Inc.	22.77
3	Wrigley (William) Jr. Co.	27.90
4	Hershey Foods Corp.	27.99
5	Topps Co. Inc. (The)	38.24

YIELD (%)

RANK	COMPANY	'94 AMT
1	Topps Co. Inc. (The)	4.31
2	Hershey Foods Corp.	2.02
3	Tootsie Roll Industries, Inc.	1.26
4	Wrigley (William) Jr. Co.	1.11
5	Grist Mill Co.	...

12-MONTH PRICE SCORE

RANK	COMPANY	'94 AMT
1	Tootsie Roll Industries, Inc.	106.59
2	Hershey Foods Corp.	104.47
3	Topps Co. Inc. (The)	95.25
4	Wrigley (William) Jr. Co.	91.62
5	Grist Mill Co.	89.36

7-YEAR PRICE SCORE

RANK	COMPANY	'94 AMT
1	Wrigley (William) Jr. Co.	127.70
2	Grist Mill Co.	119.90
3	Tootsie Roll Industries, Inc.	101.80
4	Hershey Foods Corp.	100.80
5	Topps Co. Inc. (The)	44.70

Publication, Editorial and Executive Offices, 99 Church Street, New York, NY 10007

CANDY & GUM (Cont'd.)

COMPOSITE STOCK PRICE MOVEMENTS

STANDARD & POOR'S
industry surveys

Copyright © 1995 by Standard & Poor's   USPS No. 517-780
ISSN 0196-4666

Industry References 14

The Outlook 15

Processed Foods 17

Commodities 22

Beverages 25

Tobacco 32

Composite Industry Data 35

Comparative Company Analysis 38

AUGUST 24, 1995 (Vol. 163, No. 34, Sec. 1)   Replaces Basic Analysis dated August 18, 1994

Slow growth continues

Standard & Poor's projects that inflation-adjusted Gross Domestic Product (GDP) will increase 2.8%, year to year, in 1995, following a 4.1% rise in 1994. Although slowing, the U.S. economy appears to remain in fairly good shape, increasing the likelihood of a "soft-landing" rather than a recession. Non-farm employment is expected to increase by close to one million jobs in 1995 and personal disposable income is forecast to rise 6%, slightly outpacing the prior year's rate of growth. Although consumer expenditures for food tend to remain steady during periods of both recession and prosperity, continuing gains in disposable income should nevertheless contribute to an estimated 1% inflation-adjusted increase in food spending in 1995.

Spending for food consumed both at home and away from home in the U.S. totaled $588 billion in 1994, according to the U.S. Department of Agriculture (USDA), up an inflation-adjusted 3.0% from the prior year. The increase in real spending in 1994 was primarily a reflection of growth in the U.S. population, and, to a lesser extent, the willingness of consumers to spend a bit more at the grocery store. Spending for food eaten at home by families and individuals totaled $389 billion in 1994, up 4.1%, year to year, while spending for meals and snacks eaten away from home rose to $199 billion, a year-to-year gain of 6.2%. In real terms (adjusted for retail food price increases), spending for food away from home rose 4.4% in 1994, well above the 1.2% increase in expenditures for food at home.

Greater spending for food eaten away from home is attributable to a number of long-term trends: the increasing amount of time that many of today's workers spend away from home on business travel, the ongoing entry of women into the work force; and the increasing affluence of the U.S. population. The trends suggest that growth in spending for food consumed away from home will continue to rise over the long-term, although short-term fluctuations in spending will still occur in response to the ups and downs of the economy.

Spending on meals away from home tends to drop quickly in troubled economic times. For example, during 1992's economic slump, spending for food consumed at home rose slightly more than food away from home. Families may eat at home more often during uncertain economic times in order to save money, while corporations might spend less on business meals in order to pare costs. In 1995, we expect total food expenditures to grow 3% to 4%, paced by an approximate 2% to 3% increase in spending for food at home, and a 4% to 5% increase in spending for food away from home.

Industry profits seen continuing upward trend

Most U.S. food companies benefited from low ingredient costs and an improving economy in 1994. Through the first half of 1995, however, the opposite appears to be true: most cost components are on the rise, especially for agricultural commodities and packaging, and the economy is showing signs of slowing. As a result, it is likely that aggregate food industry sales and profits will increase only modestly in 1995.

Over the years, most of the major U.S. packaged food and beverage companies have effectively broadened their sales base to include operations around the world, thereby reducing their dependence on the ups and downs of the U.S.

economy. Thus, U.S.-based companies with substantial international operations will probably fare best in 1995, as favorable economic conditions abroad offset sluggish economic growth at home. Weakness in the U.S. dollar *vis-à-vis* certain foreign currencies may also benefit American companies with international operations.

The longer-term prospects for the international operations of U.S.-based food and beverage manufacturers are bright and will benefit from population growth and rising per capita income in developing nations around the world. Over a period of many years, major U.S. food and beverage companies, such as H.J. Heinz and Coca-Cola, have successfully expanded into relatively untapped markets around the globe. Greater liberalization of trade policies and the growing adoption of progressive economic systems around the world will also benefit large U.S. food and beverage makers.

Outlook by category

● **Processed foods.** Shifting demographics and increasing ethnic diversity offer today's U.S. food companies significant opportunities in this relatively mature industry. In addition, changing patterns of consumption and lifestyle open new markets, particularly for food products that are convenient to prepare, high in nutritional value, or both. While overall industry growth prospects in the United States are generally tied to gains in population, greater access to markets outside the United States will present new opportunities for growth.

● **Nonalcoholic beverages.** Further expansion into non-traditional beverages, such as ready-to-drink teas and coffees, fruit juices, bottled water, and sports drinks, and continued growth in underdeveloped global markets should help offset slowing growth in maturing market segments. New labeling laws may cause a shift in consumption trends.

● **Alcoholic beverages.** Consumers' health concerns and government efforts to reduce the number of alcohol-related deaths will continue to force this contracting industry into

Kenneth Shea, Food, Beverages & Tobacco Analyst

Income share spent for food
(In billions of dollars)

Year	Disposable personal income	Expenditures for food			% share of income		
		At home	Away from home	Total	At home	Away from home	Total
1994	4,959.6	389.3	198.9	588.2	7.8	4.0	11.9
1993	4,688.7	374.0	187.3	561.3	8.0	4.0	12.0
1992	4,505.8	361.9	176.9	538.8	8.0	3.9	12.0
1991	4,236.6	361.8	172.1	533.8	8.5	4.1	12.6
1990	4,050.5	352.8	167.7	520.4	8.7	4.1	12.8
1989	3,787.0	329.6	155.5	485.1	8.7	4.1	12.8
1985	2,943.0	270.6	113.5	384.1	9.2	3.9	13.1
1980	1,952.9	212.0	77.4	289.4	10.9	4.0	14.8
1975	1,150.9	139.4	45.3	184.7	12.1	3.9	16.0
1970	722.0	92.2	27.5	119.7	12.8	3.8	16.6

Source: Bureau of Labor Statistics.

7

further decline. The ability to increase share in this mature market will remain the key to growth.

● **Tobacco.** The declining social acceptance of tobacco use, and of cigarettes in particular, will continue to challenge U.S. tobacco manufacturers' in domestic markets. Growing opposition to tobacco use and the influence of this opposition on tobacco excise tax increases will continue to pose significant challenges to this shrinking U.S. industry for years to come. Present strong demand for American-blend cigarettes internationally, however, should partially offset weakness in the U.S. marketplace. ∎

Food spending on the rise

Buoyed by a healthy U.S. economy, consumer spending for food eaten both at home and away from home rose 4.0%, year to year, in 1994. Although disposable personal income was up 5.8%, year to year, food spending as a percentage of disposable income declined to 11.9% in 1994 from 12.0% in 1993. Food spending had accounted for 14.8% of disposable income as recently as 1980. This steady decline reflects the inelastic nature of the aggregate demand for food; *i.e.*, as income rises, the proportion of that income spent for food declines.

Food prices post slight increases

Consumer food prices for food eaten both at home and away from home rose an average of 2.4%, year to year, in 1994. The increase was slightly below the 2.6% rise in the Consumer Price Index (CPI) for all goods and services in 1994 and was the fourth consecutive year that food inflation rose at a slower pace than the CPI.

Food prices at supermarkets and other grocery stores rose faster than at eating places for the second year in a row in 1994. Food prices at grocery stores rose 2.9%, year to year, due primarily to higher prices for fresh fruits, cereals, and bakery goods, while prices for restaurant meals ad-

vanced only 1.8%, the same as the gain in 1993. The modest rise in restaurant prices in 1994 was the smallest increase since 1964 and was attributable in part to lower beef prices, which enabled hamburger chains like McDonald's and Burger King to cut prices and offer lower-priced "value meals". This, in turn, forced fast-food restaurants that serve fare such as pizza and chicken to hold down their prices as well.

Labor costs take biggest bite

According to the U.S. Department of Agriculture (USDA), labor remained the largest component of food production costs in 1994. Labor costs for the U.S. food processing industry totaled approximately $189 billion and represented about 37 cents of every consumer dollar spent for food. Labor costs rose 6.5%, year to year, in 1994, moderately faster than in 1993. The increase in 1994 reflected growing industry employment as well as higher wages and increased benefits.

Commodities, the food processing industry's second-largest expense, accounted for 21% of total costs in 1994, down from 22% in 1993. Commodity costs as a percentage of total food processing costs have declined steadily for more than

FOOD PRICE INDEXES VS. THE CPI
(1967=10)

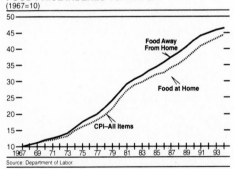

Source: Department of Labor.

FOOD EXPENDITURES AS A PERCENTAGE OF DISPOSABLE INCOME

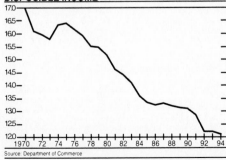

Source: Department of Commerce

WHERE THE FOOD DOLLAR GOES–1994

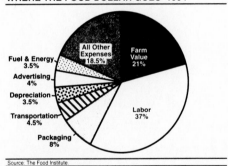

Source: The Food Institute.

FOOD PRICE INDEXES
(1982=100)

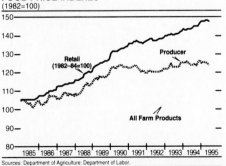

Sources: Department of Agriculture; Department of Labor.

two decades. In 1970, for example, commodities accounted for 32% of food processing costs.

The steady decline in the proportion of commodities costs relative to overall production costs is due to the increasing amount spent on marketing. (The USDA defines marketing expenditures as those costs not related to commodities. Thus, under the USDA, marketing includes not just advertising and other promotion, but also labor, packaging, and the like.) The ongoing increase in marketing expenses should continue to reduce the cost of commodities as a proportion of total food production costs.

Packaging remained the third-largest food manufacturing cost in 1994. Packaging costs for the U.S. food processing industry totalled $41 billion in 1994, accounting for about eight cents of every food dollar spent by consumers. The price of food containers and packaging materials rose about 4%, year to year, in 1994, largely due to increased use of shipping boxes, food containers, and plastic materials. The combination of greater packaging and container use and moderate price increases in the cost of packaging drove packaging costs up during the year.

Transportation costs totalled $23 billion in 1994 and accounted for about 4.5% of food manufacturers' total expenses for the year. Grain shippers were forced to pay higher barge rates, which increased about 10%, year to year, in 1994, due to equipment shortages. Manufacturers of finished food products, on the other hand, which rely more heavily on truck and rail transportation, fared better. Truck rates were down modestly in 1994, aided by ongoing industry deregulation. Railroad freight rates also declined modestly.

Demographics spur new products

Continued growth in the number of two income families has led to a variety of new food products and marketing techniques over the past 15 years. Roughly three-quarters of all American families are headed by two wage earners or by a single working parent. Dual-income and single parent families tend to buy more expensive prepared meals. In addition, the time constraints with which such families must cope have increased the demand for foods that are easy to prepare and serve. Food marketers estimate that the average American is willing to spend no more than 15 minutes preparing an ordinary meal, a estimate that would seem to be supported by another statistic: 86% of American households own a microwave oven.

During the 1980s, food manufacturers responded to the rise of dual-income and single-parent families by introducing products tailored to the increasing demand for convenience, nutrition, and variety. Traditional offerings, such as frozen dinners, were expanded to included frozen breakfast and lunch foods. Products specifically designed for microwave cooking have also proliferated. So-called "shelf stable" meals, foods packaged in aseptic material that keeps contents fresh for long periods of time without preservatives or refrigeration, were introduced as a convenience to busy families.

Although convenience, nutrition, and variety remain priorities, value is at least equally important for the '90s consumer. The recession of the early 1990s brought the free spending 1980s to an abrupt halt. Warehouse club stores sprung up to cater to this decade's more value-conscious consumer. Manufacturers of all manner of brand name consumer products, including food manufacturers, are attempting to satisfy consumers that demand more for their money.

Everything old is new again

Processed food makers continue to introduce products that they believe will appeal to today's value-conscious consumer. Soup is one segment that, while hardly new, is popular with consumers because of its nutritive value and ease of preparation. Spice Island's *Quick Meal* dehydrated soup mix is among the most successful new soup brands. *Hamburger Helper*, an old favorite of frugal cooks that remains quite popular today, has led to line extensions,

Wholesale food price indexes
(1982=100)

Food group	1989	1990	1991	1992	1993	1994
Meats	104.8	117.0	113.5	106.7	110.6	104.7
Poultry	120.4	113.6	109.9	109.0	111.7	114.7
Fish	142.9	147.2	149.5	156.1	156.6	161.5
Eggs	119.6	117.6	110.7	94.1	105.9	97.8
Dairy	110.6	117.2	114.6	117.9	118.2	119.5
Fats & oils	116.6	123.2	116.5	115.1	122.9	138.6
Proc. fruits & veg.	119.9	124.7	119.6	120.8	118.2	121.2
Sugar & sweets	120.1	123.1	128.4	127.7	127.9	132.5
Cereal & bakery prods.	131.1	134.2	137.9	144.2	147.6	151.1
Beverages	118.4	120.8	124.1	124.4	124.8	127.7
All food	117.8	123.2	122.2	120.9	123.7	125.1
Industrial commodities	111.6	115.8	116.5	117.4	119.0	120.7

Source: Department of Labor

Price changes for food and non-food items
(Consumer Price Indexes, year-to-year percent change)

Year	Food	Food at home	Food away from home	All items	All items less food
1994	2.4	2.9	1.8	2.6	2.6
1993	2.2	2.4	1.8	3.0	3.1
1992	1.2	0.7	2.0	3.0	3.5
1991	2.9	2.6	3.4	4.2	4.5
1990	5.8	6.5	4.7	5.4	5.3
1989	5.8	6.5	4.6	4.8	4.6
1988	4.1	4.2	4.1	4.1	4.1
1987	4.1	4.3	4.0	3.6	3.5
1986	3.2	2.9	3.9	1.9	1.7
1985	2.3	1.5	3.9	3.6	3.8

Source: Bureau of Labor Statistics

Major food category annual price changes

	Percent change		
	1992	1993	1994
All Food	1.2	2.2	2.4
Food at home	0.7	2.4	2.9
Meats	(1.4)	3.0	0.5
Beef & veal	(0.1)	3.6	(0.8)
Pork	(4.7)	3.1	1.7
Poultry	(0.1)	4.2	3.4
Fish & seafood	2.3	3.2	4.5
Eggs	(10.6)	8.1	(2.4)
Dairy products	2.7	0.7	2.0
Fresh fruits	(5.0)	2.5	6.6
Fresh vegetables	2.3	6.6	2.3
Processed fruits & vegetables	2.7	(1.6)	2.7
Cereals & bakery products	3.9	3.4	4.1
Sugar & sweets	2.9	0.2	1.4
Fats & oils	(1.4)	0.2	2.7
Nonalcoholic beverages	0.2	0.3	7.5
Other prepared foods	2.2	2.6	2.6
Food away from home	2.0	1.8	1.7

Sources: Bureau of Labor Statistics; Economic Research Service.

such as General Mill's *Betty Crocker Helpers*, which are available for tuna and chicken dishes.

Aging consumers a growing segment

Food makers are introducing products that cater to older consumers, an important and growing segment of the U.S. population. Individuals aged 65 years and older currently represent only about 12% of the population, but their ranks are continuing to swell. This group is expected to comprise 20% of the population by the year 2030, an increase of 65% over the next 35 years, according to the American Association of Retired Persons and the Administration on Aging.

For older shoppers, nutrition is a high priority. The amount of salt and sugar in a food product is among this group's top concerns, as are cholesterol and fat levels. Cereal marketers have been the most aggressive in their efforts to serve this market over the years and have introduced cereals and other new products that are high in fiber and low in sugar, salt, and fat.

"Take two TV dinners and call me in the morning"

Food manufacturers believe that the industry may be on the verge of an exciting new era in processed food. For decades, the processed food industry has fortified products with vitamins and other nutrients and has capitalized on trends in healthy eating by offering products that are high in fiber and low in fat. According to today's food makers, the next step may be to compete with the pharmaceutical industry and to offer what the industry dubs "nutritional foods", processed food products that would take the place of vitamin supplements and other dietary aids and that, the industry hopes one day to prove, can actually prevent or reverse diseases.

Judging by the industry's current research, food marketers have some lofty goals. Food companies are currently examining the role that soy proteins play in inhibiting cancer and heart disease. Other companies are investigating a potential link between the antioxidant vitamins—vitamin C, vitamin E and beta carotene—and the prevention of cancer, cardiovascular disease, and cataracts. Although such links have yet to be demonstrated, nor is it clear that the Food & Drug Administration would allow food companies to claim, for example, that a particular food will prevent cancer or heart disease, food companies are clearly quite excited about the prospects of this new and potentially lucrative niche and believe that such products will have broad appeal with an aging American population.

FINANCES

Profits mixed in 1994

The U.S. food industry's results were mixed in 1994. Food processors enjoyed a strong year in 1994. (For the purpose of this analysis, we define food processors as firms engaged in the processing of raw grains and/or live animals for sale to others.) Record U.S. corn and soybean harvests in the fall of 1994 resulted in a sharp decline in the prices of both of these important grains in late 1994 and into early 1995. Archer-Daniels-Midland Co. (ADM), a major processor of grains for use in the production of consumer foods and beverages, was among the major beneficiaries of the drop in corn and soybeans prices, the company's two most important raw materials. As a result, ADM's profits have risen sharply since mid-1994.

Lower grain prices were also a boon to companies in the meat and poultry segment. Falling prices for corn and

U.S. population projections*

Age group	1995 Number (thous.)	1995 % of total	2000 Number (thous.)	2000 % of total	2005 Number (thous.)	2005 % of total
Under 5 yrs.	19,553	7.4	18,908	6.9	18,959	6.6
5 to 14 yrs.	38,120	14.5	39,982	14.5	40,086	14.0
15 to 19 yrs.	18,024	6.9	19,758	7.2	20,982	7.3
20 to 24 yrs.	17,885	6.8	18,161	6.6	19,845	6.9
25 to 29 yrs.	18,994	7.2	17,836	6.5	18,072	6.3
30 to 34 yrs.	21,850	8.3	19,580	7.1	18,423	6.4
35 to 39 yrs.	22,267	8.5	22,168	8.1	19,894	6.9
40 to 44 yrs.	20,233	7.7	22,494	8.2	22,390	7.8
45 to 49 yrs.	17,440	6.6	19,824	7.2	22,041	7.7
50 to 54 yrs.	13,642	5.2	17,230	6.3	19,569	6.8
55 to 64 yrs.	21,153	8.1	23,988	8.7	29,647	10.4
65 yrs. & over	33,594	12.8	34,886	12.7	36,414	12.7
All Ages	262,755	100.0	274,815	100.0	286,322	100.0

*Includes Armed Forces abroad.
Source: Department of Commerce, Population Series P-25.

New product totals

Food category	1991	1992	1993	1994	% chg. 1993–94
Baby food	95	53	7	45	542.9
Bakery products	1,631	1,508	1,420	1,636	15.2
Baking ingredients	335	346	383	544	42.0
Beverages	1,367	1,538	1,842	2,250	22.1
Breakfast cereal	108	122	99	110	11.1
Candy, gum, snacks	1,885	2,068	2,043	2,461	20.5
Condiments	2,787	2,555	3,147	3,271	3.9
Dairy	1,111	1,320	1,099	1,323	20.4
Desserts	124	93	158	215	36.1
Entrees	808	698	631	694	10.0
Fruits & vegetables	356	276	407	487	19.7
Pet food	202	179	276	161	(41.7)
Processed meat	798	785	453	565	24.7
Side dishes	530	560	680	980	44.1
Soups	265	211	248	264	6.5
Total	12,402	12,312	12,893	15,006	16.4

Source: *Prepared Foods* magazine.

Average household food spending–1993
(In dollars)

Item	All households	Household income before taxes $5,000-$9,999	Household income before taxes $15,000-$19,999	Household income before taxes $30,000-$39,999
Average number of persons per household	2.5	1.8	2.3	2.7
Household income after taxes	31,890	7,367	16,713	31,953
Annual food expenditures	4,520	2,564	3,505	4,706
Food at home	2,784	1,974	2,465	2,802
Cereal products	162	110	152	167
Bakery products	279	188	224	285
Beef	227	159	219	227
Pork	154	126	168	132
Other meat	99	74	91	97
Poultry	129	105	103	119
Fish & seafood	88	58	82	81
Eggs	31	25	35	34
Fresh milk & cream	132	95	124	139
Other dairy products	172	103	152	184
Fresh fruit	140	100	110	135
Fresh vegetables	134	98	129	123
Processed Fruit	98	64	79	96
Processed vegetables	80	71	74	77
Sugar & sweets	119	141	105	123
Fats & oils	79	63	81	85
Miscellaneous food	381	226	305	409
Nonalcoholic beverages	232	156	205	243
Food away from home	1736	590	1,040	1,904
Share of income spent for food (%)	14.2	34.8	21.0	14.7

Source: Bureau of Labor Statistics.

FOOD COMPANIES' PROFIT MARGIN
(In percent)

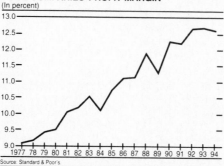

Source: Standard & Poor's.

soybeans, the primary ingredients in animal feed, lowered feed costs, encouraging ranchers to expand their herds. The result was plentiful supplies of live cattle. IBP, Inc., the world's largest meat packer, was able to operate its beef and pork processing facilities at nearly full capacity during 1994. The company's net income more than doubled in 1994 and profits in 1995 are expected to rise another 40%. Profits for Tyson Foods, Inc., the United States' largest chicken processor, also benefited substantially from lower feed costs.

Food packagers enjoyed a modestly positive year in 1994. (For the purpose of this analysis, we define food packagers as firms that produce finished food items for the retail consumer.) Although commodity costs fell during the year, the effect on total costs was not dramatic due to the ongoing decline in the cost of commodities relative to overall food processing costs.

Limited pricing flexibility restrained profit growth for packaged food companies in 1994, due in part to the growth of warehouse club stores in recent years. As a result, marketers of branded food products have been forced to keep price increases to a minimum, thereby pressuring profit margins. This margin pressure has caused many of

Top 25 food companies
(Ranked by 1994 food & beverage sales, in millions of dollars)

	Company	1993	1994	% chg.
1.	Philip Morris Cos.	34,526	35,966	4.2
2.	ConAgra Inc.	16,499	18,119	9.8
3.	PepsiCo	15,665	17,952	14.6
4.	Coca-Cola	13,937	16,140	15.8
5.	IBP Inc.	11,671	12,075	3.5
6.	Anheuser-Busch	10,792	11,364	5.3
7.	RJR Nabisco	7,025	7,699	9.6
8.	Sara Lee	7,206	7,562	4.9
9.	H.J. Heinz	7,103	7,047	(0.8)
10.	Campbell Soup	6,586	6,691	1.6
11.	Kellogg	6,295	6,562	4.2
12.	CPC International	5,636	6,203	10.1
13.	Quaker Oats	5,731	5,955	3.9
14.	Seagram Co.	5,227	5,563	6.4
15.	General Mills	5,397	5,554	2.9
16.	Tyson Foods	4,707	5,110	8.6
17.	Chiquita Brands	4,083	3,962	(3.0)
18.	Hershey Foods	3,488	3,606	3.4
19.	Dole Foods	3,108	3,498	12.5
20.	Procter & Gamble	3,271	3,290	0.6
21.	Hormel Food	2,854	3,065	7.4
22.	Dean Foods	2,243	2,406	7.3
23.	Multifoods	2,224	2,225	0.0
24.	Ralston Purina	4,526	1,794	(60.4)
25.	Coors Co.	1,582	1,663	5.1

Source: Prepared Foods.

the major U.S. food manufacturers to cut costs over the past few years. In 1994, sales growth for most of the major U.S. food manufacturers was limited to the mid-single-digits. Net income (before special items) grew at about a 10% rate in 1994. Earnings grew at a slightly faster rate than sales, due largely to cost-cutting efforts. Among U.S. companies with significant international operations, such as Kellogg, Wrigley, and Sara Lee, sales and profit margins in 1994 also benefited from favorable currency translations due to the weak U.S. dollar.

Most food manufacturers benefited from generally favorable agricultural commodity costs, recent cost cutting actions, and, for those companies with significant international sales, favorable currency exchange translations in the first half of 1995. Food companies are expected to face increasing pressure from rising grain costs in the latter half of 1995, which, combined with higher packaging costs and a slowing economy, will make it difficult for food makers to increase prices. Although continued attention to productivity enhancement will be a key theme, profit growth for U.S. food companies in 1995 may slow to the mid-single digits.

Rightsizing initiatives continue

In an effort to create critical mass and operating leverage in the mature U.S. food industry, packaged food companies went on a collective shopping spree in the 1980s. Consolidation, however, failed to produce the results that the industry had anticipated, due largely to a severe loss of pricing flexibility. As a result, the food packaging industry reversed course in the 1990s. Today, packaged food companies believe that the best way to sustain profitable growth is to maintain a portfolio of exceptional brand name products. Companies that have jumped on the "rightsizing" bandwagon in 1994 include General Mills, which spun-off of its Darden Restaurants subsidiary. Quaker Oats shuffled its business portfolio, acquiring Snapple Beverage Corp. while shedding its pet food, chocolate, and canned beans operations. H.J. Heinz decided to focus on only four distinct global businesses—baby food, frozen food, pet food, and condiments—by purchasing a number of "add on" businesses to bolster these sectors.

We expect the packaged food industry to continue to rightsize through the remainder of this decade. By focusing only on market-leading brands, a food processor gains both the pricing flexibility necessary to succeed in an increasingly competitive industry and the high-profile shelf space a product requires in order to catch the fickle consumer's eye.

Foreign ownership on the rise

The weakness of the U.S. dollar *vis-à-vis* certain foreign currencies has made investment in American food companies highly attractive to companies based outside the United States. In 1994, direct foreign investment in the U.S. food industry totalled $20.9 billion, up from $8.3 billion only a decade earlier.

The European Union (EU) collectively held the largest investment stake in U.S. food companies, which, according to the U.S. Department of Commerce, was valued at $11.1 billion in 1994. Companies based in the Netherlands account for about half of all EU investments in U.S. food makers. Netherlands-based Unilever N.V., the world's third-largest food processor after Nestle S.A. and the Philip Morris Cos., has acquired numerous U.S. assets and interests over the years. Unilever owns such popular and familiar brands as *Lipton* tea, *Ragu* spaghetti sauce, and *Wishbone* salad dressing.

Vegetarianism on rise at colleges

According to American Demographics, the number of U.S. college students that have adopted a vegetarian diet is on the rise. Driven by an increased awareness of the hazards of a diet high in fat, many college students, particularly women, are becoming vegetarians. In fact, a recent study undertaken by the National Restaurant Association found that about 15% of the nation's 15 million college students eat a vegetarian diet during a typical day, about two to three times higher than the share of the overall population believed to be vegetarian.

Fast-food restaurants have so far failed to capitalize on this growth in the number of young vegetarians. In 1993, for example, both McDonald's and Burger King tested meatless hamburgers with little success. However, U.S. food manu-facturers believe that demand for foods without meat will continue to rise, driven by health-conscious baby boomers and elderly adults who are watching their fat and cholesterol intake. Grand Metropolitan Plc's Pillsbury subsidiary, for example, has been successfully marketing *The Green Giant Harvest Burger,* a frozen vegetarian burger patty, since 1991. Food processor ConAgra introduced a line of frozen meatless dishes called "Life Choice", which were developed upon the recommendations of a cardiologist who was re-tained as a consultant by the company. Other food manufac-turers are likely to monitor the sales of these and other vegetarian products in order to determine whether or not to participate in this market. ∎

Investment in the U.S. food processing industry by Euro-pean countries that are not part of the EU was valued at $2.3 billion in 1994. Major non-EU companies with signifi-cant investments in the U.S. include Switzerland's Nestle S.A., maker of such widely known products as *Stauffers* frozen foods, *Nestle* candy bars, and *Carnation* instant drink products. Canadian companies hold $7.4 billion in assets of U.S. food companies. Companies based in Japan and in other Asian and Pacific Rim countries account for the remaining investment in U.S. food makers.

Foreign investment in U.S. food manufacturing is likely to continue to grow in the future, in part because such companies desire access to the United States' large and comparatively well-heeled consumer base. A dispropor-tionate share of investment in U.S. food processing compa-nies has been made by firms based in the United Kingdom, which can write off goodwill without an impact on earnings. U.S. companies, on the other hand, must dilute reported earnings following an acquisition. British-based Grand Metropolitan Plc, for example, owns a variety of consumer franchises, including *Smirnoff* vodka and *Pillsbury* food products, as well as the Burger King restaurant chain. The company has consistently acquired U.S. food assets over many years. Grand Met's most recent investment was the January 1995 acquisition of Pet Inc. for $2.6 billion. Pet Inc. makes a wide array of grocery items, including the *Old El Paso* line of Mexican foods and *Progresso* canned soups. Prior to the Pet Inc. investment, Grand Met's last major acquisition in the United States was the $5.7 billion pur-chase of Pillsbury Co. ∎

	COMPOSITE INDUSTRY DATA

COMPOSITE

INDUSTRY DATA

*Per share data based

on Standard & Poor's

group stock price indexes

FOODS
The companies used for this series are:
Archer-Daniels-Midland; Borden (through1993); Campbell Soup; Con Agra; CPC International; General Mills; Gerber (through 1993); Heinz; Hershey Foods; Kellogg; Kraft Inc. (1987).

		1987	1988	1989	1990	1991	1992	R1993	P1994
Sales		488.87	540.85	677.77	716.87	761.26	798.47	826.87	887.40
Operating Income		54.47	64.26	76.36	87.91	94.61	101.08	104.81	111.68
Profit Margin%		11.14	11.88	11.27	12.26	12.21	12.66	12.68	12.59
Depreciation		11.48	12.84	15.56	17.70	20.28	23.08	24.54	25.28
Taxes		17.35	17.57	18.33	22.13	24.74	23.52	24.75	24.94
Cash Flow		34.72	40.38	42.79	50.72	59.81	62.17	64.86	65.74
Earnings		23.24	27.53	27.72	33.02	39.53	39.17	40.40	37.80
Dividends		8.75	9.74	12.46	14.22	15.31	17.68	17.98	21.24
Earnings as a % of Sales		4.75	5.09	4.09	4.61	4.99	4.91	4.89	4.49
Dividends as % of Earnings		37.65	35.38	44.95	43.06	38.31	45.14	44.50	53.37
Price (1941–43 = 10)	—High	424.03	360.79	596.61	619.32	874.14	871.87	873.27	838.00
	—Low	308.54	324.09	435.09	500.82	567.41	721.93	688.45	705.17
Price-Earnings Ratios	—High	19.00	13.11	21.52	18.76	22.86	22.26	21.62	21.06
	—Low	13.95	11.77	15.70	15.17	14.84	18.43	17.04	17.72
Dividend Yield %	—High	2.70	3.01	2.86	2.84	2.58	2.45	2.61	3.01
	—Low	1.98	2.70	2.30	1.68	2.03	2.06	2.53	
Book Value		110.56	100.05	88.88	155.34	180.10	177.82	162.80	144.49
Return on Book Value %		21.02	27.52	31.19	21.26	35.02	22.03	24.82	27.55
†Working Capital		31.77	37.92	43.33	38.84	31.63	30.98	30.63	31.97
Capital Expenditures		26.02	29.62	33.85	41.70	37.26	38.42	38.63	36.55

SOFT DRINKS
The companies used for this series are:
Coca-Cola; Harcourt General (1981 to 1988); MEI Corp. (through 1986); PepsiCo.

TOBACCO
The companies used for this series are:
American Brands; Phillip Morris; RJR Nabisco (through 1988); UST Corp. (from 1987).

1987	1988	1989	1990	1991	1992	1993	1994			1987	1988	1989	1990	1991	1992	1993	1994
286.85	348.14	382.27	447.17	498.58	563.42	629.08	731.96	Sales		395.11	486.81	746.04	845.31	913.37	980.25	995.25	1,064.16
46.47	58.89	70.49	83.74	94.28	109.91	125.93	145.46	Operating Income		81.97	100.13	155.55	180.22	202.97	229.59	202.48	226.81
16.20	16.92	18.44	18.73	18.91	19.51	20.02	19.87	Profit Margin%		20.75	20.57	20.85	21.32	22.22	23.42	20.34	21.31
10.61	12.83	15.05	17.73	20.30	24.07	28.02	32.08	Depreciation		11.55	15.24	21.68	25.27	27.76	29.63	32.28	33.61
12.56	14.15	16.16	19.29	21.68	23.49	29.61	33.72	Taxes		24.40	29.78	42.20	53.13	57.93	71.48	54.27	71.78
33.46	40.57	47.88	56.87	63.46	75.35	89.07	103.29	Cash Flow		43.33	54.93	81.34	94.16	107.19	129.75	108.72	135.82
22.88	27.77	32.84	39.15	43.15	51.28	61.05	71.20	Earnings		31.78	39.69	59.65	68.89	79.44	100.12	76.45	102.21
8.78	9.89	11.45	13.35	16.04	18.40	22.14	25.63	Dividends		13.47	16.53	23.82	28.93	35.51	43.49	47.77	55.45
7.98	7.98	8.59	8.76	8.65	9.10	9.70	9.73	Earnings as a % of Sales		8.04	8.15	8.00	8.15	8.70	10.21	7.68	9.60
38.37	35.61	34.87	34.10	37.17	35.88	36.27	36.00	Dividends as % of Earnings		42.39	41.65	39.93	41.99	44.70	43.44	62.49	54.25
460.29	413.25	701.39	848.79	1,280.72	1,458.55	1,480.71	1,594.21	Price (1941–43=10) —High		494.99	503.79	830.04	953.58	1,414.74	1,507.10	1,355.34	1,147.79
330.56	332.06	408.89	603.06	764.78	1,173.47	1,269.94	1,230.37	—Low		334.68	335.73	499.40	688.86	886.84	1,272.81	861.30	882.21
20.12	14.88	21.36	21.68	29.68	28.44	24.25	22.39	Price-Earnings Ratios —High		15.58	12.69	13.92	13.84	17.81	15.05	17.73	11.23
14.45	11.96	12.45	15.40	17.72	22.88	20.80	17.28	—Low		10.53	8.46	8.37	10.00	11.16	12.71	11.27	8.63
2.66	2.98	2.80	2.21	2.10	1.57	1.74	2.08	Dividend Yield % —High		4.02	4.92	4.77	4.20	4.00	3.42	5.55	6.29
1.91	2.39	1.63	1.57	1.25	1.26	1.50	1.61	—Low		2.72	3.28	2.87	3.03	2.51	2.89	3.52	4.83
66.69	59.45	22.23	40.81	59.80	30.82	39.87	59.11	Book Value		56.36	N.A.	N.A.	N.A.	def	def	def	def
34.31	46.71	...	95.93	72.16	...	...	...	Return on Book Value %		56.39	...	...	...	def	def	def	def
7.48	d2.21	d3.08	d13.44	13.92	-8.72	-34.66	-19.23	†Working Capital		38.32	N.A.	N.A.	N.A.	N.A.	N.A.	N.A.	N.A.
20.16	18.60	22.19	29.79	37.03	42.88	45.42	51.32	Capital Expenditures		16.93	23.24	24.45	26.60	29.09	30.95	31.47	33.31

Definitions for the statistics found in the Comparative Company Analysis tables

Operating revenues—Net sales and other operating revenues. Excludes interest income if such income is "non-operating." Includes franchise/leased department income for retainers and royalties for publishers and oil and mining companies. Excludes excise taxes for tobacco, liquor, and oil companies.

Net income—Profits derived from all sources, after deductions of expenses, taxes, and fixed charges, but before any discontinued operations, extraordinary items, and dividend payments (preferred and common).

Return on revenues (%)—Net income divided by operating revenues.

Return on assets (%)—Net income divided by average total assets. Used in industry analysis and as a measure of asset-use efficiency.

Return on equity (%)—Net income, less preferred dividend requirements, divided by average common shareholder's equity. Generally used to measure performance and to make industry comparisons.

Current ratio—Current assets divided by current liabilities. It is a measure of liquidity. Current assets are those assets expected to be realized in cash or used up in the production of revenue within one year. Current liabilities generally include all debts/obligations falling due within one year.

Debt/capital ratio—Long-term debt (excluding current portion) divided by total invested capital. It indicates how highly "leveraged" a company might be. Long-term debt are those debts/obligations due after one year, including bonds, notes payable, mortgages, lease obligations, and industrial revenue bonds. Other long-term debt, when reported as a separate account, is excluded; this account generally includes pension and retirement benefits. Total invested capital is the sum of stockholders' equity, long-term debt, capital lease obligations, deferred income taxes, investment credits, and minority interest.

Debt as a percent of net working capital—Long-term debt (excluding current portion) divided by the difference between current assets and current liabilities. It is an indicator of a company's liquidity.

Price-earnings ratio (high-low)—The ratio of market price to earnings, obtained by dividing the stock's high and low market price for the year by earnings per share (before extraordinary items). It essentially indicates the value investors place on a company's earnings.

Dividend payout ratio—This is the percentage of earnings paid out in dividends. It is calculated by dividing the annual dividend by the earnings. Dividends are generally total cash payments per share over a twelve-month period. Although payments are usually calculated from the ex-dividend rates, they may also be reported on a declared basis where this has been established to be a company's payout policy.

Yield (high %-low %)—The total cash dividend payments divided by the year's high and low market prices for the stock.

Earnings per share—The amount a company reports as having been earned for the year (based on generally accepted accounting standards), divided by the number of shares outstanding. Amounts reported in Industry Surveys exclude extraordinary items.

Tangible book value per share—This measure indicates the theoretical dollar amount per common share one might expect to receive should liquidation take place. Generally, book value is determined by adding the stated (or par) value of the common stock, paid-in capital, and retained earnings, then subtracting intangible assets, preferred stock at liquidating value, and unamortized debt discount. This amount is divided by the number of outstanding shares to get book value per common share.

Share price (high-low)—This shows the calendar-year high and low of a stock's market price.

In addition to the footnotes that appear at the bottom of each page, you will notice some or all of the following:
NA—Not available.
NM—Not meaningful.
NR—Not reported.
AF—Annual figure. Data are presented on an annual basis.
CF—Combined figure. In this case, data are not available because one or more components are combined with other items.

COMPARATIVE COMPANY ANALYSIS — Food, Beverages & Tobacco

Company	Yr. End	Operating Revenues — Million $							Compound Growth Rate (%)			Index Basis (1984 = 100)				
		1984	1989	1990	1991	1992	1993	1994	1-Yr.	5-Yr.	10-Yr.	1990	1991	1992	1993	1994
FOOD																
AMERICAN MAIZE-PRODS -CL A	DEC	414.3A,C	504.8D	501.5	533.6	542.2	538.5	604.0	12.2	3.7	3.8	121	129	131	130	146
ARCHER-DANIELS-MIDLAND CO	JUN	4907.0	7928.8A	7751.3A	8468.2A	9231.5A	9811.4A	11374.3A	15.9	7.5	8.8	158	173	188	200	232
CPC INTERNATIONAL INC	DEC	4373.3	5103.1A	5781.1A	6189.1A,C	6599.0A	6738.0A	7425.0A	10.2	7.8	5.4	132	142	151	154	170
CAGLE'S INC -CL A	MAR	148.0D	193.4	192.7	208.8	280.1	312.7	349.8	11.8	12.6	6.4	130	141	189	211	236
CAMPBELL SOUP CO	JUL	3657.4	5672.1	6205.8	6204.1	6263.2	6586.2C	6690.0	1.6	3.4	6.2	170	170	171	180	183
CHIQUITA BRANDS INTL	DEC	3220.3	3822.8	4272.7	4627.4	2723.5D	2532.9	3961.7C	56.4	0.7	2.1	133	144	85	79	123
CONAGRA INC	MAY	5498.1A,C	15501.2C	19504.7A	21219.0A	21519.1	23512.2C	NA	NA	NA	NA	355	386	391	428	NA
DEAN FOODS CO	MAY	923.1	1987.5A	2158.0A	2289.4	2274.3	2431.2A	NA	NA	NA	NA	234	248	246	263	NA
DOLE FOOD CO INC	DEC	1520.1A,C	2717.8A	3003.2A	3216.0	3375.5	3430.5A	3841.6A	12.0	7.2	9.7	198	212	222	226	253
FLOWERS INDUSTRIES INC	JUN	603.0A	782.6	835.1	824.8	879.2	962.1	989.8	2.9	4.8	5.1	138	137	146	160	164
GENERAL MILLS INC	MAY	4285.2D	6448.3D	7153.2	7777.8	8134.6	8516.9	5026.7D	-41.0	-4.9	1.6	167	182	190	199	117
HEINZ (H J) CO	APR	4047.9	6085.7A	6647.1A	6581.9A	7103.4	7046.7	8086.8A	14.8	5.9	7.2	164	163	175	174	200
HERSHEY FOODS CORP	DEC	1892.5	2421.0	2715.6	2899.2	3219.8	3488.2	3606.3	3.4	8.3	6.7	144	153	170	184	191
HORMEL FOODS CORP	OCT	1454.5A	2340.5	2681.2	2836.2	2813.7	2854.0	3064.8	7.4	5.5	7.7	184	195	193	196	211
IBP INC	DEC	6592.9	9128.6	10185.2	10387.6	11128.4	11671.3	12075.4A	3.5	5.8	6.2	154	158	169	177	183
INTL MULTIFOODS CORP	FEB	1211.2	2074.9A	2191.9A	2281.4A	2223.9	2224.7	2295.1A	3.2	2.0	6.6	181	188	184	184	190
KELLOGG CO	DEC	2602.4	4651.7	5181.4	5786.6	6190.6	6295.4	6562.0	4.2	7.1	9.7	199	222	238	242	252
MCCORMICK & CO	NOV	788.4A	1246.1C	1323.0	1427.9	1471.4	1556.6	1694.8	8.9	6.3	8.0	168	181	187	197	215
PIONEER HI-BRED INTERNATIONL	AUG	716.1	867.3D	964.5A	1124.9	1261.8A	1343.4	1478.7	10.1	11.3	7.5	135	157	176	188	207
QUAKER OATS CO	JUN	3344.1A	5724.2	5030.6D	5491.2	5576.4	5730.6	5955.0	3.9	0.8	5.9	150	164	167	171	178
RALSTON PURINA-CONSOLIDATED	SEP	4980.1	6658.3D	7101.4C	7375.8	7752.4	7902.2	7705.3	-2.5	3.0	4.5	143	148	156	159	155
RYKOFF-SEXTON INC	APR	853.0	1407.1	1461.6	1519.0A	1488.1	1524.7	1569.0A,C	2.9	2.2	6.3	171	178	174	179	164
SARA LEE CORP	JUN	7000.3	11717.6A	11605.9	12381.4	13243.0	14580.0A	15536.0A	6.6	5.8	8.3	166	177	189	208	222
SEABOARD CORP	DEC	353.2A,C	518.8C	557.3	875.9	1053.7	1142.1	983.8	-13.9	13.7	10.8	158	248	298	323	279
SMUCKER (JM) CO -CL A	APR	230.5	422.4	455.0	483.5	491.3	511.5A	628.3	22.8	8.3	10.5	197	210	213	222	273
TASTY BAKING CO	DEC	222.4	269.5	277.6	288.0	297.1	137.8D	142.1	3.1	-12.0	-4.4	125	129	134	62	64
TOOTSIE ROLL INDS	DEC	93.1	179.3	194.3	207.9	245.4	259.6A	296.9	14.4	10.6	12.3	209	223	264	279	319
TYSON FOODS INC -CL A	SEP	750.1	2538.2A	3825.3	3922.1	4168.8	4707.4A	5110.3	8.6	15.0	21.2	510	523	556	628	681
UNIVERSAL FOODS CORP	SEP	432.5A,C	837.3A	838.9A	834.3A	883.4A	891.6	929.9	4.3	2.1	8.0	194	193	204	206	215
WRIGLEY (WM) JR CO	DEC	590.5	992.9	1110.6	1148.9	1286.9	1428.5	1596.6	11.8	10.0	10.5	188	195	218	242	270
BREWERS																
ANHEUSER-BUSCH COS INC	DEC	6501.2	9481.3A	10743.6	10996.3	11393.7	11505.3C	12053.8	4.8	4.9	6.4	165	169	175	177	185
BASS PLC -ADR	SEP	NA	6516.1A	8357.7A	7679.0A	7662.2	6658.7	7020.8	5.4	1.5	NA	NA	**	**	**	**
COORS (ADOLPH) -CL B	DEC	1132.6	1763.9	1863.4	1917.4	1550.8D	1581.8	1662.7	5.1	-1.2	3.9	165	169	137	140	147
DISTILLERS																
BROWN-FORMAN -CL B	APR	928.4	1016.6	1118.9	1260.1A	1414.5A	1401.4	1420.2	1.3	6.9	4.3	121	136	152	151	153
GRAND MET PLC -ADR	SEP	NA	14575.7A,C	17108.8A,C	14977.8A,C	13733.8A,C	11068.9A,C	11343.3A,C	2.5	-4.9	NA	**	**	**	**	**
SEAGRAM CO LTD	JAN	2005.7F	4508.3A,F	5031.0F	5278.0F	5214.0F	5227.0F	5563.0F	6.4	4.3	10.7	251	263	260	261	277
SOFT DRINKS & OTHER BEVERAGES																
COCA-COLA BTLNG CONS	DEC	197.1A	384.3A	431.0	464.7A	655.8	687.0	723.9	5.4	13.5	13.9	219	236	333	349	367
COCA-COLA CO	DEC	7364.0	8965.8A,C	10236.3	11571.6	13073.8	13957.0	16172.0	15.9	12.5	8.2	139	157	178	190	220
COCA-COLA ENTERPRISES	DEC	NA	3881.9	4034.0	4050.8A	5127.0A	5465.0A	6011.0A	10.0	9.1	NA	NA	**	**	**	**
PEPSICO INC	DEC	7698.7D	15242.4A,C	17802.7D	19607.9	21970.0C	25020.7	28472.4	13.8	13.3	14.0	231	255	285	325	370
TOBACCO																
AMERICAN BRANDS INC/DE	DEC	4475.0	7264.7	8270.3A	8379.0	8840.3	8287.5	7489.7D	-9.6	0.6	5.3	185	187	198	185	167
BROOKE GROUP LTD	DEC	NA	437.2A	959.3A	999.4	572.4D	546.1	347.5D	-36.4	-4.5	NA	NA	**	**	**	**
CULBRO CORP	NOV	936.9F	856.3F	828.1H	997.9F	1044.3F	1229.5A,F	179.9C,F	-85.4	-26.8	-15.2	88	107	111	131	19
PHILIP MORRIS COS INC	DEC	10137.7	39011.0	44323.0A	48064.0	50095.0	50621.0	53776.0	6.2	6.6	18.2	437	474	494	499	530
RJR NABISCO HLDGS CORP	DEC	9915.0D	12764.0A,C	13879.0	14989.0	15734.0	15104.0	15366.0	1.7	3.8	4.5	140	151	159	152	155

(cont'd)

Data by Standard & Poor's Compustat, A Division of The McGraw-Hill Companies

Operating Revenues

Data by Standard & Poor's Compustat. A Division of The McGraw-Hill Companies

Company	Yr. End	Million $							Compound Growth Rate (%)			Index Basis (1984 = 100)				
		1984	1989	1990	1991	1992	1993	1994	1-Yr.	5-Yr.	10-Yr.	1990	1991	1992	1993	1994
TOBACCO (cont'd)																
* UST INC	DEC	441.4	669.8	750.6	879.5C	1012.7	1080.4	1197.7	10.9	12.3	10.5	170	199	229	245	271
UNIVERSAL CORP/VA	JUN	1019.5	2920.3F	2815.1F	2896.5D.F	2989.0F	3047.2A.F	2975.1F	-2.4	0.4	11.3	276	284	293	299	292

Note: Data as originally reported. A - This year's data reflect an acquisition or merger. C - This year's data reflect an accounting change. F - Includes other (non-operating) income. † - Of the following calendar year. H - Some or all data is not available due to a fiscal year change. * Company included in the Standard & Poor's 500. D - Data exclude discontinued operations.

Net Income

Company	Yr. End	Million $							Compound Growth Rate (%)			Index Basis (1984 = 100)				
		1984	1989	1990	1991	1992	1993	1994	1-Yr.	5-Yr.	10-Yr.	1990	1991	1992	1993	1994
FOOD																
AMERICAN MAIZE-PRODS -CL A	DEC	10.0	12.8	16.2	12.8	10.0	0.2	26.9	NM	16.1	10.4	162	128	100	2	269
* ARCHER-DANIELS-MIDLAND CO	JUN	117.7	424.7	483.5	466.7	503.8	534.5	484.1	-9.4	2.7	15.2	411	396	428	454	411
* CPC INTERNATIONAL INC	DEC	193.4	327.5	373.9	404.2	430.6	454.5	345.0	-24.1	1.0	6.0	193	209	223	235	178
CAGLE'S INC -CL A	†MAR	-0.4	1.8	1.8	1.9	5.2	8.7	13.8	59.1	50.1	NM	NM	NM	NM	NM	NM
* CAMPBELL SOUP CO	JUL	191.2	13.1	4.4	401.5	490.5	257.2	630.0	144.9	117.0	12.7	2	210	257	135	330
CHIQUITA BRANDS INTL	DEC	21.0	67.8	93.9	128.5	-221.7	-51.1	-48.7	NM	NM	NM	446	610	-1053	-243	-231
* CONAGRA INC	†MAY	91.7	231.7	311.2	372.4	391.5	437.1	NA	NA	NA	NA	339	406	427	477	NA
DEAN FOODS CO	†MAY	26.5	61.2	72.5	62.0	68.4	70.8	NA	NA	NA	NA	274	234	259	267	NA
DOLE FOOD CO INC	DEC	1.1	94.9	120.5	133.7	65.2	77.9	67.9	-12.8	-6.5	50.9	NM	NM	5870	7011	6110
FLOWERS INDUSTRIES INC	JUN	22.1	29.6	34.3	24.0	31.7	39.2	29.5	-24.7	-0.0	2.9	155	109	143	177	133
* GENERAL MILLS INC	†MAY	115.4	373.7	464.2	505.6	506.1	469.7	259.7	-44.7	-7.0	8.5	402	438	439	407	225
* HEINZ (H J) CO	†APR	266.0	504.5	568.0	638.3	529.9	602.9	591.0	-2.0	3.2	8.3	214	240	199	227	222
* HERSHEY FOODS CORP	DEC	108.7	171.1	215.9	219.5	242.6	297.2	184.2	-38.0	1.5	5.4	199	202	223	273	170
* HORMEL FOODS CORP	OCT	29.5	70.1	77.1	86.4	95.2	100.8	118.0	17.1	11.0	14.3	262	293	323	342	400
IBP INC	DEC	49.9	35.3	48.3	1.4	63.6	77.5	182.3	135.3	38.8	13.8	97	3	128	155	365
INTL MULTIFOODS CORP	†FEB	21.7	25.3	35.2	39.1	41.2	-13.4	57.0	NM	17.6	10.1	162	180	190	-62	263
* KELLOGG CO	DEC	250.5	422.1	502.8	606.0	682.8	680.7	705.4	3.6	10.8	10.9	201	242	273	272	282
* MCCORMICK & CO	NOV	54.6	52.5	69.4	80.9	95.2	99.7	61.2	-38.6	3.1	1.1	127	148	174	183	112
PIONEER HI-BRED INTERNATIONL	AUG	69.1	81.9	72.7	104.2	152.2	137.5	212.7	54.7	21.0	11.9	105	151	220	199	308
* QUAKER OATS CO	JUN	138.7	203.0	228.9	235.8	247.6	286.8	231.5	-19.3	2.7	5.3	165	170	179	207	167
RALSTON PURINA-CONSOLIDATED	SEP	242.7	351.2	396.3	391.9	320.7	341.3	218.4	-36.0	-9.1	-1.1	163	161	132	141	90
RYKOFF-SEXTON INC	†APR	11.2	11.3	13.8	12.6	-19.7	7.4	9.4	27.4	-3.7	-1.8	123	113	-176	66	84
* SARA LEE CORP	†JUN	188.4	411.5	470.3	535.0	761.0	704.0	234.0	-66.8	-10.6	2.2	250	284	404	374	124
SEABOARD CORP	DEC	15.7	18.7	30.0	2.2	31.1	15.8	35.2	122.6	13.5	8.4	192	136	198	101	225
SMUCKER (JM) CO -CL A	†APR	15.9	30.2	31.7	34.1	37.4	30.5	36.3	19.0	3.8	8.6	200	215	236	192	229
TASTY BAKING CO	DEC	2.9	9.6	1.9	7.9	8.6	5.7	5.8	2.0	-9.5	7.0	66	267	291	193	197
TOOTSIE ROLL INDS	DEC	8.8	20.2	22.6	26.5	32.0	35.4	37.9	7.0	13.4	15.7	255	300	362	401	429
* TYSON FOODS INC -CL A	SEP	18.2	100.6	120.0	145.5	160.5	180.3	-2.1	-100.0	NM	NM	661	801	884	993	309
UNIVERSAL FOODS CORP	SEP	18.5	20.6	41.7	45.8	41.7	60.6	50.9	-10.0	5.0	12.0	300	351	853	844	412
* WRIGLEY (WM) JR CO	DEC	39.7	106.1	117.4	128.7	148.6	174.9	230.5	31.8	16.8	19.2	296	324	375	441	581
BREWERS																
* ANHEUSER-BUSCH COS INC	DEC	391.5	767.2	842.4	939.8	994.2	594.5	1032.1	73.6	6.1	10.2	215	240	254	152	264
BASS PLC -ADR	SEP	NA	599.0	721.3	644.7	608.4	469.7	550.4	17.2	-1.7	NA	NA	**	**	**	**
COORS (ADOLPH) -CL B	DEC	44.7	13.1	21.3	23.9	35.7	-41.9	58.1	NM	34.6	2.7	87	53	80	-94	130
DISTILLERS																
* BROWN-FORMAN -CL B	†APR	81.7	81.0	145.2	146.4	156.2	161.1	148.6	-7.7	12.9	6.2	178	179	191	197	182
GRAND MET PLC -ADR	SEP	NA	821.0	1188.7	1153.7	1111.0	617.8	709.7	14.9	-2.9	NA	NA	**	**	**	**
SEAGRAM CO LTD	†JAN	383.6	710.6	756.0	727.0	474.0	379.0	811.3	114.0	2.7	7.8	197	190	124	99	211

Net Income

Company	Yr. End	Million $ 1984	1989	1990	1991	1992	1993	1994	Index Basis (1984 = 100) 1990	1991	1992	1993	1994	Compound Growth Rate (%) 1-Yr.	5-Yr.	10-Yr.
SOFT DRINKS & OTHER BEVERAGES																
• COCA-COLA BTLNG CONS	DEC	9.4	-2.9	0.2	2.9	2.1	14.8	14.1	2	31	22	158	150	-4.6	NM	4.2
* COCA-COLA CO	DEC	628.8	1192.8	1381.9	1618.0	1883.8	2188.0	2554.0	220	257	300	348	406	16.7	16.4	15.0
* COCA-COLA ENTERPRISES	DEC	NA	71.7	93.4	-82.4	-15.0	-15.0	69.0	**	**	**	**	**	NM	-0.8	NA
* PEPSICO INC	DEC	206.7	901.4	1090.6	1080.2	1301.7	1587.9	1784.0	528	523	630	768	863	12.4	14.6	24.1
TOBACCO																
* AMERICAN BRANDS INC/DE	DEC	414.1	630.8	596.0	806.1	883.8	668.2	885.1	144	195	213	161	214	32.5	7.0	7.9
BROOKE GROUP LTD	DEC	NA	25.5	375.9	-149.6	-32.3	-7.2	-18.0	NA	**	**	**	**	NM	0.9	NA
CULBRO CORP	NOV	13.7	1.1	3.1	3.2	1.9	1.0	1.2	23	23	14	7	8	12.9	0.9	-21.9
* PHILIP MORRIS COS INC	DEC	888.5	2946.0	3540.0	3927.0	4939.0	3568.0	4725.0	398	442	556	402	532	32.4	9.9	18.2
* RJR NABISCO HLDGS CORP	DEC	843.0	-1172.0	-462.0	368.0	776.0	-3.0	764.0	-55	44	92	-0	91	NM	NM	-1.0
* UST INC	DEC	83.7	190.5	223.3	265.9	312.6	368.9	387.5	267	318	373	441	463	5.1	15.3	16.6
UNIVERSAL CORP/VA	JUN	38.3	54.0	37.1	56.4	70.7	80.2	38.6	97	147	185	210	101	-51.9	-6.5	0.1

Note: Data as originally reported. * Company included in the Standard & Poor's 500. † Of the following calendar year.

Return on Revenues (%)

Company	Yr. End	1990	1991	1992	1993	1994
FOOD						
AMERICAN MAIZE-PRODS -CL A	DEC	3.2	2.4	1.8	0.0	4.5
* ARCHER-DANIELS-MIDLAND CO	JUN	6.2	6.5	5.5	5.4	4.3
* CPC INTERNATIONAL INC	DEC	6.5	6.5	6.5	6.7	4.6
CAGLE'S INC -CL A	†MAR	0.9	0.9	1.9	2.8	3.9
* CAMPBELL SOUP CO	JUL	0.1	6.5	7.8	3.9	9.4
CHIQUITA BRANDS INTL	DEC	2.2	2.8	NM	NM	NM
* CONAGRA INC	†MAY	1.6	1.8	1.8	2.9	NA
DEAN FOODS CO	†MAY	3.4	2.7	3.0	2.9	NA
DOLE FOOD CO INC	DEC	4.0	4.2	1.9	2.3	1.8
FLOWERS INDUSTRIES INC	JUN	4.1	2.9	3.6	4.1	3.0
* GENERAL MILLS INC	†MAY	6.5	6.5	6.2	5.5	5.2
* HEINZ (H J) CO	†APR	8.5	9.7	7.5	8.6	7.3
* HERSHEY FOODS CORP	DEC	8.0	7.6	7.5	8.5	5.1
HORMEL FOODS CORP	OCT	2.9	3.0	3.4	3.5	3.9
IBP INC	DEC	0.5	0.0	0.6	0.7	1.5
INTL MULTIFOODS CORP	†FEB	1.6	1.7	1.9	NM	2.5
* KELLOGG CO	DEC	9.7	10.5	11.0	10.8	10.8
MCCORMICK & CO	NOV	5.2	5.7	6.5	6.4	3.6
PIONEER HI-BRED INTERNATIONL	AUG	7.5	9.3	12.1	10.2	14.4
* QUAKER OATS CO	JUN	4.6	4.3	4.4	5.0	3.9
* RALSTON PURINA-CONSOLIDATED	SEP	5.6	5.3	4.1	4.3	2.8
RYKOFF-SEXTON INC	†APR	0.9	0.8	NM	0.5	0.6
* SARA LEE CORP	JUN	4.1	4.3	5.7	0.8	3.6
SEABOARD CORP	DEC	5.4	2.4	1.4	1.4	1.6
SMUCKER (JM) CO -CL A	†APR	7.0	7.1	7.6	6.0	5.8
TASTY BAKING CO	DEC	0.7	2.7	2.9	4.1	4.1
TOOTSIE ROLL INDS	DEC	11.6	12.8	13.1	13.7	12.8
* TYSON FOODS INC -CL A	SEP	3.1	3.7	3.9	3.8	NM
UNIVERSAL FOODS CORP	SEP	5.9	6.9	4.7	6.3	5.5
* WRIGLEY (WM) JR CO	DEC	10.6	11.2	11.5	12.2	14.4
BREWERS						
* ANHEUSER-BUSCH COS INC	DEC	7.8	8.5	8.7	5.2	8.6

(cont'd)

Return on Assets (%)

Company	Yr. End	1990	1991	1992	1993	1994
AMERICAN MAIZE-PRODS -CL A	DEC	3.8	2.9	2.1	0.0	5.2
ARCHER-DANIELS-MIDLAND CO	JUN	9.5	8.0	7.3	6.7	5.6
CPC INTERNATIONAL INC	DEC	9.1	9.0	8.9	8.9	6.4
CAGLE'S INC -CL A	†MAR	3.7	3.5	3.5	9.7	17.4
CAMPBELL SOUP CO	JUL	0.1	9.7	11.5	5.6	12.7
CHIQUITA BRANDS INTL	DEC	5.0	4.8	NM	NM	NM
CONAGRA INC	†MAY	4.4	3.9	4.0	4.2	NA
DEAN FOODS CO	†MAY	9.3	7.4	7.8	7.1	NA
DOLE FOOD CO INC	DEC	5.1	5.1	2.2	2.4	1.9
FLOWERS INDUSTRIES INC	JUN	7.7	5.5	7.1	8.2	5.6
GENERAL MILLS INC	†MAY	12.9	12.3	11.3	9.5	6.1
HEINZ (H J) CO	†APR	12.1	11.7	8.7	9.1	8.1
HERSHEY FOODS CORP	DEC	11.1	9.9	9.7	10.8	6.4
HORMEL FOODS CORP	OCT	10.1	10.4	10.8	10.0	10.3
IBP INC	DEC	3.4	0.1	4.3	5.1	10.7
INTL MULTIFOODS CORP	†FEB	4.3	5.0	5.2	NM	6.9
KELLOGG CO	DEC	14.1	15.8	17.2	16.5	16.2
MCCORMICK & CO	NOV	7.7	8.2	8.8	8.2	4.2
PIONEER HI-BRED INTERNATIONL	AUG	7.6	10.0	13.2	11.3	17.2
QUAKER OATS CO	JUN	7.0	7.4	8.2	9.8	7.9
RALSTON PURINA-CONSOLIDATED	SEP	9.0	8.7	6.6	6.7	4.5
RYKOFF-SEXTON INC	†APR	3.6	2.8	NM	1.6	2.1
SARA LEE CORP	JUN	6.8	6.8	6.6	6.8	5.3
SEABOARD CORP	DEC	7.6	4.8	6.6	2.8	9.1
SMUCKER (JM) CO -CL A	†APR	13.3	12.9	13.1	9.1	9.1
TASTY BAKING CO	DEC	1.6	6.0	6.5	5.1	6.5
TOOTSIE ROLL INDS	DEC	15.2	15.4	15.7	13.5	12.4
TYSON FOODS INC -CL A	SEP	4.7	5.7	6.1	5.7	6.8
UNIVERSAL FOODS CORP	SEP	9.5	9.6	9.6	7.9	6.8
WRIGLEY (WM) JR CO	DEC	22.1	21.6	22.2	22.9	25.7
ANHEUSER-BUSCH COS INC	DEC	9.0	9.6	9.7	5.6	9.4

Return on Equity (%)

Company	Yr. End	1990	1991	1992	1993	1994
AMERICAN MAIZE-PRODS -CL A	DEC	10.9	8.3	6.1	0.1	11.9
ARCHER-DANIELS-MIDLAND CO	JUN	14.6	12.5	12.0	11.4	9.8
CPC INTERNATIONAL INC	DEC	27.4	25.8	25.9	26.4	19.5
CAGLE'S INC -CL A	†MAR	9.3	23.0	25.7	28.4	35.0
CAMPBELL SOUP CO	JUL	0.3	23.0	25.7	13.8	34.1
CHIQUITA BRANDS INTL	DEC	16.3	NM	NM	NM	NM
CONAGRA INC	†MAY	20.0	17.2	17.1	19.3	NA
DEAN FOODS CO	†MAY	18.6	14.6	15.1	14.1	NA
DOLE FOOD CO INC	DEC	13.7	13.6	6.4	7.6	6.4
FLOWERS INDUSTRIES INC	JUN	16.1	11.4	14.9	15.7	10.6
GENERAL MILLS INC	†MAY	48.3	40.7	39.1	39.6	40.2
HEINZ (H J) CO	†APR	27.3	27.5	22.6	25.9	24.6
HERSHEY FOODS CORP	DEC	18.3	17.0	17.3	20.7	12.9
HORMEL FOODS CORP	OCT	15.7	15.7	15.5	16.6	19.2
IBP INC	DEC	9.6	0.3	12.5	13.5	26.2
INTL MULTIFOODS CORP	†FEB	11.2	12.3	12.9	NM	21.0
KELLOGG CO	DEC	28.4	29.8	33.3	37.2	40.1
MCCORMICK & CO	NOV	19.5	15.7	23.0	22.0	12.8
PIONEER HI-BRED INTERNATIONL	AUG	11.4	15.7	20.6	16.9	24.9
QUAKER OATS CO	JUN	20.8	24.1	27.9	40.6	45.6
RALSTON PURINA-CONSOLIDATED	SEP	53.0	54.2	41.7	56.9	48.0
RYKOFF-SEXTON INC	†APR	20.9	6.7	NM	19.6	4.9
SARA LEE CORP	JUN	14.7	20.6	24.7	24.7	6.1
SEABOARD CORP	DEC	17.8	9.3	12.2	5.5	10.8
SMUCKER (JM) CO -CL A	†APR	17.8	17.0	17.3	13.4	14.7
TASTY BAKING CO	DEC	3.5	14.4	14.6	12.5	18.4
TOOTSIE ROLL INDS	DEC	18.8	18.8	19.2	18.0	16.8
TYSON FOODS INC -CL A	SEP	21.6	19.6	17.8	18.4	NM
UNIVERSAL FOODS CORP	SEP	22.1	19.6	18.4	16.1	16.1
WRIGLEY (WM) JR CO	DEC	31.5	29.8	30.9	32.6	36.5
ANHEUSER-BUSCH COS INC	DEC	24.9	23.2	22.0	13.4	23.8

Data by Standard & Poor's Compustat, A Division of The McGraw-Hill Companies

Return on Revenues (%) / Return on Assets (%) / Return on Equity (%)

Company	Yr. End	RoR 1990	RoR 1991	RoR 1992	RoR 1993	RoR 1994	RoA 1990	RoA 1991	RoA 1992	RoA 1993	RoA 1994	RoE 1990	RoE 1991	RoE 1992	RoE 1993	RoE 1994
BREWERS (cont'd)																
BASS PLC -ADR	SEP	8.6	8.4	7.9	7.1	7.8	7.8	5.8	5.5	4.7	5.7	14.6	10.9	9.9	8.5	10.2
* COORS (ADOLPH) -CL B	DEC	2.1	1.2	2.3	NM	3.5	2.4	1.3	2.1	NM	4.3	3.6	2.2	4.0	NM	8.9
DISTILLERS																
* BROWN-FORMAN -CL B	†APR	13.0	11.6	11.0	11.5	10.5	13.8	12.9	12.5	12.7	11.8	23.5	21.3	20.4	25.5	30.1
GRAND MET PLC -ADR	SEP	6.9	7.7	8.1	5.6	6.3	7.7	6.8	6.8	3.9	4.7	21.9	18.7	17.6	10.1	12.8
* SEAGRAM CO LTD	†JAN	15.0	13.8	9.1	7.3	14.6	7.0	6.2	4.3	3.5	6.6	13.4	11.7	8.3	7.6	15.4
SOFT DRINKS & OTHER BEVERAGES																
COCA-COLA BTLNG CONS	DEC	0.1	0.6	0.3	2.2	2.0	0.1	0.5	0.3	2.1	2.2	NM	1.4	NM	53.5	44.5
* COCA-COLA CO	DEC	13.5	14.0	14.4	15.7	15.8	15.7	16.6	17.7	19.0	19.7	39.2	39.5	45.3	51.7	52.0
* COCA-COLA ENTERPRISES	DEC	2.3	NM		NM	NM	1.9	NM	NM	NM	0.8	5.5	NM			
* PEPSICO INC	DEC	6.1	5.5	5.9	6.3	6.3	6.8	6.0	6.6	7.1	7.4	24.8	20.7	23.9	27.2	27.0
TOBACCO																
* AMERICAN BRANDS INC/DE	DEC	7.2	9.6	10.0	8.1	11.8	4.7	5.6	5.9	4.3	6.8	17.7	20.3	20.7	15.6	19.9
BROOKE GROUP LTD	DEC	39.2	NM	NM	NM	0.6	78.7	NM	NM	NM	NM					
CULBRO CORP	NOV	0.4	0.3	0.2	0.1		0.8	0.9	0.5	0.2	0.3	2.5	2.6	1.6	0.9	1.0
* PHILIP MORRIS COS INC	DEC	8.0	8.2	9.9	7.0	8.8	8.3	8.4	10.1	7.1	9.1	32.9	32.1	39.4	29.5	38.7
RJR NABISCO HLDGS CORP	DEC	NM	2.5	4.9	NM	5.0	NM	1.1	2.4	NM	2.4	NM	3.6	9.0	NM	7.3
* UST INC	DEC	29.7	30.2	30.9	34.1	32.4	35.5	41.6	47.0	53.5	53.5	46.7	55.6	62.5	75.3	94.0
UNIVERSAL CORP/VA	JUN	1.3	1.9	2.4	2.6	1.3	3.3	4.6	5.6	5.7	2.4	9.5	14.3	20.5	22.3	9.7

Note: Data as originally reported.
* Company included in the Standard & Poor's 500.   † Of the following calendar year.

Current Ratio / Debt / Capital Ratio (%) / Debt as % of Net Working Capital

Company	Yr. End	CR 1990	CR 1991	CR 1992	CR 1993	CR 1994	D/C 1990	D/C 1991	D/C 1992	D/C 1993	D/C 1994	NWC 1990	NWC 1991	NWC 1992	NWC 1993	NWC 1994
FOOD																
AMERICAN MAIZE-PRODS -CL A	DEC	1.6	3.6	4.0	3.0	2.6	21.3	31.4	31.8	36.1	38.0	117.0	92.4	87.2	136.2	164.4
* ARCHER-DANIELS-MIDLAND CO	JUN	3.4	3.0	3.4	4.1	3.5	15.9	18.3	23.9	27.8	27.0	46.1	58.5	68.6	68.9	72.6
* CPC INTERNATIONAL INC	DEC	1.1	1.3	1.2	1.2	1.1	36.6	35.2	34.5	32.0	31.7	620.4	235.5	275.1	231.1	692.1
CAGLE'S INC -CL A	†MAR	2.1	1.8	2.2	2.1	1.7	36.1	39.1	36.2	23.3	23.8	97.6	122.0	92.3	59.9	86.6
* CAMPBELL SOUP CO	JUL	1.3	1.2	1.2	0.9	1.0	28.9	27.1	22.9	19.0	19.4	219.3	321.2	343.4	NM	NM
CHIQUITA BRANDS INTL	DEC	1.6	2.4	1.8	1.5	1.4	43.1	55.9	67.7	70.5	67.9	119.1	124.7	292.6	539.1	516.2
CONAGRA INC	†MAY	1.1	1.1	1.1	1.1	NA	49.1	45.1	47.3	45.1	NA	819.2	732.8	1008.5	565.1	NA
DEAN FOODS CO	†MAY	2.0	1.9	2.0	1.3	NA	25.0	24.8	22.4	18.8	NA	75.6	84.7	76.2	146.5	NA
DOLE FOOD CO INC	DEC	1.4	1.7	1.5	1.7	1.9	36.3	43.2	42.9	44.6	51.8	209.3	197.4	294.4	240.2	242.6
FLOWERS INDUSTRIES INC	JUN	1.6	1.6	1.4	1.3	1.5	26.9	28.0	27.7	10.3	22.9	189.7	244.4	216.7	113.6	170.2
* GENERAL MILLS INC	†MAY	0.9	0.8	0.7	0.6	0.7	35.9	33.8	43.1	44.6	71.5	NM	NM	NM	NM	NM
* HEINZ (H J) CO	†APR	1.5	0.8	0.9	1.4	1.1	21.5	6.2	28.6	40.0	45.2	103.9	NM	NM	288.2	898.5
* HERSHEY FOODS CORP	DEC	1.9	1.6	1.3	1.1	1.2	16.4	15.8	9.5	9.5	8.8	85.3	103.4	85.8	220.6	103.1
HORMEL FOODS CORP	OCT	2.5	2.7	2.9	2.7	2.7	4.3	3.6	1.1	1.0	1.5	8.4	6.6	6.6	1.5	2.3
IBP INC	DEC	1.5	1.6	1.9	1.9	1.6	47.0	48.6	46.0	40.0	29.6	216.3	214.1	154.9	136.8	100.7
INTL MULTIFOODS CORP	†FEB	1.4	1.4	1.7	1.5	1.5	24.3	23.8	32.6	41.4	37.1	99.9	81.3	96.9	141.9	117.6
* KELLOGG CO	DEC	0.9	0.9	1.2	1.0	1.2	11.6	0.6	12.9	21.5	26.4	NM	NM	190.2	1710.2	289.7
* MCCORMICK & CO	NOV	1.3	1.2	1.4	1.4	1.4	34.0	31.8	28.8	40.6	42.4	205.3	244.4	414.4	235.2	658.6
PIONEER HI-BRED INTERNATIONL	AUG	1.8	2.1	2.5	2.7	3.2	2.8	8.9	8.4	7.6	6.9	7.7	21.7	17.7	14.9	12.9
* QUAKER OATS CO	JUN	1.3	1.4	1.2	1.0	1.0	35.5	35.5	36.5	49.2	58.3	216.0	211.7	341.6		
RALSTON PURINA-CONSOLIDATED	SEP	1.2	1.4	1.0	1.1	1.0	69.8	65.1	67.4	71.1	71.0	796.1	430.1	6032.3	1088.8	2584.4
RYKOFF-SEXTON INC	†APR	2.4	2.2	2.1	2.1	2.0	31.6	40.8	45.8	45.6	40.2	55.0	85.4	96.1	94.6	90.7
* SARA LEE CORP	JUN	1.2	1.2	1.1	0.9	0.9	31.6	27.0	23.5	19.8	25.1	395.3	355.6	351.6	NM	NM
SEABOARD CORP	DEC	2.7	2.8	3.2	3.2	3.3	22.5	21.7	20.2	37.5	32.7	60.4	42.0	0.0	70.4	68.5
SMUCKER (JM) CO -CL A	†APR	2.8	3.0	3.0	2.1	2.4	2.1	1.7	0.0	17.0	20.3	4.7	3.5		54.9	59.9
TASTY BAKING CO (cont'd)	DEC	1.9	2.1	2.1	1.8	2.0	30.6	29.4	24.9	27.0	18.6	82.8	73.9	60.1	104.0	60.9

Data by Standard & Poor's Compustat, A Division of The McGraw-Hill Companies

Current Ratio · Debt / Capital Ratio (%) · Debt as % of Net Working Capital

Company	Yr. End	Current Ratio 1990	1991	1992	1993	1994	Debt/Capital 1990	1991	1992	1993	1994	Debt % NWC 1990	1991	1992	1993	1994
FOOD (cont'd)																
TOOTSIE ROLL INDS	DEC	3.5	4.8	5.8	2.2	4.5	0.0	0.0	3.9	11.2	10.0	0.0	0.0	7.0	45.0	29.7
TYSON FOODS INC -CL A	SEP	1.2	1.2	1.6	1.5	2.3	47.1	40.4	33.8	33.8	44.2	925.4	755.8	339.4	322.9	191.5
UNIVERSAL FOODS CORP	SEP	1.7	1.8	1.6	1.8	1.7	31.3	32.6	33.9	34.6	33.3	129.1	120.0	145.2	125.0	126.9
WRIGLEY (WM) JR CO	DEC	2.8	3.2	3.0	3.2	3.0	0.0	0.0	0.0	0.0	0.0	0.0	0.0	0.0	0.0	0.0
BREWERS																
* ANHEUSER-BUSCH COS INC	DEC	1.0	1.2	1.2	1.0	1.1	38.3	30.8	30.9	35.8	35.2	21855.0	1176.0	742.3	NM	1598.3
BASS PLC -ADR	SEP	0.9	1.4	1.6	1.4	1.1	32.9	26.7	28.7	29.1	24.8	NM	275.5	227.9	387.0	697.1
COORS (ADOLPH) -CL B	DEC	1.6	1.3	1.4	1.0	0.9	8.0	14.9	22.3	20.3	14.9	54.7	199.2	195.9	243.6	NM
DISTILLERS																
† BROWN-FORMAN -CL B	APR	3.3	3.0	3.4	2.3	2.4	12.9	11.9	14.3	34.6	27.2	26.0	26.1	30.3	81.1	59.9
GRAND MET PLC -ADR	SEP	1.2	1.4	1.5	1.5	1.3	46.4	44.0	39.4	44.3	39.2	507.5	335.5	217.9	250.8	239.6
† SEAGRAM CO LTD	JAN	1.3	2.3	1.9	1.3	1.0	25.0	31.1	33.3	36.8	33.9	242.6	123.9	139.6	382.6	3342.4
SOFT DRINKS & OTHER BEVERAGES																
COCA-COLA BTLNG CONS	DEC	0.8	0.8	0.7	0.7	0.8	58.0	68.9	80.4	79.8	77.8	NM	NM	NM	NM	NM
* COCA-COLA CO	DEC	1.0	1.0	0.8	0.9	0.8	11.5	17.6	22.0	23.3	20.8	NM	NM	NM	NM	NM
COCA-COLA ENTERPRISES	DEC	0.5	0.5	0.5	0.7	0.7	50.0	66.3	55.4	56.9	54.7	NM	3692.4	NM	NM	NM
* PEPSICO INC	DEC	0.9	1.2	1.1	0.8	1.0	50.2	54.1	53.1	47.1	50.0	NM	924.9	1537.9	NM	NM
TOBACCO																
* AMERICAN BRANDS INC/DE	DEC	NA	NA	NA	NA	1.5	37.5	35.9	34.6	36.2	24.1	NA	NA	NA	NA	97.2
BROOKE GROUP LTD	DEC	1.1	0.6	0.9	0.5	0.6	145.7	932.5	NM	NM	131.3	870.4	NM	NM	NM	NM
CULBRO CORP	NOV	2.3	2.5	2.0	2.4	3.9	55.1	50.3	52.6	58.1	45.9	145.7	147.5	134.4	138.0	126.3
* PHILIP MORRIS COS INC	DEC	NA	NA	NA	NA	NA	52.4	48.7	48.0	50.6	48.1	NM	NM	1829.2	5943.1	NA
RJR NABISCO HLDGS CORP	DEC	0.8	1.0	1.2	1.1	0.8	67.7	51.4	51.7	48.3	37.7	NM	7969.1			NM
* UST INC	DEC	3.9	3.2	4.1	3.1	2.4	0.6	0.0	0.0	7.8	25.4	1.6	0.0	0.0	17.5	56.5
UNIVERSAL CORP/VA	JUN	1.6	1.3	1.4	1.4	1.4	25.1	27.7	36.4	38.3	43.0	54.6	71.6	69.6	93.8	93.7

Note: Data as originally reported.   * Company included in the Standard & Poor's 500.   † Of the following calendar year.

Price-Earnings Ratio (High-Low) · Dividend Payout Ratio (%) · Yield (High % - Low %)

Company	Yr. End	P-E 1990	1991	1992	1993	1994	Payout 1990	1991	1992	1993	1994	Yield 1990	1991	1992	1993	1994
FOOD																
AMERICAN MAIZE-PRODS -CL A	DEC	9- 6	12- 8	17- 13	NM- NM	10- 6	26	32	41	NM	25	3.0- 4.2	2.8- 3.8	2.5- 3.2	2.7- 4.5	2.5- 4.1
* ARCHER-DANIELS-MIDLAND CO	JUN	16- 11	22- 12	20- 14	18- 13	23- 15	5	6	6	6	7	0.3- 0.4	0.3- 0.5	0.3- 0.4	0.3- 0.5	0.3- 0.4
* CPC INTERNATIONAL INC	DEC	18- 13	18- 14	19- 14	18- 14	23- 20	41	42	43	43	61	2.4- 3.2	2.4- 3.1	2.3- 3.0	2.5- 3.2	2.5- 3.1
CAGLE'S INC -CL A	†MAR	11- 6	8- 6	8- 3	8- 4	8- 4	0	0	6	5	4	0.3- 0.4	0.8- 2.1	1.6- 2.3	2.0- 2.6	0.5- 1.2
* CAMPBELL SOUP CO	JUL	28- 17	28- 17	23- 16	44- 35	18- 14	NM	35	36	90	43	1.6- 2.3	1.3- 2.1	1.6- 2.3	2.0- 2.6	2.4- 3.2
CHIQUITA BRANDS INTL	DEC	14- 7	20- 12	NM- NM	NM- NM	NM- NM	16	22	NM	NM	NM	1.1- 2.2	1.1- 1.9	1.1- 2.4	4.3	1.0- 1.8
† CONAGRA INC	†MAY	18- 11	24- 15	23- 16	19- 13	NA- NA	31	35	38	38	NA	1.7- 2.9	1.4- 2.3	1.7- 2.1	2.1- 3.1	2.0- 2.7
DEAN FOODS CO	†MAY	15- 11	18- 13	18- 13	19- 16	NA- NA	28	37	35	36	NA	1.8- 2.4	1.7- 2.6	1.9- 2.6	2.8- 3.8	2.0- 2.7
DOLE FOOD CO INC	DEC	21- 12	24- 18	23- 16	19- 15	31- 20	5	18	37	31	35	0.3- 0.5	0.8- 1.5	1.0- 1.5	1.5- 2.2	1.0- 1.8
FLOWERS INDUSTRIES INC	JUN					25- 20	60	92	76	69	97	2.8- 5.0	3.8- 5.1	3.6- 4.5	3.6- 4.5	3.8- 4.8
* GENERAL MILLS INC	†MAY	18- 11	24- 14	24- 19	25- 19	38- 30	45	49	54	64	115	2.5- 4.1	2.0- 3.4	2.6- 3.3	2.9- 3.8	3.0- 3.8
* HEINZ (H J) CO	†APR	17- 13	20- 13	22- 17	17- 13	16- 13	44	44	57	55	59	2.2- 3.4	2.2- 3.4	2.5- 2.7	2.9- 3.8	3.0- 4.6
* HERSHEY FOODS CORP	DEC	17- 12	18- 14	18- 14	17- 13	25- 19	41	39	38	34	59	2.5- 3.5	2.1- 2.7	1.7- 2.2	1.7- 2.2	1.9- 2.7
HORMEL FOODS CORP	OCT	22- 15	20- 14	20- 14	16- 11	19- 12	26	29	29	34	32	1.3- 1.9	1.3- 1.9	1.5- 2.1	0.8- 1.1	1.9- 3.0
IBP INC	DEC	NM- NM	NM- NM	14- 11	16- 11	9- 6	59	NM	22	12	5	2.8- 4.1	2.3- 4.7	2.7- 3.4	0.8- 1.1	0.6- 0.9
INTL MULTIFOODS CORP	†FEB	14- 9	16- 11	14- 11	16- 11	6- 5	45	40	38	NM	25	3.3- 5.1	2.5- 3.8	3.4- 5.1	3.6- 4.6	4.2- 5.3
* KELLOGG CO	DEC	19- 14	27- 14	26- 18	23- 16	19- 15	46	43	42	45	44	1.6- 2.6	1.6- 3.1	2.2- 3.4	1.9- 2.8	2.9- 3.0
MCCORMICK & CO	NOV	16- 11	27- 13	24- 16	24- 16	33- 24	28	33	24	36	64	1.1- 1.9	1.1- 1.9	1.7- 2.4	2.0- 2.2	1.7- 2.2
PIONEER HI-BRED INTERNATIONL	AUG	20- 13	22- 10	18- 12	26- 16	17- 12	50	34	24	33	25	1.6- 3.0	1.6- 3.0	1.3- 2.3	2.1- 3.2	1.5- 2.0
QUAKER OATS CO	JUN	20- 14	25- 16	23- 15	20- 15	25- 18	48	51	53	49	63	2.1- 3.3	2.1- 3.3	2.5- 3.4	2.5- 3.2	2.5- 3.6

Data by Standard & Poor's Compustat, A Division of The McGraw-Hill Companies

Price-Earnings Ratio (High-Low) · Dividend Payout Ratio (%) · Yield (High % - Low %)

Company	Yr. End	P/E 1990	P/E 1991	P/E 1992	P/E 1993	P/E 1994	Payout 1990	Payout 1991	Payout 1992	Payout 1993	Payout 1994	Yield 1990	Yield 1991	Yield 1992	Yield 1993	Yield 1994
FOOD (cont'd)																
RALSTON PURINA-CONSOLIDATED	SEP	17-12	18-14	21-15	NA-NA	NA-NA	28	31	41	NA	NA	1.7-2.3	1.7-2.3	2.0-2.9	1.8-2.5	NA-NA
RYKOFF-SEXTON INC	†APR	20-12	22-14	NM-NM	NA-NA	28-22	50	55	NM	0	5	2.5-4.2	2.5-3.9	1.5-2.3	0.0-0.0	0.2-0.2
* SARA LEE CORP	JUN	17-13	27-14	21-15	22-15	59-44	42	43	40	40	142	2.4-3.4	1.6-3.1	1.9-2.6	1.8-2.7	2.4-3.2
SEABOARD CORP	DEC	7-5	12-8	9-5	24-16	9-7	2	4	2	7	4	0.4-0.5	0.3-0.5	0.3-0.4	0.3-0.4	0.5-0.6
* SMUCKER (JM) CO -CL A	†APR	22-15	34-17	31-19	31-19	21-16	32	33	33	44	40	1.5-2.1	1.0-1.9	1.1-1.7	1.4-2.3	1.9-2.4
TASTY BAKING CO	DEC	63-30	16-9	14-11	23-12	16-13	219	56	57	70	56	3.5-7.4	3.5-6.2	4.1-5.1	3.1-5.8	3.4-4.4
TOOTSIE ROLL INDS	DEC	21-13	28-13	27-19	25-19	21-15	10	9	9	11	12	0.5-0.7	0.3-0.7	0.3-0.5	0.4-0.6	0.6-0.8
TYSON FOODS INC -CL A	SEP	22-13	22-13	21-13	22-16	19-13	2	3	3	3	NM	0.1-0.2	0.1-0.2	0.2-0.3	0.2-0.2	0.3-0.4
UNIVERSAL FOODS CORP	SEP	17-12	19-13	25-17	17-14	18-13	35	35	54	41	47	2.0-3.4	1.9-2.7	2.6-3.2	2.4-2.9	2.7-3.5
* WRIGLEY (WM) JR CO	DEC	20-15	25-15	31-19	31-20	27-19	50	50	49	50	45	2.5-3.4	2.0-3.4	1.6-2.5	2.2-2.5	1.7-2.4
BREWERS																
* ANHEUSER-BUSCH COS INC	DEC	15-11	19-12	17-12	28-20	14-12	32	33	34	63	39	2.1-2.8	1.7-2.7	2.0-2.3	2.3-3.2	2.7-3.2
* BASS PLC -ADR	SEP	10-7	13-9	16-9	18-12	15-12	127	52	63	66	62	12.-18.3	4.1-5.8	3.8-5.5	3.7-5.3	4.2-5.1
* COORS (ADOLPH) -CL B	DEC	26-16	38-27	24-16	NM-NM	14-10	48	78	53	NM	33	1.8-2.9	2.1-2.9	2.2-3.2	2.2-3.3	2.4-3.4
DISTILLERS																
* BROWN-FORMAN -CL B	†APR	18-11	16-12	15-13	15-13	15-12	41	44	46	45	45	2.4-3.9	2.8-3.6	2.9-3.6	3.1-3.8	3.0-3.7
* GRAND MET PLC -ADR	†SEP	NA-NA	14-10	17-11	24-19	22-17	36	43	50	80	74	NA-NA	3.0-4.2	2.9-4.4	3.3-4.3	3.4-4.3
* SEAGRAM CO LTD	†JAN	12-9	15-11	25-20	30-24	15-12	23	26	43	55	27	2.0-2.6	1.7-2.5	1.8-2.2	1.8-2.3	1.8-2.2
SOFT DRINKS & OTHER BEVERAGES																
* COCA-COLA BTLNG CONS	DEC	NM-NM	NM-68	NM-NM	26-11	25-16	NM	367	NM	55	66	3.5-5.9	3.3-5.4	4.2-5.8	2.1-5.2	2.7-4.2
* COCA-COLA CO	DEC	24-16	34-18	32-25	27-22	27-20	39	NM	39	40	39	1.6-2.5	1.2-2.3	1.2-1.6	1.5-1.8	0.5-2.0
* COCA-COLA ENTERPRISES	DEC	26-19	NM-NM	NM-NM	38-27	38-23	8	NM	32	31	10	0.3-2.4	0.3-2.0	0.2-1.7	0.4-1.8	0.4-0.4
* PEPSICO INC	DEC	20-13	27-17	27-19	22-18	19-13	28	34	32	31	32	1.4-2.1	1.3-2.0	1.2-1.7	1.4-1.8	1.7-2.4
TOBACCO																
* AMERICAN BRANDS INC/DE	DEC	14-10	12-9	12-9	12-9	9-7	47	41	42	60	46	3.4-4.6	3.3-4.5	3.6-4.6	4.9-6.9	5.2-6.8
BROOKE GROUP LTD	DEC	1-0	NM-NM	NM-NM	81-56	NM-NM	4	NM	NM	NM	0	4.5-9.1	7.3-14.7	6.6-16.8	0.0-0.0	0.0-0.0
CULBRO CORP	NOV	50-17	35-18	49-33	19-11	65-48	111	108	186	64	0	3.8-6.4	3.1-6.0	3.8-5.6	0.0-0.0	0.0-0.0
* PHILIP MORRIS COS INC	DEC	14-9	19-11	16-13	NM-NM	12-9	40	45	43	NM	56	3.0-4.3	2.3-4.0	2.7-3.6	3.4-5.8	4.7-6.4
RJR NABISCO HLDGS CORP	DEC	NA-NA	59-25	21-14	NM-NM	20-13	NM	0	0	0	NM	NA-NA	NA-NA	0.0-0.0	0.0-0.0	0.0-0.0
* UST INC	DEC	19-13	20-14	25-18	19-14	17-13	56	56	57	56	60	3.0-4.4	1.9-4.0	2.3-3.2	2.9-3.9	3.6-4.7
UNIVERSAL CORP/VA	JUN	16-10	20-7	16-10	14-9	9-7	66	44	27	35	84	4.0-6.6	2.2-6.6	1.7-2.7	2.5-3.9	3.5-5.3

* Company included in the Standard & Poor's 500. † Of the following calendar year.

Note: Data as originally reported.

Earnings per Share · Book Value per Share · Share Price (High-Low)

Company	Yr. End	EPS 1990	EPS 1991	EPS 1992	EPS 1993	EPS 1994	Book 1990	Book 1991	Book 1992	Book 1993	Book 1994	Price 1990	Price 1991	Price 1992	Price 1993	Price 1994
FOOD																
AMERICAN MAIZE-PRODS -CL A	DEC	2.44	2.00	1.55	0.02	2.63	21.59	22.08	23.52	18.13	20.43	21.00-15.13	23.13-16.75	25.75-20.00	23.50-14.38	26.00-15.88
* ARCHER-DANIELS-MIDLAND CO	JUN	0.85	0.81	0.89	0.94	0.89	6.26	7.10	8.12	8.87	9.77	13.52-9.08	18.24-10.12	17.96-12.27	16.70-12.67	20.12-13.53
* CPC INTERNATIONAL INC	DEC	2.42	2.61	2.78	2.95	2.25	4.77	6.18	5.40	6.37	5.06	42.38-31.00	46.75-36.00	51.63-39.75	51.13-39.88	55.63-44.25
CAGLE'S INC -CL A	†MAR	0.32	0.36	0.99	1.66	2.67	3.63	4.05	5.07	6.59	8.81	3.50-1.85	3.05-2.00	7.45-2.80	12.55-7.15	22.63-10.75
* CAMPBELL SOUP CO	JUL	0.02	1.58	1.95	1.02	2.51	5.06	5.35	6.31	4.40	5.67	31.00-21.88	43.88-27.06	45.25-31.50	45.38-35.25	46.00-34.25
CHIQUITA BRANDS INTL	DEC	2.23	2.55	-4.28	-0.99	-1.07	11.53	15.38	9.14	7.89	5.86	32.13-16.00	50.75-29.38	40.13-15.25	17.75-10.00	19.38-11.25
* CONAGRA INC	†MAY	1.42	1.50	1.58	1.81	NA	-4.26	-2.12	-2.45	-1.61	NA	25.50-15.17	36.50-22.33	35.75-24.50	33.63-22.75	33.13-25.50
DEAN FOODS CO	†MAY	1.79	1.53	1.73	1.78	NA	9.36	10.00	11.11	10.64	NA	27.25-20.17	33.50-24.83	31.50-22.75	32.88-23.13	33.50-25.25
DOLE FOOD CO INC	DEC	2.03	2.24	1.09	1.30	1.14	15.58	15.58	16.80	17.54	17.97	38.63-26.25	48.00-28.00	40.00-26.00	37.88-25.88	35.50-22.50
FLOWERS INDUSTRIES INC	JUN	0.98	0.71	0.92	1.07	0.80	6.27	6.27	6.36/	7.43/	7.35/	20.88-11.88	21.25-14.75	21.25-14.75	20.50-16.38	20.25-16.00
* GENERAL MILLS INC	†MAY	2.82	3.05	3.10	2.95	1.64	6.26	7.79	7.15	6.27	0.13	52.00-31.38	73.63-43.50	75.88-58.75	74.13-56.88	62.25-49.38
* HEINZ (H J) CO	†APR	2.13	2.40	2.04	2.35	2.38	5.88	4.67	3.73	4.00	0.52	37.00-27.50	48.63-31.50	45.50-35.13	45.13-34.13	39.00-30.75
* HERSHEY FOODS CORP	DEC	2.39	2.43	2.69	3.31	2.12	9.16	10.13	11.81	10.72	11.39	39.63-28.25	44.50-35.13	48.38-38.25	55.88-43.50	53.50-41.13
HORMEL FOODS CORP	OCT	1.01	1.13	1.24	1.31	1.54	5.96	7.02	7.88	6.50	7.59	19.75-14.00	23.13-16.00	24.75-16.75	25.50-20.25	26.75-18.75
IBP INC	DEC	1.01	0.03	1.34	1.62	3.79	5.83	5.39	6.61	8.21	11.88	21.75-14.75	26.25-12.88	20.63-14.50	26.25-17.50	35.50-22.63
INTL MULTIFOODS CORP (cont d)	†FEB	1.81	2.00	2.13	-0.72	3.16	10.50	16.19/	16.64/	13.63/	16.16/	24.92-16.08	31.50-22.00	29.25-23.25	27.50-17.25	19.13-15.13

Data by Standard & Poor's Compustat, A Division of The McGraw-Hill Companies

Earnings per Share / Book Value per Share / Share Price (High-Low)

Company	Yr. End	EPS 1990	EPS 1991	EPS 1992	EPS 1993	EPS 1994	BV 1990	BV 1991	BV 1992	BV 1993	BV 1994	SP 1990	SP 1991	SP 1992	SP 1993	SP 1994
FOOD (cont'd)																
* KELLOGG CO	DEC	2.08	2.51	2.86	2.94	3.15	7.62	8.77	7.97	7.26	8.13	38.75-29.38	67.00-35.00	75.38-54.38	67.88-47.25	60.75-47.38
* MCCORMICK & CO	NOV	0.83	0.98	1.16	1.22	0.75	3.61	4.00	4.36	4.15	3.62	13.25-9.00	26.50-12.25	30.25-20.50	29.75-20.00	24.75-17.75
* PIONEER HI-BRED INTERNATIONL	AUG	0.78	1.15	1.68	1.53	2.40	6.92	7.28	8.54	8.92	9.96	15.63-10.42	24.75-11.83	30.25-19.75	35.50-24.13	40.50-29.50
* QUAKER OATS CO	JUN	1.47	1.53	1.63	1.97	1.68	3.64	2.98	2.82	0.86	-0.36	29.75-20.50	37.88-23.88	37.19-25.13	38.50-30.19	42.50-29.69
RALSTON PURINA-CONSOLIDATED	SEP	3.23	3.34	2.82	NA	NA	0.51	2.69	-0.64	-1.35	-1.70	54.19-38.88	60.13-46.00	58.88-40.88	52.13-37.88	NA-NA
† RYKOFF-SEXTON INC	†APR	0.95	0.87	-1.35	0.50	0.64	12.86/	13.09/	11.50/	11.91/	14.15/	19.30-11.40	19.20-12.30	16.90-11.10	17.80-10.80	18.00-14.10
* SARA LEE CORP	JUN	0.96	1.08	1.54	1.40	0.44	4.97	5.48	7.05	7.32	6.92	16.69-12.06	29.06-14.81	32.44-23.31	31.13-21.00	26.00-19.38
SEABOARD CORP	DEC	20.19	14.28	20.89	10.63	23.67	147.01	160.79	181.17	204.37	232.58	140-100	169-108	187-114	257-174	205-158
* SMUCKER (JM) CO -CL A	†APR	1.08	1.16	1.27	1.05	1.25	5.68	6.47	6.76	5.99	6.08	23.19-16.06	38.88-20.00	39.00-24.50	23.38-20.25	26.00-20.50
TASTY BAKING CO	DEC	0.32	1.30	1.41	0.93	0.94	8.45	9.08	9.75	4.93	5.37	20.25-9.50	20.50-11.75	19.50-15.63	21.38-11.38	15.50-12.00
* TOOTSIE ROLL INDS	DEC	1.01	1.19	1.43	1.58	1.70	3.67	4.75	6.11	4.96	6.35	21.57-13.37	33.32-15.85	38.66-27.34	39.29-30.40	36.41-26.21
* TYSON FOODS INC -CL A	SEP	0.91	1.05	1.16	1.22	-0.01	-0.89	0.43	1.72	2.96	3.77	17.69-11.38	23.25-14.00	24.88-15.25	27.13-19.25	25.00-18.75
* UNIVERSAL FOODS CORP	SEP	1.95	2.18	1.57	2.15	1.95	6.10	7.38	7.42	7.49	6.89	33.88-23.25	40.38-28.63	39.50-26.63	37.25-30.38	34.38-26.13
* WRIGLEY (WM) JR CO	DEC	1.00	1.09	1.27	1.50	1.98	3.42	3.95	4.27	4.94	5.92	19.75-14.58	27.00-16.38	39.88-22.13	46.13-29.50	53.88-38.13
BREWERS																
* ANHEUSER-BUSCH COS INC	DEC	2.96	3.26	3.48	2.17	3.91	11.14	13.75	14.78	14.08	15.28	45.25-34.00	62.00-39.25	60.75-51.75	60.25-43.00	55.38-47.13
BASS PLC -ADR	SEP	2.05	1.62	1.41	1.09	1.26	15.48	14.74	13.77	11.76	12.94	21.38-14.25	20.50-14.50	23.25-16.25	19.38-13.50	18.50-15.13
* COORS (ADOLPH) -CL B	DEC	1.05	0.64	0.95	-1.10	1.52	28.59	28.64	17.81	16.21	17.06	27.38-17.38	24.25-17.38	22.88-15.50	22.63-15.00	20.88-14.75
DISTILLERS																
* BROWN-FORMAN -CL B	†APR	1.74	1.76	1.88	2.04	2.15	5.33	5.78	6.37	2.54	3.94	30.58-18.67	28.17-21.58	30.00-24.00	29.58-24.33	32.50-26.13
GRAND MET PLC -ADR	SEP	2.40	2.32	2.18	1.02	1.36	4.05	3.30	4.34	2.25	2.26	NA-NA	32.88-23.38	37.25-24.38	29.00-22.38	30.00-23.13
* SEAGRAM CO LTD	†JAN	2.01	1.92	1.26	1.02	2.18	11.66	13.00	9.09	9.28	10.58	23.50-18.00	29.50-20.41	30.88-25.13	30.38-24.50	32.63-26.25
SOFT DRINKS & OTHER BEVERAGES																
COCA-COLA BTLNG CONS	DEC	-0.03	0.24	-0.23	1.60	1.52	-12.94	-40.28	-56.60	-33.39	-31.61	25.00-15.00	26.50-16.25	20.75-15.25	41.50-17.00	37.25-24.00
* COCA-COLA CO	DEC	1.02	1.22	1.43	1.68	1.98	2.62	3.10	-2.68	3.11	3.59	24.50-16.31	40.88-21.31	45.38-35.56	45.13-37.50	53.50-38.88
* COCA-COLA ENTERPRISES	DEC	0.65	-0.79	-0.11	0.52	0.52	-14.55	-21.41	9.70/	9.53/	10.14/	16.88-12.25	20.38-11.75	16.25-11.25	15.88-11.75	19.50-14.00
* PEPSICO INC	DEC	1.37	1.35	1.61	1.96	2.22	-1.19	-0.49	-2.01	-1.99	-1.25	27.88-18.00	36.50-23.50	43.38-30.50	43.63-34.50	41.13-29.25
TOBACCO																
* AMERICAN BRANDS INC/DE	DEC	2.99	3.91	4.29	3.30	4.38	2.83	3.83	5.33	2.51	5.33	41.63-30.88	47.63-35.63	49.88-39.00	40.63-28.50	38.38-29.38
BROOKE GROUP LTD	DEC	15.69	-6.91	-2.46	-0.74	1.02	-1.06	-22.10	-26.73	-34.28	-20.90	12.50-6.13	9.63-4.75	6.38-2.50	6.13-1.25	5.38-1.25
CULBRO CORP	NOV	0.72	4.24	5.45	4.06	5.45	23.53	-22.44	-22.92	-22.76	21.60	32.25-12.50	25.88-13.25	22.25-14.38	19.50-14.38	17.50-12.88
* PHILIP MORRIS COS INC	DEC	3.83	1.10	2.75	-0.25	2.05						52.00-36.00	65.00-27.50	86.63-69.50	77.63-45.00	64.50-47.25
* RJR NABISCO HLDGS CORP	DEC	-5.95					-178	-63.41	-60.68	-60.62	-42.56	NA	NA	58.75-39.38	46.25-21.88	40.63-26.56
* UST INC	DEC	0.98	1.18	1.41	1.71	1.87	2.19	2.22	2.38	2.20	1.79	18.25-12.38	34.00-16.38	35.38-25.25	32.75-24.38	31.50-23.63
UNIVERSAL CORP/VA	JUN	1.11	1.72	2.15	2.39	1.09	11.10	11.43	8.83	7.81	6.46	18.06-11.00	34.00-11.81	34.25-22.25	33.75-21.75	26.25-17.50

Note: Data as originally reported.

* Company included in the Standard & Poor's 500.   † Of the following calendar year.   I - This amount includes intangibles that cannot be identified.

Information has been obtained from sources believed to be reliable, but its accuracy and completeness, and that of the opinions based thereon, are not guaranteed. Printed in the United States of America. Industry Surveys is a publication of Standard & Poor's Equity Research Department. This Department operates independently of, and has no access to information obtained by, S&P's Corporate Bond Rating Department, which may, through its regular operations, obtain information of a confidential nature.

Data by *Standard & Poor's Compustat, A Division of The McGraw-Hill Companies*

Tootsie Roll Industries   2242P

NYSE Symbol **TR**

12-SEP-95 **Industry:** Food

Summary: This company is a major manufacturer and distributor of candy, sold primarily under the Tootsie Roll brand name, and is the largest U.S. confectioner of lollipops.

Quantitative Evaluations	
Outlook (1 Lowest—5 Highest) • **3**	
Fair Value • **39¼**	
Risk • **Low**	
Earn./Div. Rank • **A**	
Technical Eval. • **Bullish** since 7/95	
Rel. Strength Rank (1 Lowest—99 Highest) • **68**	
Insider Activity • **NA**	

Recent Price • 39¼   Yield • 0.6%
52 Wk Range • 41-26¼   12-Mo. P/E • 22.6

Earnings vs. Previous Year
▲=Up ▼=Down ▶=No Change

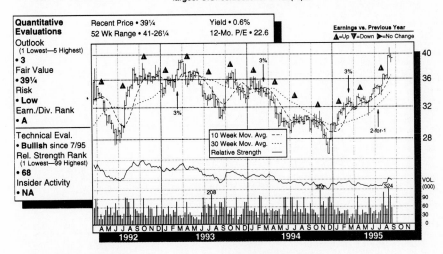

10 Week Mov. Avg. – – –
30 Week Mov. Avg. · · · ·
Relative Strength —

2-for-1

Business Profile - 12-SEP-95

This conservatively managed candy producer has reported 18 consecutive annual sales increases, and has distributed an annual stock dividend for 30 consecutive years. Its strong balance sheet continues to improve. Future growth is expected to come from line extensions, acquisitions, and expansion in the Far East and other international markets. The shares, recently trading at 20X the analyst 1996 EPS estimate of $2.00, are at a premium to the projected EPS growth rate.

Operational Review - 12-SEP-95

Net sales in the 26 weeks ended July 1, 1995, rose 8.2%, year to year, on volume increases attributable to product line extensions and successful promotions. Substantial gains in Mexican peso sales were outweighed by the sharp decline of the peso against the dollar. Gross margins narrowed, reflecting higher ingredient and packaging costs and a shift in product mix. Despite higher investment income and a lower tax rate, net income was up only 5.6%.

Stock Performance - 08-SEP-95

In the past 30 trading days, TR's shares have increased 12%, compared to a 2% rise in the S&P 500. Average trading volume for the past five days was 13,700 shares, compared with the 40-day moving average of 25,903 shares.

Key Stock Statistics

Dividend Rate/Share	0.25	Shareholders	9,500
Shs. outstg. (M)	22.3	Market cap. (B)	$0.877
Avg. daily vol. (M)	0.030	Inst. holdings	23%
Tang. Bk. Value/Share	6.34	Insider holdings	NA
Beta	0.83		

Value of $10,000 invested 5 years ago: $ 26,409

Fiscal Year Ending Dec. 31

	1995	% Change	1994	% Change	1993	% Change
Revenues (Million $)						
1Q	60.27	7%	56.37	13%	50.00	17%
2Q	68.77	9%	62.89	17%	53.92	5%
3Q	—	—	111.0	19%	93.24	7%
4Q	—	—	66.66	7%	62.41	-3%
Yr.	—	—	296.9	14%	259.6	6%
Income (Million $)						
1Q	7.32	5%	6.96	4%	6.70	21%
2Q	8.33	6%	7.86	7%	7.35	9%
3Q	—	—	15.39	7%	14.38	10%
4Q	—	—	7.72	10%	7.02	5%
Yr.	—	—	37.93	7%	35.44	11%
Earnings Per Share ($)						
1Q	0.33	6%	0.31	3%	0.30	24%
2Q	0.37	6%	0.35	6%	0.33	10%
3Q	—	—	0.69	7%	0.65	10%
4Q	—	—	0.34	9%	0.32	5%
Yr.	—	—	1.70	7%	1.58	11%

Next earnings report expected: late October

Tootsie Roll Industries

Business Summary - 12-SEP-95

Tootsie Roll Industries, Inc. is a major candy producer. Its most important product is the Tootsie Roll, a chocolate-flavored candy of a chewy consistency, sold in several sizes and also used as a center for other products in the line, including Tootsie Pops. Products also include Tootsie Pop Drops, Tootsie Roll Flavor Rolls and Tootsie Frooties. The company makes other candies under the Mason and Tootsie labels, including Mason Dots and Mason Crows, and produces a chocolate-covered cherry confection under the Cella's trademark.

In late 1993, Cambridge Brands Inc., the chocolate and caramel confections business of Warner-Lambert Co., was acquired for $81.3 million. Brands purchased included Junior Mints, Sugar Daddy, Sugar Babies, Charleston Chew and Pom Poms. In 1988, the company acquired Charms Co., a privately owned maker of lollipops and hard candy sold under the trademarks Charms, Blow-Pop and Zip-A-Dee-Doo-Da-Pops.

TR's products are marketed in a variety of packages designed for display and sold in various retail outlets and vending machines. Some 100 candy and grocery brokers and the company itself service about 15,000 customers throughout the U.S. Customers include wholesale distributors of candy and groceries, supermarkets, variety stores, drug chains, discount chains, vending machine operators and fund-raising organizations.

The company also sells its products in Mexico and Canada, which together accounted for 9.5% of 1994 sales, and operates a manufacturing facility in Mexico.

TR's business is somewhat seasonal, with a high proportion of sales and earnings in the third quarter in anticipation of Halloween. Each year after Halloween receivables have been paid, the company invests remaining funds in short-term marketable securities, such as money-market and other, similar short-term investments.

Principal raw materials used are sugar and corn syrup. From time to time, the company changes the size of certain products, which are usually sold at standard retail prices, to reflect significant changes in ingredient costs.

Important Developments

Aug. '95—TR said that although Mexican peso sales in the 26 weeks ended July 1, 1995, were up significantly, because of price increases and volume growth, translated U.S. dollar sales in Mexico were substantially lower, as a result of the sharp devaluation of the peso against the dollar.

Capitalization

Long Term Debt: $27,500,000 (7/1/95).

Per Share Data ($) (Year Ended Dec. 31)

	1994	1993	1992	1991	1990	1989
Tangible Bk. Val.	6.34	4.97	6.11	4.76	3.68	2.70
Cash Flow	4.67	1.92	1.70	1.46	1.24	1.12
Earnings	1.70	1.58	1.43	1.18	1.01	0.90
Dividends	0.21	0.17	0.13	0.11	0.10	0.10
Payout Ratio	12%	11%	9%	9%	10%	11%
Prices - High	36 3/8	39 1/4	38 5/8	33 3/8	21 1/2	16 1/8
- Low	26 1/4	30 3/8	27 3/8	15 7/8	13 3/8	10 1/4
P/E Ratio - High	21	25	27	28	21	18
- Low	15	19	19	13	13	11

Income Statement Analysis (Million $)

	1994	%Chg	1993	%Chg	1992	%Chg	1991
Revs.	297	14%	260	6%	245	18%	208
Oper. Inc.	70.5	16%	61.0	13%	53.9	14%	47.2
Depr.	10.5	39%	7.5	26%	6.0	NM	6.0
Int. Exp.	1.6	158%	0.6	45%	0.4	120%	0.2
Pretax Inc.	61.2	6%	57.7	11%	51.9	17%	44.2
Eff. Tax Rate	38%	—	39%	—	38%	—	40%
Net Inc.	37.9	7%	35.4	11%	32.0	21%	26.5

Balance Sheet & Other Fin. Data (Million $)

	1994	1993	1992	1991	1990	1989
Cash	62.4	56.2	88.9	65.3	36.8	18.5
Curr. Assets	119	112	130	102	78.0	54.0
Total Assets	310	304	222	184	160	136
Curr. Liab.	26.3	50.9	22.5	21.2	22.6	20.7
LT Debt	27.5	27.5	7.5	Nil	Nil	Nil
Common Eqty.	240	212	182	153	130	110
Total Cap.	276	246	193	158	136	114
Cap. Exp.	8.2	52.5	12.5	6.6	5.2	3.1
Cash Flow	48.4	43.0	38.0	32.5	27.7	25.0

Ratio Analysis

	1994	1993	1992	1991	1990	1989
Curr. Ratio	4.5	2.2	5.8	4.8	3.5	2.6
% LT Debt of Cap.	10.0	11.2	3.9	Nil	Nil	Nil
% Net Inc.of Revs.	12.8	13.7	13.1	12.8	11.6	11.3
% Ret. on Assets	12.4	13.5	15.7	15.4	15.2	15.2
% Ret. on Equity	16.8	18.0	19.2	18.8	18.8	20.1

Dividend Data —Dividends have been paid since 1943. Payments are identical on the common and Class B common shares.

Amt. of Div. $	Date Decl.	Ex-Div. Date	Stock of Record	Payment Date
0.110	Dec. 07	Dec. 16	Dec. 22	Jan. 12 '95
3% Stk.	Feb. 21	Mar. 06	Mar. 10	Apr. 21 '95
0.110	Feb. 21	Mar. 06	Mar. 10	Apr. 11 '95
0.125	May. 31	Jun. 20	Jun. 22	Jul. 11 '95
2-for-1	May. 31	Jul. 12	Jun. 22	Jul. 11 '95

Data as orig. reptd.; bef. results of disc. opers. and/or spec. items. Per share data adj. for stk. divs. as of ex-div. date. E-Estimated. NA-Not Available. NM-Not Meaningful. NR-Not Ranked.

Office—7401 South Cicero Ave., Chicago, IL 60629. **Tel**—(312) 838-3400. **Chrmn & CEO**—M. J. Gordon. **Pres & COO**—E. R. Gordon. **Treas**—B. P. Bowen. **Secy**—W. Touretz. **VP-Fin**—G. H. Ember, Jr. **Dirs**—E. R. Gordon, M. J. Gordon, L. J. Lewis-Brent, C. W. Seibert, W. Touretz. **Transfer Agent & Registrar**—Chemical Bank, NYC. **Incorporated** in Virginia in 1919. **Empl**-1,700. **S&P Analyst:** Efraim Levy

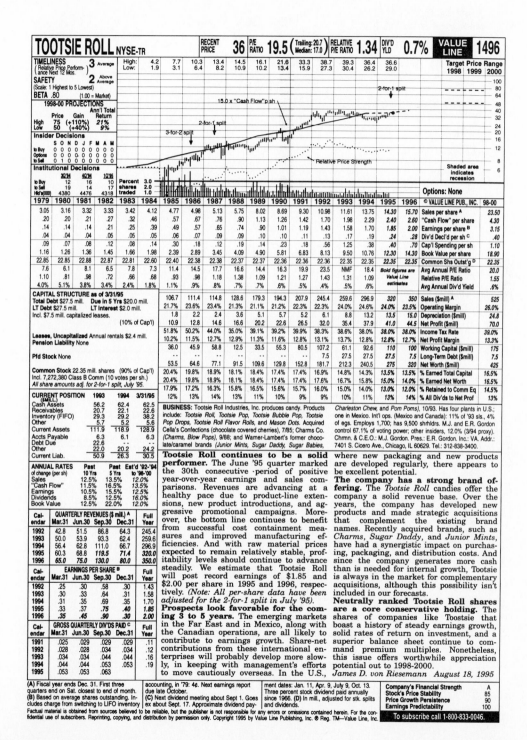

TOOTSIE ROLL NYSE-TR

| RECENT PRICE | 36 | P/E RATIO | 19.5 | (Trailing: 20.7 / Median: 17.0) | RELATIVE P/E RATIO | 1.34 | DIV'D YLD | 0.7% | VALUE LINE | 1496 |

TIMELINESS 3 Average (Relative Price Performance Next 12 Mos.)

SAFETY 2 Above Average (Scale: 1 Highest to 5 Lowest)

BETA .80 (1.00 = Market)

1998-00 PROJECTIONS

	Price	Gain	Ann'l Total Return
High	75	(+110%)	21%
Low	50	(+40%)	9%

Insider Decisions

	S	O	N	D	J	F	M	A	M
to Buy	0	0	0	0	0	0	0	0	0
Options	0	0	0	0	0	0	0	0	0
to Sell	0	1	0	0	0	0	0	0	0

Institutional Decisions

	3Q'94	4Q'94	1Q'95
to Buy	12	16	10
to Sell	19	14	17
Hld's(000)	4380	4476	4318

Percent shares traded: 3.0 / 2.0 / 1.0

High: 4.2 7.7 10.3 13.4 14.5 16.1 21.6 33.3 38.7 39.3 36.4 36.6
Low: 1.9 3.1 6.4 8.2 10.9 10.2 13.4 15.9 27.3 30.4 26.2 29.0

Target Price Range 1998 1999 2000

15.0 x "Cash Flow" p sh
2-for-1 split
3-for-2 split
Relative Price Strength
Shaded area indicates recession

Options: None

1979	1980	1981	1982	1983	1984	1985	1986	1987	1988	1989	1990	1991	1992	1993	1994	1995	1996	© VALUE LINE PUB., INC.	98-00
3.05	3.16	3.32	3.33	3.42	4.12	4.77	4.98	5.13	5.75	8.02	8.69	9.30	10.98	11.61	13.75	14.30	15.70	Sales per share ᴬ	23.50
.20	.20	.21	.27	.32	.46	.57	.67	.76	.90	1.13	1.26	1.42	1.70	1.98	2.29	2.40	2.60	"Cash Flow" per share	4.30
.14	.14	.14	.21	.25	.39	.49	.57	.65	.74	.90	1.01	1.19	1.43	1.58	1.70	1.85	2.00	Earnings per share ᴮ	3.15
.04	.04	.04	.05	.05	.05	.06	.07	.09	.09	.10	.10	.11	.13	.17	.19	.24	.28	Div'd Decl'd per sh ᶜ	.40
.09	.07	.08	.12	.08	.14	.30	.18	.12	.19	.14	.23	.18	.56	1.25	.38	.40	.70	Cap'l Spending per sh	1.10
1.16	1.26	1.36	1.45	1.66	1.98	2.39	2.89	3.45	4.09	4.90	5.61	6.83	8.13	9.50	10.76	14.30	18.90	Book Value per share	
22.85	22.85	22.88	22.87	22.81	22.60	22.40	22.38	22.38	22.37	22.37	22.36	22.36	22.36	22.35	22.35	22.35	22.35	Common Shs Outst'g ᴰ	22.35
7.6	6.1	8.1	6.5	7.8	7.3	11.4	14.5	17.7	16.6	14.4	16.3	19.9	23.5	NMF	18.4	Bold figures are Value Line estimates		Avg Annual P/E Ratio	20.0
1.10	.81	.98	.72	.66	.68	.93	.98	1.18	1.38	1.09	1.21	1.27	1.43	1.31	1.09			Relative P/E Ratio	1.55
4.0%	5.1%	3.8%	3.4%	2.4%	1.8%	1.1%	.9%	.8%	.7%	.7%	.6%	.5%	.4%	.5%	.6%			Avg Annual Div'd Yield	.6%

CAPITAL STRUCTURE as of 3/31/95

Total Debt $27.5 mill. **Due in 5 Yrs** $20.0 mill.
LT Debt $27.5 mill. **LT Interest** $2.0 mill.
Incl. $7.5 mill. capitalized leases.

(10% of Cap'l)

Leases, Uncapitalized Annual rentals $2.4 mill.
Pension Liability None

Pfd Stock None

Common Stock 22.35 mill. shares (90% of Cap'l)
Incl. 7,272,380 Class B Comm (10 votes per sh.)
All share amounts adj. for 2-for-1 split, July '95.

	106.7	111.4	114.8	128.6	179.3	194.3	207.9	245.4	259.6	296.9	320	350	Sales ($mill) ᴬ	525
	21.7%	23.6%	23.4%	21.3%	21.1%	21.2%	22.3%	22.3%	24.0%	24.6%	24.0%	23.5%	Operating Margin	26.0%
	1.8	2.2	2.4	3.6	5.1	5.7	5.2	6.1	8.8	13.2	13.5	15.0	Depreciation ($mill)	24.8
	10.9	12.8	14.6	16.6	20.2	22.6	26.5	32.0	35.0	37.9	41.0	44.5	Net Profit ($mill)	70.0
	51.8%	50.2%	44.0%	35.0%	39.1%	39.2%	39.9%	38.3%	38.6%	38.0%	38.0%	38.0%	Income Tax Rate	39.0%
	10.2%	11.5%	12.7%	12.9%	11.3%	11.6%	12.8%	13.1%	13.7%	12.8%	12.8%	12.7%	Net Profit Margin	13.3%
	36.0	45.9	58.8	12.5	33.5	55.3	80.5	107.2	61.1	92.6	110	175	Working Capital ($mill)	175
	--	--	--	--	--	--	--	7.5	27.5	27.5	27.5	7.5	Long-Term Debt ($mill)	7.5
	53.5	64.6	77.1	91.5	109.6	129.8	152.8	181.7	212.3	240.5	275	320	Net Worth ($mill)	425
	20.4%	19.8%	18.9%	18.1%	18.4%	17.4%	17.4%	16.9%	14.8%	14.3%	13.5%	13.5%	% Earned Total Capital	16.5%
	20.4%	19.8%	18.9%	18.1%	18.4%	17.4%	17.4%	17.6%	16.7%	15.8%	15.0%	14.0%	% Earned Net Worth	16.5%
	17.9%	17.2%	16.3%	15.8%	16.5%	15.6%	15.7%	16.0%	15.0%	14.0%	13.0%	12.0%	% Retained to Comm Eq	14.5%
	12%	13%	14%	13%	11%	10%	9%	9%	10%	11%	13%	14%	% All Div'ds to Net Prof	13%

CURRENT POSITION (SMILL.)

	1993	1994	3/31/95
Cash Assets	56.2	62.4	62.5
Receivables	20.7	22.1	22.6
Inventory (FIFO)	29.3	29.2	38.2
Other	5.7	5.2	5.6
Current Assets	111.9	118.9	128.9
Accts Payable	6.3	6.1	6.3
Debt Due	22.6	--	--
Other	22.0	20.2	24.2
Current Liab.	50.9	26.3	30.5

ANNUAL RATES

of change (per sh)	Past 10 Yrs	Past 5 Yrs	Est'd '92-'94 to '98-'00
Sales	12.5%	13.5%	12.0%
"Cash Flow"	11.5%	16.5%	13.5%
Earnings	10.5%	15.5%	12.5%
Dividends	8.5%	12.5%	16.0%
Book Value	12.5%	22.0%	12.5%

QUARTERLY REVENUES ($ mill.) ᴬ

Calendar	Mar.31	Jun.30	Sep.30	Dec.31	Full Year
1992	42.8	51.5	86.8	64.3	245.4
1993	50.0	53.9	93.3	62.4	259.6
1994	56.4	62.8	111.0	66.7	296.9
1995	60.3	68.8	119.5	71.4	320.0
1996	65.0	75.0	130.0	80.0	350.0

EARNINGS PER SHARE ᴮ

Calendar	Mar.31	Jun.30	Sep.30	Dec.31	Full Year
1992	.25	.30	.58	.30	1.43
1993	.30	.33	.64	.31	1.58
1994	.31	.35	.69	.35	1.70
1995	.33	.37	.75	.40	1.85
1996	.35	.45	.90	.30	2.00

GROSS QUARTERLY DIV'DS PAID ᶜ

Calendar	Mar.31	Jun.30	Sep.30	Dec.31	Full Year
1991	.025	.029	.029	.029	.11
1992	.028	.028	.034	.034	.12
1993	.034	.034	.044	.044	.16
1994	.044	.044	.053	.053	.19
1995	.053	.053	.063		

BUSINESS: Tootsie Roll Industries, Inc. produces candy. Products include: Tootsie Roll, Tootsie Pop, Tootsie Bubble Pop, Tootsie Pop Drops, Tootsie Roll Flavor Rolls, and Mason Dots. Acquired Cella's Confections (chocolate covered cherries), 7/85; Charms Co. (Charms, Blow Pops), 9/88; and Warner-Lambert's former chocolate/caramel brands (Junior Mints, Sugar Daddy, Sugar Babies, Charleston Chew, and Pom Poms), 10/93. Has four plants in U.S.; one in Mexico. Int'l ops. (Mexico and Canada): 11% of '93 sls., 4% of egs. Employs 1,700; has 9,500 shrhldrs. M.J. and E.R. Gordon control 67.1% of voting power; other insiders, 12.0% (3/94 proxy). Chrmn. & C.E.O.: M.J. Gordon. Pres.: E.R. Gordon. Inc.: VA. Addr.: 7401 S. Cicero Ave., Chicago, IL 60629. Tel.: 312-838-3400.

Tootsie Roll continues to be a solid performer. The June '95 quarter marked the 30th consecutive period of positive year-over-year earnings and sales comparisons. Revenues are advancing at a healthy pace due to product-line extensions, new product introductions, and aggressive promotional campaigns. Moreover, the bottom line continues to benefit from successful cost containment measures and improved manufacturing efficiencies. And with raw material prices expected to remain relatively stable, profitability levels should continue to advance steadily. We estimate that Tootsie Roll will post record earnings of $1.85 and $2.00 per share in 1995 and 1996, respectively. (Note: All per-share data have been adjusted for the 2-for-1 split in July '95.)

Prospects look favorable for the coming 3 to 5 years. The emerging markets in the Far East and in Mexico, along with the Canadian operations, are all likely to contribute to earnings growth. Share-net contributions from these international enterprises will probably develop more slowly, in keeping with management's efforts to move cautiously overseas. In the U.S., where new packaging and new products are developed regularly, there appears to be excellent potential.

The company has a strong brand offering. The Tootsie Roll candies offer the company a solid revenue base. Over the years, the company has developed new products and made strategic acquisitions that complement the existing brand names. Recently acquired brands, such as Charms, Sugar Daddy, and Junior Mints, have had a synergistic impact on purchasing, packaging, and distribution costs. And since the company generates more cash than is needed for internal growth, Tootsie is always in the market for complementary acquisitions, although this possibility isn't included in our forecasts.

Neutrally ranked Tootsie Roll shares are a core conservative holding. The shares of companies like Tootsie that boast a history of steady earnings growth, solid rates of return on investment, and a superior balance sheet continue to command premium multiples. Nonetheless, this issue offers worthwhile appreciation potential out to 1998-2000.

James D. von Riesemann August 18, 1995

(A) Fiscal year ends Dec. 31. First three quarters end on Sat. closest to end of month. (B) Based on average shares outstanding. Includes charge from switching to LIFO inventory accounting, in '79: 4¢. Next earnings report due late October. (C) Next dividend meeting about Sept. 1. Goes ex about Sept. 17. Approximate dividend payment dates: Jan. 11, Apr. 9, July 9, Oct. 13. Three percent stock dividend paid annually since 1966. (D) In mill., adjusted for stk. splits and dividends.

Company's Financial Strength	A
Stock's Price Stability	85
Price Growth Persistence	90
Earnings Predictability	100

STANDARD & POOR'S

STOCK REPORTS

Hershey Foods

1132

NYSE Symbol **HSY**

In S&P 500

27-SEP-95   Industry:
Food

Summary: Hershey is the leading U.S. producer of chocolate and confectionery products. Through its Hershey Pasta Group, it is also the second largest U.S. pasta maker.

S&P Opinion: Accumulate (★★★★)	Recent Price • 63½	Yield • 2.3%
	52 Wk Range • 64¾-44⅛	12-Mo. P/E • 27.6

Quantitative Evaluations

Outlook
(1 Lowest—5 Highest)
• **2+**

Fair Value
• **59**

Risk
• **Low**

Earn./Div. Rank
• **A**

Technical Eval.
• **Neutral** since 9/95

Rel. Strength Rank
(1 Lowest—99 Highest)
• **74**

Insider Activity
• **Neutral**

Earnings vs. Previous Year
▲=Up ▼=Down ▶=No Change

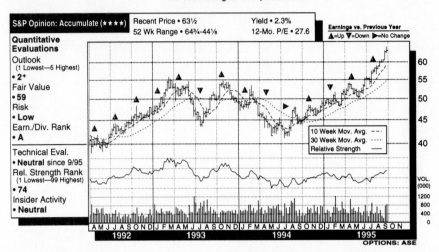

10 Week Mov. Avg. – – –
30 Week Mov. Avg. ·······
Relative Strength ——

VOL.
(000)

OPTIONS: ASE

Overview - 27-SEP-95

Net sales are projected to rise at an approximate 5% to 10% annual pace through 1996, driven primarily by core product volume gains and, to a lesser extent, selected price increases. Near-term cost levels should benefit from 1994's restructuring actions and increased throughput from highly efficient new manufacturing capacity. These benefits, in addition to controlled levels of promotions and advertising for core confectionery brands, should contribute to operating margin expansion. Decreased emphasis on dilutive international expansion and an increasingly aggressive share buyback policy will also contribute to our earnings-per-share growth (before unusual items) forecast of 10% to 14% annually over the next few years.

Valuation - 27-SEP-95

Given our projection of steady, 10% to 14% annual earnings-per-share growth over the next few years, we believe that the shares are attractively valued at current levels. The shares have over the years commanded a premium to the S&P 500's P/E multiple (and HSY's EPS growth rate) because of the company's long record of earnings growth, and relatively conservative level of indebtedness. With expectations of a somewhat soft U.S. economy through 1996, these defensive shares should continue to trade at a premium to the market for the foreseeable future. These high-quality, low-risk shares are principally suited for conservative, long-term growth accounts.

Key Stock Statistics

S&P EPS Est. 1995	3.40	Tang. Bk. Value/Share	11.73
P/E on S&P Est. 1995	18.7	Beta	1.15
S&P EPS Est. 1996	3.85	Shareholders	34,300
Dividend Rate/Share	1.44	Market cap. (B)	$ 4.9
Shs. outstg. (M)	77.7	Inst. holdings	33%
Avg. daily vol. (M)	0.111	Insider holdings	NA

Value of $10,000 invested 5 years ago: $ 20,217

Fiscal Year Ending Dec. 31

	1995	% Change	1994	% Change	1993	% Change
Revenues (Million $)						
1Q	867.5	-2%	883.9	-2%	897.8	12%
2Q	722.3	7%	676.0	9%	618.4	NM
3Q	—	—	966.5	3%	935.7	13%
4Q	—	—	1,080	4%	1,036	7%
Yr.	—	—	3,606	3%	3,488	8%
Income (Million $)						
1Q	60.63	14%	53.02	-50%	105.1	78%
2Q	33.32	32%	25.33	-3%	26.03	-25%
3Q	—	—	81.06	10%	73.97	11%
4Q	—	—	24.82	-73%	92.18	12%
Yr.	—	—	184.2	-38%	297.2	23%
Earnings Per Share ($)						
1Q	0.70	15%	0.61	-47%	1.16	78%
2Q	0.38	31%	0.29	NM	0.29	-26%
3Q	E1.05	13%	0.93	13%	0.82	11%
4Q	E1.27	NM	0.29	-72%	1.04	14%
Yr.	E3.40	60%	2.12	-36%	3.31	23%

Next earnings report expected: late October

Business Summary - 26-SEP-95

Hershey Foods Corporation, primarily through its Hershey Chocolate U.S.A., Hershey International and Hershey Pasta Group divisions and its Hershey Canada Inc. subsidiary, produces and distributes a broad line of chocolate, confectionery and pasta products.

The company makes chocolate and confectionery products in various packaged forms and markets them under more than 50 brands. Principal chocolate and confectionery products in the U.S. are: Hershey's, Hershey's with almonds and Cookies 'N' Mint bars; Hugs and Kisses (both also with almonds) chocolates; Kit Kat wafer bars; Mr. Goodbar chocolate bars; Reese's Pieces candies; Rolo caramels in milk chocolate; Skor toffee bars; Y&S Twizzlers licorice; and Amazin' Fruit gummy bears fruit candy. Grocery products include Hershey's chocolate chips, cocoa and syrup; and Reese's peanut butter and peanut butter chips. Hershey's chocolate milk is produced and sold under license by about 20 independent dairies throughout the U.S., using a chocolate milk mix manufactured by HSY. The most significant raw material used in the production of the company's chocolate and confectionery products is cocoa beans.

HSY also makes pasta products throughout most of the U.S. and markets its products on a regional basis under several brand names, including San Giorgio, Ronzoni, Skinner, P&R, Light 'n Fluffy and American Beauty.

The company has various international arrangements, the investment in which changes from time to time, but which in the aggregate are not material to HSY.

Important Developments

Aug. '95—HSY purchased 9,049,773 shares (about 10%) of its common stock outstanding from Hershey Trust Co., for approximately $500 million. The Hershey Trust retained 99.4% of all Class B common shares (which carry 10 votes per share), giving the trust 76.1% voting power of both classes of common stock (from 77.1%).

Jul. '95—Sales and operating income in 1995's first half rose 2% and 19%, respectively, against the same period a year earlier. HSY attributed most of the profit gain to manufacturing efficiencies associated with higher sales at Hershey Chocolate North America and Hershey Pasta Group, and continued productivity improvements.

Jan. '95—HSY said new confectionery products, international acquisitions and pasta price increases were primary sources of sales growth for the company in 1994.

Capitalization

Long Term Debt: $154,089,000 (7/2/95).

Class B Stock: 15,242,979 shs. ($1 par); 10 votes each; div. about 10% lower than com.
Milton Hershey School owns 99%.

Per Share Data ($)
(Year Ended Dec. 31)

	1994	1993	1992	1991	1990	1989
Tangible Bk. Val.	11.39	10.72	11.81	10.13	9.16	8.25
Cash Flow	3.60	4.43	3.63	3.24	3.08	2.50
Earnings	2.12	3.31	2.69	2.43	2.39	1.90
Dividends	1.25	1.14	1.03	0.94	0.99	0.74
Payout Ratio	59%	34%	38%	39%	41%	39%
Prices - High	53½	55⅞	48⅜	44½	39⅝	36⅞
- Low	41⅛	43½	38¼	35⅛	28¼	24¾
P/E Ratio - High	25	17	18	18	17	19
- Low	19	13	14	14	12	13

Income Statement Analysis (Million $)

	1994	%Chg	1993	%Chg	1992	%Chg	1991
Revs.	3,606	3%	3,488	8%	3,220	11%	2,899
Oper. Inc.	604	8%	557	9%	513	11%	463
Depr.	129	29%	100	18%	84.4	16%	72.7
Int. Exp.	40.3	15%	34.9	-17%	41.8	5%	39.7
Pretax Inc.	333	-35%	511	27%	401	10%	363
Eff. Tax Rate	45%	—	42%	—	40%	—	40%
Net Inc.	184	-38%	297	22%	243	10%	220

Balance Sheet & Other Fin. Data (Million $)

	1994	1993	1992	1991	1990	1989
Cash	27.0	16.0	203	71.0	27.0	52.0
Curr. Assets	949	889	940	744	662	568
Total Assets	2,891	2,855	2,673	2,342	2,079	1,814
Curr. Liab.	796	814	737	471	341	286
LT Debt	157	166	174	283	273	216
Common Eqty.	1,441	1,412	1,465	1,335	1,244	1,117
Total Cap.	1,792	1,751	1,843	1,790	1,671	1,475
Cap. Exp.	139	212	250	226	179	162
Cash Flow	313	397	327	292	278	226

Ratio Analysis

	1994	1993	1992	1991	1990	1989
Curr. Ratio	1.2	1.1	1.3	1.6	1.9	2.0
% LT Debt of Cap.	8.8	9.5	9.5	15.8	16.4	14.7
% Net Inc.of Revs.	5.1	8.5	7.5	7.6	7.9	7.1
% Ret. on Assets	6.4	10.9	9.7	9.9	11.1	9.6
% Ret. on Equity	13.0	21.0	17.3	17.0	18.3	16.1

Dividend Data
—Dividends have been paid since 1930. A dividend reinvestment plan is available.

Amt. of Div. $	Date Decl.	Ex-Div. Date	Stock of Record	Payment Date
0.325	Nov. 01	Nov. 15	Nov. 21	Dec. 15 '94
0.325	Feb. 07	Feb. 17	Feb. 24	Mar. 15 '95
0.325	Apr. 24	May. 17	May. 23	Jun. 15 '95
0.360	Aug. 01	Aug. 23	Aug. 25	Sep. 15 '95

Data as orig. reptd.; bef. results of disc. opers. and/or spec. items. Per share data adj. for stk. divs. as of ex-div. date.
E-Estimated. NA-Not Available. NM-Not Meaningful. NR-Not Ranked.

Office—100 Crystal A Drive, Hershey, PA 17033. **Tel**—(717) 534-6799. **Chrmn & CEO**—K. L. Wolfe. **Pres**—J. P. Viviano. **Sr VP-Fin**—W. F. Christ. **Investor Contact**—James A. Edris. **Dirs**—H. O. Beaver Jr., T. C. Graham, B. Guiton Hill, J. C. Jamison, S. C. Mobley, F. I. Neff, R. J. Pera, J. M. Pietruski, V. A. Sarni, J. P. Viviano, K. L. Wolfe. **Transfer Agent & Registrar**—Chemical Bank, NYC. **Incorporated** in Delaware in 1927. **Empl**-15,600. **S&P Analyst:** Kenneth A. Shea

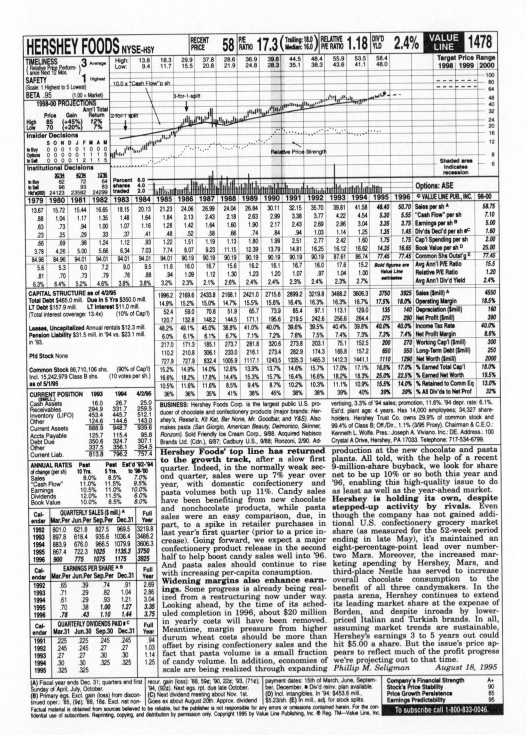

HERSHEY FOODS NYSE-HSY

RECENT PRICE	**58**	P/E RATIO	**17.3**	(Trailing: 18.0 / Median: 16.0)	RELATIVE P/E RATIO	**1.18**	DIV'D YLD	**2.4%**	VALUE LINE	**1478**

TIMELINESS 3 Average
(Relative Price Perform-ance Next 12 Mos.)

SAFETY 1 Highest
(Scale: 1 Highest to 5 Lowest)

BETA .95 (1.00 = Market)

1998-00 PROJECTIONS

	Price	Gain	Ann'l Total Return
High	85	(+45%)	12%
Low	70	(+20%)	7%

Insider Decisions

	S	O	N	D	J	F	M	A	M
to Buy	0	0	0	1	0	1	0	0	0
Options	0	0	0	0	0	1	1	1	5
to Sell	0	0	0	1	2	1	1	1	5

Institutional Decisions

	3Q'94	4Q'94	1Q'95
to Buy	62	72	64
to Sell	96	93	83
Hld'(000)	24123	23582	24299

Percent shares traded: 6.0 / 4.0 / 2.0

High/Low price range:
13.8/9.4, 18.3/11.7, 29.9/15.5, 37.8/20.8, 28.6/21.9, 36.9/24.8, 39.6/28.3, 44.5/35.1, 48.4/38.3, 55.9/43.6, 53.5/41.1, 58.4/48.0

10.0 x "Cash Flow" p sh
3-for-1-split
2-for-1 split

Relative Price Strength

Shaded area indicates recession

Target Price Range 1998 1999 2000

Options: ASE

© VALUE LINE PUB., INC.

1979	1980	1981	1982	1983	1984	1985	1986	1987	1988	1989	1990	1991	1992	1993	1994	1995	1996		98-00
13.67	15.72	15.44	16.65	18.15	20.13	21.23	24.06	26.99	24.04	26.84	30.11	32.15	35.70	39.81	41.58	48.40	50.70	Sales per sh A	58.75
.88	1.04	1.17	1.35	1.48	1.64	1.84	2.13	2.43	2.18	2.63	2.99	3.38	3.77	4.22	4.54	5.30	5.55	"Cash Flow" per sh	7.10
.63	.73	.94	1.00	1.07	1.16	1.28	1.42	1.64	1.60	1.90	2.17	2.43	2.69	2.86	3.04	3.35	3.75	Earnings per sh B	5.00
.23	.25	.29	.33	.37	.41	.48	.52	.58	.66	.74	.84	.94	1.03	1.14	1.25	1.35	1.45	Div'ds Decl'd per sh C	1.60
.66	.69	.98	1.24	1.12	.93	1.22	1.15	1.19	1.13	1.80	1.99	2.51	2.77	2.42	1.60	1.75	1.75	Cap'l Spending per sh	2.00
3.78	4.26	5.00	5.66	6.34	7.03	7.74	8.07	9.23	11.15	12.39	13.79	14.81	16.25	16.12	16.62	14.35	16.65	Book Value per sh D	25.00
84.96	84.96	94.01	94.01	94.01	94.01	94.01	90.19	90.19	90.19	90.19	90.19	90.19	90.19	87.61	86.74	77.45	77.45	Common Shs Outst'g E	77.45
5.6	5.3	6.0	7.2	9.0	9.5	11.6	16.0	16.7	15.6	16.2	16.1	16.7	16.0	17.6	15.2	Bold figures are Value Line estimates		Avg Ann'l P/E Ratio	15.5
.81	.70	.73	.79	.76	.88	.94	1.09	1.12	1.30	1.23	1.20	1.07	.97	1.04	1.00			Relative P/E Ratio	1.20
6.3%	6.4%	5.2%	4.6%	3.8%	3.8%	3.2%	2.3%	2.1%	2.6%	2.4%	2.4%	2.3%	2.4%	2.3%	2.7%			Avg Ann'l Div'd Yield	2.4%

CAPITAL STRUCTURE as of 4/2/95
Total Debt $465.0 mill. Due in 5 Yrs $350.0 mill.
LT Debt $157.9 mill. LT Interest $11.0 mill.
(Total interest coverage: 13.4x) (10% of Cap'l)

Leases, Uncapitalized Annual rentals $12.3 mill.
Pension Liability $31.5 mill. in '94 vs. $23.1 mill. in '93.

Pfd Stock None

Common Stock 86,710,106 shs. (90% of Cap'l)
Incl. 15,242,979 Class B shs. (10 votes per sh.)
as of 5/1/95

	1996.2	2169.6	2433.8	2168.1	2421.0	2715.6	2899.2	3219.8	3488.2	3606.3	3750	3925	Sales ($mill) A	4550
	14.9%	15.2%	15.0%	14.7%	15.5%	15.6%	16.4%	16.3%	16.3%	16.7%	17.5%	18.0%	Operating Margin	18.5%
	52.4	59.0	70.6	51.9	65.7	73.9	85.4	97.1	113.1	129.0	135	140	Depreciation ($mill)	160
	120.7	132.8	148.2	144.5	171.1	195.6	219.5	242.6	256.6	264.4	275	290	Net Profit ($mill)	390
	48.2%	49.1%	45.0%	38.8%	41.0%	40.0%	39.6%	39.5%	40.4%	39.8%	40.0%	40.0%	Income Tax Rate	40.0%
	6.0%	6.1%	6.1%	6.7%	7.1%	7.2%	7.6%	7.5%	7.4%	7.3%	7.3%	7.4%	Net Profit Margin	8.6%
	217.0	171.3	185.1	273.7	281.8	320.6	273.8	203.1	75.1	152.5	200	270	Working Cap'l ($mill)	300
	110.2	210.8	306.1	296.9	216.1	273.4	282.9	174.3	165.8	157.2	650	550	Long-Term Debt ($mill)	250
	727.9	727.9	832.4	1005.9	1117.1	1243.5	1335.3	1465.3	1412.3	1441.1	1110	1290	Net Worth ($mill)	2000
	15.2%	14.9%	14.0%	12.8%	13.9%	13.7%	14.9%	15.7%	17.0%	17.1%	16.5%	17.0%	% Earned Total Cap'l	18.0%
	16.6%	18.2%	17.8%	14.4%	15.3%	15.7%	16.4%	16.6%	18.2%	18.3%	25.0%	22.5%	% Earned Net Worth	19.5%
	10.5%	11.6%	11.6%	8.5%	9.4%	8.7%	10.2%	10.3%	11.1%	10.9%	15.5%	14.0%	% Retained to Comm Eq	13.0%
	36%	36%	35%	41%	38%	45%	38%	38%	39%	40%	39%	39%	% All Div'ds to Net Prof	32%

CURRENT POSITION ($MILL.)

	1993	1994	4/2/95
Cash Assets	16.0	26.7	25.0
Receivables	294.9	331.7	259.5
Inventory (LIFO)	453.4	445.7	512.1
Other	124.6	144.6	143.0
Current Assets	888.9	948.7	939.6
Accts Payable	125.7	115.4	95.8
Debt Due	350.6	324.7	307.1
Other	337.5	356.1	354.5
Current Liab.	813.8	796.2	757.4

ANNUAL RATES of change (per sh)

	Past 10 Yrs.	Past 5 Yrs.	Est'd '92-'94 to '98-'00
Sales	8.0%	8.5%	7.0%
"Cash Flow"	11.0%	11.5%	9.5%
Earnings	10.5%	11.0%	10.0%
Dividends	12.0%	11.5%	6.0%
Book Value	10.0%	8.5%	8.0%

QUARTERLY SALES ($ mill.) A

Calendar	Mar.Per	Jun.Per	Sep.Per	Dec.31	Full Year
1992	801.0	621.8	827.5	969.5	3219.8
1993	897.8	618.4	935.6	1036.4	3488.2
1994	883.9	676.0	966.5	1079.9	3606.3
1995	867.4	722.3	1025	1135.3	3750
1996	900	775	1075	1175	3925

EARNINGS PER SHARE A B

Calendar	Mar.Per	Jun.Per	Sep.Per	Dec.31	Full Year
1992	.65	.39	.74	.91	2.69
1993	.71	.29	.82	1.04	2.86
1994	.61	.29	.93	1.21	3.04
1995	.70	.38	1.00	1.27	3.35
1996	.78	.43	1.10	1.44	3.75

QUARTERLY DIVIDENDS PAID B C

Calendar	Mar.31	Jun.30	Sep.30	Dec.31	Full Year
1991	.225	.225	.245	.245	.94
1992	.245	.245	.27	.27	1.03
1993	.27	.27	.30	.30	1.14
1994	.30	.30	.325	.325	1.25
1995	.325	.325			

BUSINESS: Hershey Foods Corp. is the largest public U.S. producer of chocolate and confectionery products (major brands: Hershey's, Reese's, Kit Kat, Bar None, Mr. Goodbar, and Y&S). Also makes pasta (San Giorgio, American Beauty, Delmonico, Skinner, Ronzoni). Sold Friendly Ice Cream Corp., 9/88. Acquired Nabisco Brands Ltd. (Cdn.), 6/87; Cadbury U.S., 9/88; Ronzoni, 2/90. Advertising, 3.3% of '94 sales; promotion, 11.6%. '94 depr. rate: 6.1%. Est'd. plant age: 4 years. Has 14,000 employees; 34,327 shareholders. Hershey Trust Co. owns 29.9% of common stock and 99.4% of Class B; Off./Dir., 1.1% (3/95 Proxy). Chairman & C.E.O.: Kenneth L. Wolfe. Pres.: Joseph A. Viviano. Inc.: DE. Address.: 100 Crystal A Drive, Hershey, PA 17033. Telephone: 717-534-6799.

Hershey Foods' top line has returned to the growth track, after a slow first quarter. Indeed, in the normally weak second quarter, sales were up 7% year over year, with domestic confectionery and pasta volumes both up 11%. Candy sales have been benefiting from new chocolate and nonchocolate products, while pasta sales were an easy comparison, due, in part, to a spike in retailer purchases in last year's first quarter (prior to a price increase). Going forward, we expect a major confectionery product release in the second half to help boost candy sales well into '96. And pasta sales should continue to rise with increasing per-capita consumption.

Widening margins also enhance earnings. Some progress is already being realized from a restructuring now under way. Looking ahead, by the time of its scheduled completion in 1996, about $20 million in yearly costs will have been removed. Meantime, margin pressure from higher durum wheat costs should be more than offset by rising confectionery sales and the fact that pasta volume is a small fraction of candy volume. In addition, economies of scale are being realized through expanding production at the new chocolate and pasta plants. All told, with the help of a recent 9-million-share buyback, we look for share net to be up 10% or so both this year and '96, enabling this high-quality issue to do as least as well as the year-ahead market.

Hershey is holding its own, despite stepped-up activity by rivals. Even though the company has not gained additional U.S. confectionery grocery market share (as measured for the 52-week period ending in late May), it's maintained an eight-percentage-point lead over number-two Mars. Moreover, the increased marketing spending by Hershey, Mars, and third-place Nestle has served to increase overall chocolate consumption to the benefit of all three candymakers. In the pasta arena, Hershey continues to extend its leading market share at the expense of Borden, and despite inroads by lower-priced Italian and Turkish brands. In all, assuming market trends are sustainable, Hershey's earnings 3 to 5 years out could hit $5.00 a share. But the issue's price appears to reflect much of the profit progress we're projecting out to that time.

Phillip M. Seligman   *August 18, 1995*

(A) Fiscal year ends Dec. 31; quarters end first Sunday of April, July, October.
(B) Primary eqs. Excl. gain (loss) from discontinued oper.: '85, 19¢, 18¢. Excl. net non-recur. gain (loss): '88, 59¢; '90, 22¢; '93, (71¢); '94, (92¢). Next eqs. rpt. due late October.
(C) Next dividend meeting about Nov. 1st. Goes ex about August 20th. Approx. dividend payment dates: 15th of March, June, September, December. ■ Div'd reinv. plan available.
(D) Incl. intangibles. In '94 $453.6 mill., $5.23/sh. (E) In mill., adj. for stock splits.

Factual material is obtained from sources believed to be reliable, but the publisher is not responsible for any errors or omissions contained herein. For the confidential use of subscribers. Reprinting, copying, and distribution by permission only. Copyright 1995 by Value Line Publishing, Inc. ® Reg. TM—Value Line, Inc.

Company's Financial Strength	A+
Stock's Price Stability	90
Price Growth Persistence	85
Earnings Predictability	95

To subscribe call 1-800-833-0046.

Wrigley (Wm.) Jr.　2506

NYSE Symbol **WWY**

In S&P 500

07-AUG-95　Industry:
Food

Summary: This company is the world's largest producer of chewing gum, with about 50% of the U.S. market. The Wrigley family controls 51% of the supervoting Class B stock.

S&P Opinion: Hold (★★★)	Recent Price • 44½	Yield • 1.3%
	52 Wk Range • 49⅝–39½	12-Mo. P/E • 23.9

Quantitative Evaluations

Outlook
(1 Lowest—5 Highest)
• **1**⁻

Fair Value
• **35½**

Risk
• **Low**

Earn./Div. Rank
• **A+**

Technical Eval.
• **Bearish** since 7/95

Rel. Strength Rank
(1 Lowest—99 Highest)
• **26**

Insider Activity
• **Favorable**

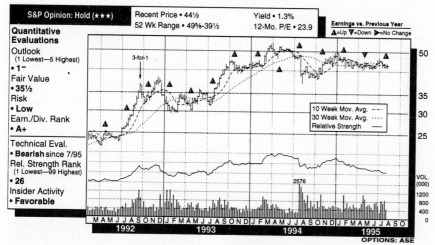

Earnings vs. Previous Year
▲=Up ▼=Down ▶=No Change

10 Week Mov. Avg. – – –
30 Week Mov. Avg. ····
Relative Strength —

OPTIONS: ASE

Overview - 07-AUG-95

Net sales are projected to rise about 10% annually through 1996, driven principally by unit volume growth of 1% to 2% in the U.S., and 7% to 10% in international markets. Selling price increases and favorable currency translations should also contribute modestly to sales growth in the near-term. Operating margins should be sustained, as manufacturing efficiencies help offset a mix shift toward less-profitable international sales, as well as continued heavy marketing spending associated with expansion abroad. Higher foreign tax credits may allow a slight easing in the effective tax rate in 1995. Overall, we expect EPS (excluding special items) to advance at a 12% to 15% annual rate through 1996.

Valuation - 07-AUG-95

Despite our bullish earnings outlook for the company through 1996, the stock appears to be fairly valued at current levels. In recent years, WWY shares have commanded a large premium relative to the P/E multiple of the S&P 500 Index (25% to 75%), reflecting WWY's steady, mid-teen EPS growth and low risk profile during this time period. The shares are currently in the middle of this range, and, given our expectations of a slight slowing of EPS gains, we foresee only average performance over the next six to 12 months. However, these high-quality shares remain suitable for long-term investors seeking above-average capital appreciation with relatively low risk.

Key Stock Statistics

S&P EPS Est. 1995	1.95	Tang. Bk. Value/Share	6.29
P/E on S&P Est. 1995	22.8	Beta	1.04
S&P EPS Est. 1996	2.20	Shareholders	24,100
Dividend Rate/Share	0.56	Market cap. (B)	$ 5.2
Shs. outstg. (M)	116.2	Inst. holdings	24%
Avg. daily vol. (M)	0.143	Insider holdings	NA

Value of $10,000 invested 5 years ago: $ 27,840

Fiscal Year Ending Dec. 31

	1995	% Change	1994	% Change	1993	% Change
Revenues (Million $)						
1Q	410.2	8%	378.6	14%	332.0	7%
2Q	470.6	11%	423.0	10%	386.2	14%
3Q	—	—	404.1	12%	360.5	7%
4Q	—	—	390.9	12%	349.5	16%
Yr.	—	—	1,597	12%	1,429	11%
Income (Million $)						
1Q	55.28	-27%	75.94	79%	42.36	42%
2Q	63.90	10%	58.35	9%	53.56	20%
3Q	—	—	61.62	25%	49.11	19%
4Q	—	—	34.62	16%	29.86	17%
Yr.	—	—	230.5	32%	174.9	18%
Earnings Per Share ($)						
1Q	0.48	-26%	0.65	81%	0.36	13%
2Q	0.55	10%	0.50	9%	0.46	21%
3Q	E0.57	—	0.53	26%	0.42	20%
4Q	E0.35	—	0.30	15%	0.26	18%
Yr.	E1.95	—	1.98	32%	1.50	18%

Next earnings report expected: mid August

Standard NYSE Stock Reports　　**August 14, 1995**　　Vol. 62/No. 156/Sec. 39

Wrigley (Wm.) Jr.

2506
07-AUG-95

Business Summary - 07-AUG-95

Wrigley is the world's largest manufacturer of chewing gum, accounting for about 50% of total chewing gum sales volume in the U.S. Principal products include Wrigley's Spearmint, Doublemint, Juicy Fruit, Big Red and Winterfresh. Other products include Freedent, Orbit, Hubba Bubba (bubble gum) and Extra. Chewing gum accounts for over 90% of total sales and earnings.

By geographical area, sales and profit contributions in 1994 were derived as follows:

	Sales	Profits
U.S.	55%	50%
Europe	33%	30%
Asia, Pacific & Other	12%	20%

Three associated domestic companies produce certain other products. Amurol Products Co. primarily manufactures novelty gum products and, to a lesser extent, hard candies and mints. L.A. Dreyfus Co. makes chewing gum base for Wrigley and other customers, as well as industrial coatings and adhesives. Northwestern Flavors, Inc. processes flavorings and refines mint oil for Wrigley and for food-related industries. The Wrico Packaging division produces a large portion of the company's domestic printed and other wrapping supplies. Major markets abroad include Australia, Canada, Germany, the Philippines, Taiwan and the U.K. WWY brands are sold in 121 countries and territories.

Important Developments

Jul. '95—WWY attributed a 10% year to year increase in net sales during 1995's first half primarily to international volume gains, currency translation gains due to a relatively weaker U.S. dollar, and selective selling price increases.

Jan. '95—WWY's 12% sales increase in 1994 reflected 9% greater unit volume growth of chewing gum, and higher selling prices. In North America, U.S. unit volumes of Wrigley brands rose 3%, led by new Winterfresh product contributions. Overseas, unit volume climbed 15%, on strong shipments in Eastern and Central Europe, the U.K. and Germany. Asia/Pacific 1994 unit volume gains were relatively small; a decline in the Philippines following a selling price hike offset volume increases in China and other markets.

Capitalization

Long Term Debt: None (3/95).

Class B Common Stock: 24,996,373 shs. (no par). 10 votes per sh.; ea. conv. into one com.; restricted transferability.

The Wrigley family controls 51%.

Stockholders: 24,078.

Per Share Data ($)

	(Year Ended Dec. 31)					
	1994	1993	1992	1991	1990	1989
Tangible Bk. Val.	5.92	4.94	4.27	3.95	3.42	2.91
Cash Flow	2.33	1.80	1.52	1.34	1.22	1.11
Earnings	1.98	1.50	1.27	1.09	1.00	0.90
Dividends	0.90	0.75	0.62	0.55	0.49	0.45
Payout Ratio	45%	50%	49%	50%	49%	50%
Prices - High	53⅞	46⅛	39⅞	27	19¾	18
- Low	38⅛	29½	22⅛	16⅜	14⅝	11⅞
P/E Ratio - High	27	31	31	25	20	20
- Low	19	20	17	15	15	13

Income Statement Analysis (Million $)

	1994	%Chg	1993	%Chg	1992	%Chg	1991
Revs.	1,597	12%	1,429	11%	1,287	12%	1,149
Oper. Inc.	331	9%	303	22%	249	10%	227
Depr.	41.1	19%	34.6	16%	29.8	4%	28.7
Int. Exp.	149	NM	1.5	29%	1.2	-15%	1.4
Pretax Inc.	353	27%	279	20%	232	12%	208
Eff. Tax Rate	35%	—	37%	—	36%	—	38%
Net Inc.	231	32%	175	17%	149	16%	129

Balance Sheet & Other Fin. Data (Million $)

	1994	1993	1992	1991	1990	1989
Cash	230	190	182	145	114	109
Curr. Assets	623	502	449	403	357	308
Total Assets	979	815	711	625	564	499
Curr. Liab.	210	159	149	127	127	148
LT Debt	Nil	Nil	Nil	Nil	Nil	Nil
Common Eqty.	688	575	499	463	401	343
Total Cap.	704	598	512	471	410	351
Cap. Exp.	87.0	63.1	66.7	45.2	45.5	45.4
Cash Flow	272	209	178	157	144	131

Ratio Analysis

	1994	1993	1992	1991	1990	1989
Curr. Ratio	3.0	3.2	3.0	3.2	2.8	2.1
% LT Debt of Cap.	Nil	Nil	Nil	Nil	Nil	Nil
% Net Inc.of Revs.	14.4	12.2	11.5	11.2	10.6	10.7
% Ret. on Assets	25.7	23.0	22.3	21.7	22.1	22.7
% Ret. on Equity	36.5	32.6	31.0	29.8	31.6	32.8

Dividend Data

(For many years quarterly dividends have been supplemented by a substantial year-end extra. Dividends have been paid since 1913. A dividend reinvestment plan is available. Payments on the common and Class B common in the past 12 months were:)

Amt. of Div. $	Date Decl.	Ex-Div. Date	Stock of Record	Payment Date
0.120	Aug. 19	Oct. 07	Oct. 14	Nov. 01 '94
0.440	Oct. 26	Dec. 09	Dec. 15	Dec. 31 '94
0.140	Oct. 26	Jan. 09	Jan. 13	Feb. 01 '95
0.140	Mar. 09	Apr. 10	Apr. 17	May. 01 '95
0.140	Jun. 14	Jul. 13	Jul. 17	Aug. 01 '95

Data as orig. reptd.; bef. results of disc. opers. and/or spec. items. Per share data adj. for stk. divs. as of ex-div. date. E-Estimated. NA-Not Available. NM-Not Meaningful. NR-Not Ranked.

Office—410 North Michigan Ave., Chicago, IL 60611. **Tel**—(312) 644-2121. **Pres & CEO**—W. Wrigley. **VP & Treas**—D. Petrovich. **Investor Contact**—Christopher J. Perille. **Dirs**—C. F. Allison III, L. P. Bell, R. P. Billingsley, R. D. Ewers, G. E. Gardner, P. S. Pritzker, R. K. Smucker, W. Wrigley, W. Wrigley, Jr. **Transfer Agent & Registrar**—First Chicago Trust Co. of New York, NYC. **Incorporated** in Delaware in 1927. **Empl**-7,000. **S&P Analyst:** Kenneth A. Shea

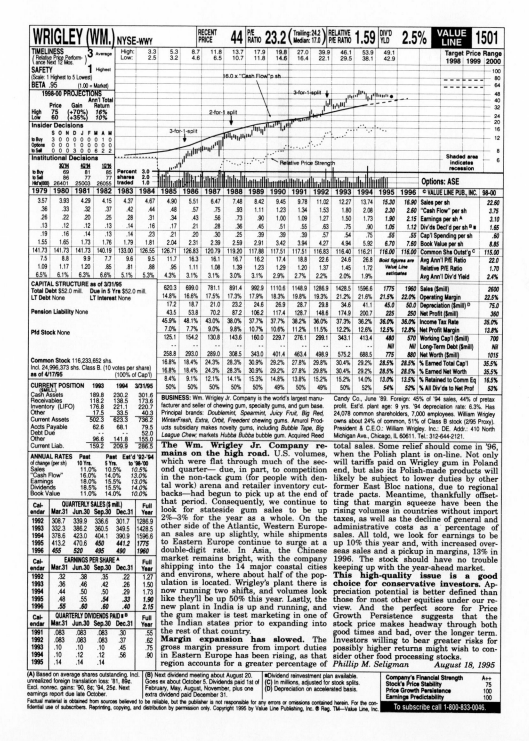

WRIGLEY (WM.) NYSE-WWY

RECENT PRICE	44	P/E RATIO	23.2	(Trailing: 24.2 / Median: 17.0)	RELATIVE P/E RATIO	1.59	DIV'D YLD	2.5%	VALUE LINE	1501

TIMELINESS 3 Average
(Relative Price Perform-)
(ance Next 12 Mos.)

SAFETY 1 Highest
(Scale: 1 Highest to 5 Lowest)

BETA .95 (1.00 = Market)

| High: | 3.3 | 5.3 | 8.7 | 11.8 | 13.7 | 17.9 | 19.8 | 27.0 | 39.9 | 46.1 | 53.9 | 49.1 |
| Low: | 2.5 | 3.2 | 4.6 | 6.5 | 10.7 | 11.8 | 14.6 | 16.4 | 22.1 | 29.5 | 38.1 | 42.9 |

Target Price Range 1998 1999 2000

16.0 x "Cash Flow" p sh
3-for-1 split
2-for-1 split
3-for-1 split

1998-00 PROJECTIONS
	Price	Gain	Ann'l Total Return
High	75	(+70%)	16%
Low	60	(+35%)	10%

Insider Decisions
	S	O	N	D	J	F	M	A	M
to Buy	3	0	0	0	0	0	1	0
Options	0	0	0	1	0	0	0	0
to Sell	0	0	3	0	0	6	2	2

Institutional Decisions
	3Q'94	4Q'94	1Q'95
to Buy	69	81	85
to Sell	86	77	77
Hld's(000)	26401	25003	26055

Percent 3.0 / shares 2.0 / traded 1.0

Relative Price Strength

Shaded area indicates recession

Options: ASE

1979	1980	1981	1982	1983	1984	1985	1986	1987	1988	1989	1990	1991	1992	1993	1994	1995	1996	© VALUE LINE PUB., INC.	98-00
3.57	3.93	4.29	4.15	4.37	4.67	4.90	5.51	6.47	7.48	8.42	9.45	9.78	12.27	13.74	15.30	16.90	Sales per sh	22.60
.36	.33	.32	.37	.42	.44	.48	.57	.75	.93	1.11	1.23	1.34	1.53	1.80	2.08	2.30	2.60	"Cash Flow" per sh	3.75
.26	.22	.20	.25	.28	.31	.34	.43	.56	.73	.90	1.00	1.09	1.27	1.50	1.73	1.90	2.15	Earnings per sh A	3.10
.13	.12	.12	.13	.14	.16	.17	.21	.28	.36	.45	.51	.55	.63	.75	.90	1.05	1.12	Div'ds Decl'd per sh B ■	1.65
.19	.16	.14	.13	.14	.23	.21	.20	.30	.25	.39	.39	.39	.57	.54	.75	.55	.55	Cap'l Spending per sh	.60
1.55	1.65	1.73	1.76	1.79	1.81	2.04	2.31	2.39	2.59	2.91	3.42	3.94	4.27	4.94	5.92	6.70	7.60	Book Value per sh	8.85
141.73	141.73	141.73	140.19	133.00	126.55	126.71	126.83	120.79	119.20	117.88	117.51	117.51	116.83	116.40	116.21	116.00	116.00	Common Shs Outst'g C	115.00
7.5	8.8	9.9	7.7	9.6	9.5	11.7	16.3	16.1	16.7	16.2	17.4	18.8	22.6	24.6	26.8			Avg Ann'l P/E Ratio	22.0
1.09	1.17	1.20	.85	.81	.88	.95	1.11	1.08	1.39	1.23	1.29	1.20	1.37	1.45	1.72			Relative P/E Ratio	1.70
6.5%	6.1%	6.3%	6.6%	5.1%	5.3%	4.3%	3.1%	3.1%	3.0%	3.1%	2.9%	2.7%	2.2%	2.0%	1.9%			Avg Ann'l Div'd Yield	2.4%

Bold figures are Value Line estimates

CAPITAL STRUCTURE as of 3/31/95
Total Debt $52.0 mill. **Due in 5 Yrs** $52.0 mill.
LT Debt None **LT Interest** None

Pension Liability None

Pfd Stock None

Common Stock 116,233,652 shs.
Incl. 24,996,373 shs. Class B. (10 votes per share)
as of 4/17/95 (100% of Cap'l)

	620.3	699.0	781.5	891.4	992.9	1110.6	1148.9	1286.9	1428.5	1596.6	1775	1960	Sales ($mill)	2600
	14.8%	16.6%	17.5%	17.3%	17.9%	18.3%	19.8%	19.3%	21.2%	21.6%	21.5%	22.0%	Operating Margin	22.5%
	17.2	18.7	21.0	23.2	24.6	26.9	28.7	29.8	34.6	41.1	45.0	50.0	Depreciation ($mill) D	75.0
	43.5	53.8	70.2	87.2	106.2	117.4	128.7	148.6	174.9	200.7	225	250	Net Profit ($mill)	360
	45.9%	48.1%	43.0%	38.0%	37.7%	37.7%	38.2%	36.0%	37.3%	36.2%	36.0%	36.0%	Income Tax Rate	35.0%
	7.0%	7.7%	9.0%	9.8%	10.7%	10.6%	11.2%	11.5%	12.2%	12.6%	12.5%	12.8%	Net Profit Margin	13.8%
	125.1	154.2	130.8	143.6	160.0	229.7	276.1	299.1	343.1	413.4	480	570	Working Cap'l ($mill)	700
	--	--	--	--	--	--	--	--	--	--	Nil	Nil	Long-Term Debt ($mill)	Nil
	258.8	293.0	289.0	308.5	343.0	401.4	463.4	498.9	575.2	688.5	775	880	Net Worth ($mill)	1015
	16.8%	18.4%	24.3%	28.3%	30.9%	29.2%	27.8%	29.8%	30.4%	29.2%	28.5%	28.5%	% Earned Total Cap'l	35.5%
	16.8%	18.4%	24.3%	28.3%	30.9%	29.2%	27.8%	29.8%	30.4%	29.2%	28.5%	28.5%	% Earned Net Worth	35.5%
	8.4%	9.1%	12.1%	14.1%	15.3%	14.8%	13.8%	15.2%	15.2%	14.0%	13.0%	13.5%	% Retained to Comm Eq	16.5%
	50%	50%	50%	50%	50%	50%	49%	50%	50%	52%	54%	52%	% All Div'ds to Net Prof	53%

CURRENT POSITION ($MILL.)
	1993	1994	3/31/95
Cash Assets	189.8	230.2	301.6
Receivables	118.2	138.5	173.6
Inventory (LIFO)	176.8	221.1	220.7
Other	17.5	33.5	40.3
Current Assets	502.3	623.3	736.2
Accts Payable	62.6	68.1	79.5
Debt Due	--	--	52.0
Other	96.6	141.8	155.0
Current Liab.	159.2	209.9	286.5

ANNUAL RATES
of change (per sh)	Past 10 Yrs.	Past 5 Yrs.	Est'd '92-'94 to '98-'00
Sales	11.0%	10.5%	10.5%
"Cash Flow"	16.0%	14.0%	13.0%
Earnings	18.0%	15.5%	13.0%
Dividends	18.5%	15.5%	14.0%
Book Value	11.0%	14.0%	10.0%

QUARTERLY SALES ($ mill.)
Calendar	Mar.31	Jun.30	Sep.30	Dec.31	Full Year
1992	308.7	339.9	336.6	301.7	1286.9
1993	322.3	386.2	360.5	349.5	1428.5
1994	378.6	423.0	404.1	390.9	1596.6
1995	413.2	470.6	450	441.2	1775
1996	455	520	495	490	1960

EARNINGS PER SHARE A
Calendar	Mar.31	Jun.30	Sep.30	Dec.31	Full Year
1992	.32	.38	.35	.22	1.27
1993	.36	.46	.42	.26	1.50
1994	.44	.50	.50	.29	1.73
1995	.48	.55	.54	.33	1.90
1996	.55	.60	.60	.40	2.15

QUARTERLY DIVIDENDS PAID B ■
Calendar	Mar.31	Jun.30	Sep.30	Dec.31	Full Year
1991	.083	.083	.083	.30	.55
1992	.083	.083	.083	.37	.62
1993	.10	.10	.10	.45	.75
1994	.10	.12	.12	.56	.90
1995	.14	.14	.14		

BUSINESS: Wm. Wrigley Jr. Company is the world's largest manufacturer and seller of chewing gums, specialty gums, and gum base. Principal brands: *Doublemint, Spearmint, Juicy Fruit, Big Red, WinterFresh, Extra, Orbit, Freedent* chewing gums. Amurol Products subsidiary makes novelty gums, including *Bubble Tape, Big League Chew*; markets *Hubba Bubba* bubble gum. Acquired Reed Candy Co., June '89. Foreign: 45% of '94 sales, 44% of pretax profit. Est'd. plant age: 9 yrs. '94 depreciation rate: 6.3%. Has 24,078 common shareholders, 7,000 employees. William Wrigley owns about 24% of common, 51% of Class B stock (2/95 Proxy). President & C.E.O.: William Wrigley. Inc.: DE. Addr.: 410 North Michigan Ave., Chicago, IL 60611. Tel.: 312-644-2121.

The Wm. Wrigley Jr. Company remains on the high road. U.S. volumes, which were flat through much of the second quarter— due, in part, to competition in the non-tack gum (for people with dental work) arena and retailer inventory cutbacks—had begun to pick up at the end of that period. Consequently, we continue to look for stateside gum sales to be up 2%–3% for the year as a whole. On the other side of the Atlantic, Western European sales are up slightly, while shipments to Eastern Europe continue to surge at a double-digit rate. In Asia, the Chinese market remains bright, with the company shipping into the 14 major coastal cities and environs, where about half of the population is located. Wrigley's plant there is now running two shifts, and volumes look like they'll be up 50% this year. Lastly, the new plant in India is up and running, and the gum maker is test marketing in one of the Indian states prior to expanding into the rest of that country.

Margin expansion has slowed. The gross margin pressure from import duties in Eastern Europe has been rising, as that region accounts for a greater percentage of total sales. Some relief should come in '96, when the Polish plant is on-line. Not only will tariffs paid on Wrigley gum in Poland end, but also its Polish-made products will likely be subject to lower duties by other former East Bloc nations, due to regional trade pacts. Meantime, thankfully offsetting that margin squeeze have been the rising volumes in countries without import taxes, as well as the decline of general and administrative costs as a percentage of sales. All told, we look for earnings to be up 10% this year and, with increased overseas sales and a pickup in margins, 13% in 1996. The stock should have no trouble keeping up with the year-ahead market.

This high-quality issue is a good choice for conservative investors. Appreciation potential is better defined than those for most other equities under our review. And the perfect score for Price Growth Persistence suggests that the stock price makes headway through both good times and bad, over the longer term. Investors willing to bear greater risks for possibly higher returns might wish to consider other food processing stocks.

Phillip M. Seligman **August 18, 1995**

(A) Based on average shares outstanding. Incl. unrealized foreign translation loss: '81, 8¢. Excl. nonrec. gains: '90, 8¢; '94, 25¢. Next earnings report due late October.

(B) Next dividend meeting about August 20. Goes ex about October 5. Dividends paid 1st of February, May, August, November, plus one extra dividend paid December 31. ■Dividend reinvestment plan available.
(C) In millions, adjusted for stock splits.
(D) Depreciation on accelerated basis.

Company's Financial Strength	A++
Stock's Price Stability	75
Price Growth Persistence	100
Earnings Predictability	100

Tootsie Roll
Industries, Inc.

Annual Report 1994

To Our Shareholders

1994 was another year of successful operations. Our key goal of merging the Junior Mints, Charleston Chew, Sugar Daddy and Sugar Babies lines, which we acquired late in 1993, into our existing business was successfully and profitably met. These new brands were integrated into the Tootsie Roll and Charms sales, marketing, distribution and administrative organizations with little incremental staff or overhead.

We are also pleased to report that record results were once again posted in 1994. Sales grew by 14% from $260 million to $297 million, a record high for the eighteenth consecutive year.

Sales growth was primarily fueled by the full year impact of the aforementioned chocolate/caramel brands, another good Halloween season for many of our core brands and growth in our Mexican subsidiary. New flavors, pack configurations and seasonal items, developed to appeal to the ever-evolving preferences of our customers, also contributed to the sales increase.

Earnings reached $37.9 million, a record high for the thirteenth consecutive year and an increase of 7% over the $35.4 million reported in 1993. Higher sales and ongoing expense controls, partially offset by lower investment income and higher interest expense, accounted for the growth in earnings.

Earnings per share reached a record $3.50, which is a 7% increase over the $3.27 achieved in 1993. Earnings per share has grown at an annually compounded rate of 16% over the past 10 years.

We continued to rebuild our financial resources in 1994 following the significant acquisition and capital investments made in 1993. As of December 31, 1994, our cash and short-term investments, net of interest bearing debt, had reached $34.9 million, an increase of $28.8 million over the prior year end. We shall continue to prudently conserve our financial resources as we vigilantly pursue new internal and external growth opportunities.

The strengthening of our financial position was accomplished despite 1994 capital expenditures of $8.2 million, that included several projects designed to reduce cost, vertically integrate the processing of certain key ingredients, expand capacity, improve quality or enhance productivity.

In addition to capital investments, we continued to invest in our well known brands during the year. Extensive advertising and promotional programs were executed in order to sustain public awareness and increase demand across all generations in the United States, Mexico and in several emerging markets.

We recognize that superior performance is dependent upon having a high caliber organization, and acknowledge the many contributions to the company's continued success this past year made by our loyal employees, as well as those of our customers, suppliers, sales brokers and shareholders.

Tootsie Roll is fast approaching its 100th anniversary in 1996, one of the very few branded candy companies to achieve this milestone. As we are developing plans for suitable activities to celebrate and publicize our past, we remain focused on the future and committed to extend the Tootsie Roll legacy into the next century and beyond.

Melvin J. Gordon

Melvin J. Gordon
Chairman of the Board and
Chief Executive Officer

Ellen R. Gordon

Ellen R. Gordon
President and
Chief Operating Officer

Financial Highlights

	December 31,	
	1994	1993
	(in thousands except per share data)	
Net Sales	$296,932	$259,593
Net Earnings	37,931	35,442
Working Capital	92,626	61,052
Net Property, Plant and Equipment	85,648	86,699
Shareholders' Equity	240,461	212,343
Average Shares Outstanding*	10,848	10,848
Per Share Items*		
Net Earnings	$3.50	$3.27
Shareholders' Equity	22.17	19.57
Cash Dividends Paid	.42	.35

*Based on average shares outstanding adjusted for stock dividends.

Operating Report

Marketing and Sales

We attained record sales once again in 1994 as the Junior Mints, Charleston Chew, Sugar Daddy and Sugar Babies product lines became fully integrated into the company and accounted for a significant amount of the sales increase.

These new chocolate and caramel brands not only contributed directly to sales growth, but also had a synergistic impact on certain existing products lines. For instance, the theater business of Mason Dots was boosted by its joint distribution with Junior Mints, and new variety bags and off-shelf displays incorporating both new and existing items were introduced.

While our base business continued to be favorably impacted by strong Back to School and Halloween selling periods, sales of certain trend setting items, which had been unusually strong in prior years, declined from their peak and returned to more normal levels. These decreases were partially offset by increased sales in many core Tootsie Roll products.

New sales also stemmed from niche marketing strategies that deliver our products to consumers in numerous pack configurations and through every appropriate distribution channel. In 1994, an expanded assortment of seasonal packs and new candy flavors were introduced as line extensions, while bonus packs were utilized to deliver an even greater value to our consumers.

An updated package design with bolder graphics and a complimentary new assortment of tropical flavors were introduced in the Mason Dots line in anticipation of that brand's 50th anniversary in 1995. The trade received these enhancements positively.

Advertising and Public Relations

As has been our long standing practice, we employed television advertising as the chief medium to convey our message to the public in 1994. Tootsie Roll, Tootsie Pop and Charms Blow Pop advertisements ran nationally on both network and cable television, and major markets were specifically targeted through a spot campaign.

Game shows and talk shows were used to deliver the healthful message that Tootsie Rolls contain no cholesterol and far less saturated fat than other leading bars. In fact, the Commissioner of the Food and Drug Administration used Tootsie Rolls on national television to demonstrate the usefulness of the new nutritional labeling standards in distinguishing the relatively low saturated fat content of our products.

The company continued to receive favorable press coverage in national magazines, television reports and local newspapers. For instance: a clipping was received reporting that Tootsie Rolls are tucked away in "care packages" destined for Macedonia; a request came to us from the Peace Corps in Nairobi for information about Tootsie Roll's method of operation to be used in business classes for natives of East Africa; articles came in with photographs showing American soldiers sharing Tootsie Rolls and good will with the Haitians; a poignant report from several publications stated that the late Jacqueline Kennedy Onasis set an informal and friendly atmosphere for guests in her office by offering Tootsie Rolls to them.

Human interest stories such as these incorporating references to our products and our fast-approaching 100th anniversary pour in from around the world and contribute to the special place Tootsie Roll occupies in the history of America.

Manufacturing

Competing in an industry that has seen very little price movement since the late 1980's requires peak operating efficiency to keep costs in check. In this regard we have established policies to vertically integrate our operations where it is economically advantageous to do so and to keep our plants ahead of the state-of-the-art for our industry in terms of the machinery, equipment and systems we use.

In 1994, we undertook and completed numerous capital projects in regard to both of these policies. In Chicago we took action to make, rather than purchase, certain raw material blends and added more process control equipment to enhance product quality.

We added a cold storage room and made modifications to the loading docks in the Chicago warehouse facility to accommodate the distribution requirements of the new chocolate/caramel brands. We also acquired a parcel of contiguous land for future growth.

Efficiency projects were completed in our three other domestic plants. Many of these were in the Cambridge, Massachusetts plant which we acquired along with the chocolate/caramel brands in late 1993. Here we incorporated a number of ideas that had proven to provide savings or improve quality in our other operations.

In Mexico we continued the modernization efforts that have been ongoing for several years by installing upgraded cooking and wrapping equipment.

Physical Distribution

We assimilated the new chocolate/caramel brands into our distribution network in 1994. In Chicago, this necessitated the reconfiguration of our warehousing and shipping space and included the cold storage and dock modification capital projects mentioned above.

This reconfiguration was made possible by the additional space we obtained when the facility was purchased in 1993. The remaining surplus space in Chicago has been leased to third parties for terms ranging from two to nine years, including renewal options.

Our per unit distribution cost has increased somewhat since the addition of the chocolate/caramel brands to our line due to increased utilization of refrigerated storage and transportation. This increase has been partially mitigated by the efficiencies realized by larger consolidated loads and, in percentage terms, by the higher average selling prices of chocolate items.

Purchasing

Modest cost increases were seen in several key commodities during the past year, although the timing and hedging of our sugar purchases lessened the effect of the price increase in that commodity. Also, corn syrup prices eased during the summer as the midwest corn crop developed into one of the largest on record.

As the United States' economy gained momentum and strong export demand for U.S. materials developed, the capacity of packaging material suppliers began to come under pressure during the second half of 1994 and prices for paper, board, plastics, foil and other materials increased dramatically. The company was protected to some degree from these increases by having previously negotiated fixed price contracts for many of these materials. However, higher packaging costs and relatively long order lead times, which increased significantly during the latter part of 1994, are anticipated in 1995.

As we deem it to be advisable, we will continue to utilize futures and options as part of our hedging program, make opportunity buys in larger quantities when available and negotiate longer-term supply contracts where appropriate to minimize the impact of commodity and packaging price fluctuations.

International

Our Mexican and Canadian subsidiaries each reported increased sales and profits over the prior year. In Mexico, an especially strong fourth quarter was posted, reflecting another successful Christmas selling season. The majority of our Mexican sales were recorded prior to the large devaluation of the peso that occurred during the last two weeks of December, 1994.

At the year-end exchange rate our 1994 Mexican sales would have translated into approximately $9 million fewer U.S. dollars. Stabilization of the peso in the future or anticipated peso selling price increases for our goods could tend to offset this sales decline somewhat in 1995.

The peso devaluation had the further effect of reducing the stated U.S. dollar value of our net Mexican assets by approximately $5 million. In accordance with generally accepted accounting principles, whereby all assets and liabilities are translated at the year-end exchange rate, this amount was recorded as a direct reduction in shareholders' equity.

Canadian sales growth came from distribution gains for existing products and the new chocolate/caramel product lines. We also completed the realignment of our broker network there.

Our sales office in the Far East continued to expand and refine distribution and to test and advertise our products in various countries in the Pacific Rim, however, development of sales in this region is costly and will be approached cautiously.

The company is exploring markets throughout the world with great interest. Our President, Ellen R. Gordon, was recently appointed by the President of the United States to the President's Export Council.

Human Resources

As the company has grown and its operations have become more complex, we have become increasingly aware of the critical value of the human element to the success of our endeavors. A sound management team is in place to identify and direct future growth opportunities for the company. Highly qualified individuals with diverse talents and backgrounds have been carefully recruited to build strength throughout the organization.

At the same time, we have reinforced entrepreneurial values at all levels in the company so that flexibility and creative determination are preserved. It was this combination of professionalism and entrepreneurialism, along with great commitment by dedicated personnel in all departments coupled with advanced information systems, that enabled us to successfully meet the challenges posed by integrating the chocolate/caramel brands in 1993 and 1994.

Management's Discussion and Analysis of Financial Condition and Results of Operations

(in thousands except per share, percentage and ratio figures)

FINANCIAL REVIEW

This financial review discusses the company's financial condition, results of operations, liquidity and capital resources. It should be read in conjunction with the Consolidated Financial Statements and related footnotes beginning on pages 8 and 12, respectively.

FINANCIAL CONDITION

We further strengthened our financial condition in 1994 by achieving record operating results. Net earnings grew from $35,442 in 1993 to $37,931 in 1994, a 7.0% increase. As a result of using cash from operations to pay off short-term debt, working capital grew from $61,052 to $92,626, an increase of 51.7%.

Cash from operations was also used to fund $8,179 of capital expenditures and for the payment of $4,514 in dividends. This represented an increase of 22.4% in dividends paid over the prior year and marked the fifty-second consecutive year that cash dividends have been paid.

A 3% stock dividend was also distributed to shareholders in

1994. This was the thirtieth consecutive year that a stock dividend has been distributed.

The improvement in our financial position in 1994 over 1993 is reflected in the following ratios: current ratio rose from 2.2:1 to 4.5:1; quick ratio rose from 1.5:1 to 3.2:1; current liabilities to net worth decreased from 24.0% to 10.9% and debt to equity fell from 23.6% to 11.4%. Shareholders' equity increased by 13.2% to $240,461. These statistics are indicative of the company's conservative financial posture in the deployment of its assets.

RESULTS OF OPERATIONS

1994 vs. 1993

1994 represented the eighteenth consecutive year of record sales. Reaching $296,932, 1994 net sales were up 14.4% over 1993 sales of $259,593. The highest quarter, both in terms of sales dollars and in terms of dollar and percentage increase over the prior year, was the third quarter with traditionally strong Back to School and Halloween promotions.

The sales increase in 1994 was due largely to the full year impact of the new chocolate/caramel brands, Junior Mints, Charleston Chew, Sugar Daddy and Sugar Babies. Sales for these brands were, however, lower than they had been in the twelve months preceding the acquisition, as we kept with our plan of emphasizing profitable sales.

Other factors contributing to sales increases were a strong year in Mexico and growth in other established Tootsie Roll brands, offset by decreases in several newer, trend setting items which returned to more normal sales levels from their previous year peaks.

Cost of goods sold as a percentage of sales increased slightly from 51.6% to 52.4%, reflecting higher ingredient and packaging costs and increased indirect costs. Consequently, gross margin, which was $141,367 or 12.5% higher than 1993, declined slightly as a percentage of sales from 48.4% to 47.6%.

Gross margins have historically been lower in the fourth quarter due to the seasonal nature of our business and to the product mix

NET SALES
Per Share

90	$17.91
91	$19.16
92	$22.52
93	$23.93
94	$27.37

NET EARNINGS
Per Share

90	$2.08
91	$2.35
92	$2.95
93	$3.27
94	$3.50

5

sold at that time of year. This effect was lessened in 1994, with improved margins on foreign operations and due to changing sales patterns resulting from the new chocolate/caramel brands.

Operating expenses, comprising marketing, selling, physical distribution, general and administrative expenses and goodwill amortization, as a percentage of sales, were 27.4%, a decrease of .4% versus 1993. While the synergies realized through integrating the chocolate/caramel brands caused marketing and administrative costs to decline as a percent of sales, increased use of refrigerated storage and transportation caused per unit distribution costs to increase. Goodwill amortization was also higher as a result of the chocolate/caramel brands acquisition.

Other income declined by $3,014 due to lower investment income and higher interest expense. These changes had been anticipated and were the result of financing the chocolate/caramel brands acquisition and the purchase of our Chicago plant, both of which occurred toward the

end of 1993. The 1994 effective tax rate was comparable to that of 1993 at 38.0% versus 38.6%.

Consolidated net earnings rose 7.0% to a new company record of $37,931 or $3.50 per share in 1994 from the previous record of $35,442 or $3.27 per share in 1993. This represents the thirteenth consecutive year of record earnings achievement.

1993 vs. 1992

Net sales increased in 1993 to $259,593, a record level for the seventeenth consecutive year and 5.8% over 1992 sales of $245,424. Factors contributing to sales growth during the year were the chocolate/caramel brands acquisition in October, 1993, continued success of our traditional product lines, favorable results with seasonal lines and line extensions, as well as growth in our Mexican and Canadian subsidiaries.

Sales remained at the highest level in the third quarter due to successful Halloween and Back to School promotions, but declined in the fourth quarter from the prior year level due to softness in

certain market segments, partially offset by sales of the new chocolate/caramel brands.

Cost of goods sold, as a percentage of sales, was consistent with 1992 at 51.6% versus 51.8%. Raw material prices remained stable throughout the year and productivity improvements continued to mitigate modest changes in the cost of other factors of production. Gross margin grew by 6.2% to $125,615 because of increased sales and as a percentage of sales it remained constant at 48.4% versus 48.2% in 1992. Fourth quarter gross margin was lower than that of the other three quarters due to seasonality and sales mix factors.

Operating expenses declined slightly as a percentage of sales to 27.8% from 28.7% in the prior year. This favorable result demonstrates the effect of expense control programs that keep costs in check.

The effective tax rate was comparable to the 1992 rate at 38.6% versus 38.3% and other income, consisting primarily of interest and dividend income,

SHAREHOLDERS' EQUITY
Per Share

Year	Value
90	$11.97
91	$14.08
92	$16.75
93	$19.57
94	$22.17

NET EARNINGS
As a % of Sales

Year	Value
90	11.6
91	12.3
92	13.1
93	13.7
94	12.8

GROSS MARGIN
Millions of dollars

90	91	92	93	94
$91	$101	$118	$126	$141

SHAREHOLDERS' EQUITY
Millions of dollars

90	91	92	93	94
$130	$153	$182	$212	$240

NET SALES
Millions of dollars

90	91	92	93	94
$194	$208	$245	$260	$297

NET EARNINGS
Millions of dollars

90	91	92	93	94
$22.6	$26.5	$32.0	$35.4	$37.9

remained essentially even with the prior year as the decrease in our short-term investment portfolio to partially finance the acquisition, did not occur until later in the year. Consolidated earnings rose 10.6% to $35,442, a record high for the twelfth consecutive year.

Liquidity and Capital Resources

Cash flows from operating activities increased by $7,098 to $40,495 in 1994 from $33,397 in 1993 and $35,623 in 1992. Higher profits and depreciation and amortization in 1994 were partially offset by increases in working capital.

Cash flows from investing activities in 1994 reflect a net reduction in our investment portfolio, which was applied toward the repayment of debt. Capital expenditures were $19,813 lower in 1994 than in 1993 which had included the purchase of our Chicago plant, the Cambridge acquisition and the Charms expansion.

Cash flows from financing activities in 1994 include a net reduction of $22,601 in interest bearing debt. These borrowings had occurred in 1993 in connection with the purchase of the chocolate/caramel business.

Cash dividends were declared and paid in 1994 for the fifty-second consecutive year. Cash dividends declared were increased by 21.5% to $.42 per share during 1994.

Our operating results and financial condition are expressed in the following financial statements.

7

CONSOLIDATED STATEMENT OF

Earnings and Retained Earnings

TOOTSIE ROLL INDUSTRIES, INC. AND SUBSIDIARIES

(in thousands except per share data)

For the year ended December 31,

	1994	1993	1992
Net sales	$296,932	$259,593	$245,424
Cost of goods sold	155,565	133,978	127,123
Gross margin	141,367	125,615	118,301
Operating expenses:			
Marketing, selling and advertising	44,974	40,096	38,958
Distribution and warehousing	20,682	17,655	16,959
General and administrative	13,017	12,837	13,186
Amortization of the excess of cost over acquired net tangible assets	2,706	1,510	1,265
	81,379	72,098	70,368
Earnings from operations	59,988	53,517	47,933
Other income, net (Note 8)	1,179	4,193	3,989
Earnings before income taxes	61,167	57,710	51,922
Provision for income taxes (Notes 1 and 4)	23,236	22,268	19,890
Net earnings	37,931	35,442	32,032
Retained earnings at beginning of year	96,647	90,285	83,507
	134,578	125,727	115,539
Deduct (Note 5):			
Cash dividends ($.42, $.35 and $.27 per share)	4,580	3,769	2,947
Stock dividends	22,235	25,311	22,307
	26,815	29,080	25,254
Retained earnings at end of year	$107,763	$ 96,647	$ 90,285
Earnings per common share	$ 3.50	$ 3.27	$ 2.95
Average common and class B common shares outstanding (Note 5)	10,848	10,848	10,848

(The accompanying notes are an integral part of these statements.)

39

CONSOLIDATED STATEMENT OF

Financial Position

TOOTSIE ROLL INDUSTRIES, INC. AND SUBSIDIARIES

(in thousands)

Assets

	December 31,	
	1994	1993
CURRENT ASSETS:		
Cash and cash equivalents (Notes 1 and 10)	$ 16,509	$ 1,986
Investments held to maturity (Notes 1 and 10)	45,861	54,217
Accounts receivable, less allowances of $1,466 and $2,075	22,087	20,656
Inventories (Note 1):		
Finished goods and work-in-process	16,704	17,186
Raw materials and supplies	12,464	12,108
Prepaid expenses	3,094	3,667
Deferred income taxes (Notes 1 and 4)	2,168	2,094
Total current assets	118,887	111,914
PROPERTY, PLANT AND EQUIPMENT, at cost (Note 1):		
Land	6,672	4,231
Buildings	26,982	25,347
Machinery and equipment	109,438	107,685
Leasehold improvements	6	10
	143,098	137,273
Less—Accumulated depreciation and amortization	57,450	50,574
	85,648	86,699
OTHER ASSETS:		
Excess of cost over acquired net tangible assets, net of accumulated amortization of $9,966 and $7,260 (Notes 1 and 2)	98,668	101,375
Other assets	6,880	3,952
	105,548	105,327
	$310,083	$303,940

(The accompanying notes are an integral part of these statements.)

Liabilities and Shareholders' Equity

	December 31,	
	1994	1993
CURRENT LIABILITIES:		
Notes payable to banks (Notes 2, 6 and 10)	$ —	$ 22,601
Accounts payable	6,124	6,259
Dividends payable	1,219	1,026
Accrued liabilities (Note 3)	17,046	17,919
Income taxes payable	1,872	3,057
Total current liabilities	26,261	50,862
NONCURRENT LIABILITIES:		
Deferred income taxes (Notes 1 and 4)	7,716	6,364
Postretirement health care and life insurance benefits (Notes 1 and 7)	4,993	4,498
Industrial Development Bonds (Notes 6 and 10)	7,500	7,500
Term notes payable (Notes 6 and 10)	20,000	20,000
Other long term liabilities	3,152	2,373
Total noncurrent liabilities	43,361	40,735
SHAREHOLDERS' EQUITY (Notes 1 and 5):		
Common stock, $.69-4/9 par value—		
25,000 shares authorized		
7,306 and 7,069, respectively, issued	5,074	4,909
Class B common stock, $.69-4/9 par value—		
10,000 shares authorized		
3,542 and 3,465, respectively, issued	2,459	2,406
Capital in excess of par value	132,997	111,108
Retained earnings, per accompanying statement	107,763	96,647
Foreign currency translation adjustment account (Note 1)	(7,832)	(2,727)
	240,461	212,343
COMMITMENTS (Note 9)		
	$310,083	$303,940

10

41

CONSOLIDATED STATEMENT OF

Cash Flows

TOOTSIE ROLL INDUSTRIES, INC. AND SUBSIDIARIES

(in thousands)

For the year ended December 31,

	1994	1993	1992
CASH FLOWS FROM OPERATING ACTIVITIES:			
Net earnings	$37,931	$35,442	$32,032
Adjustments to reconcile net earnings to net cash provided by operating activities:			
Depreciation and amortization	10,478	8,814	6,071
Loss on retirement of fixed assets	190	34	152
Translation loss	—	—	124
Changes in operating assets and liabilities:			
Accounts receivable	(5,158)	(7,941)	113
Inventories	(1,091)	(2,727)	(3,443)
Prepaid expenses and other assets	(3,952)	(2,827)	(724)
Accounts payable and accrued liabilities	(107)	3,179	2,964
Income taxes payable and deferred	1,075	214	(3,536)
Postretirement health care and life insurance benefits	495	522	450
Other long-term liabilities	778	(432)	1,420
Other	(144)	(881)	
Net cash provided by operating activities	40,495	33,397	35,623
CASH FLOWS FROM INVESTING ACTIVITIES:			
Acquisition of Cambridge Brands	—	(81,317)	
Capital expenditures	(8,179)	(27,992)	(10,956)
Investment purchases	(72,394)	(22,854)	(86,357)
Investment sales	81,650	61,096	52,752
Net cash provided by (used in) investing activities	1,077	(71,067)	(44,561)
CASH FLOWS FROM FINANCING ACTIVITIES:			
Issuances of industrial development bonds and notes payable.	25,000	92,000	7,500
Repayments of notes payable	(47,000)	(50,000)	—
Borrowings under line of credit agreements, net of repayments	(535)	348	
Dividends paid in cash	(4,514)	(3,687)	(2,965)
Net cash provided by (used in) financing activities	(27,049)	38,661	4,535
Increase (decrease) in cash and cash equivalents	14,523	991	(4,403)
Cash and cash equivalents at beginning of year	1,986	995	5,398
Cash and cash equivalents at end of year	$16,509	$ 1,986	$ 995
Supplemental cash flow information:			
Income taxes paid	$22,817	$22,111	$23,733
Interest paid	$ 1,798	$ 653	$ 116

(The accompanying notes are an integral part of these statements.)

42

Notes to Consolidated Financial Statements *($ in thousands except per share data)*

TOOTSIE ROLL INDUSTRIES, INC. AND SUBSIDIARIES

NOTE 1—SIGNIFICANT ACCOUNTING POLICIES:

Basis of consolidation:

The consolidated financial statements include the accounts of Tootsie Roll Industries, Inc. and its wholly-owned subsidiaries (the company), which are primarily engaged in the manufacture and sale of candy products. All significant intercompany transactions have been eliminated.

Revenue recognition:

Revenues are recognized when products are shipped. Accounts receivable are unsecured.

Cash and cash equivalents:

The company considers temporary cash investments with a maturity of three months or less to be cash equivalents.

Investments:

Investments consist of various marketable securities that have maturities of less than one year. As of January 1, 1994, the company has adopted the provisions of Statement of Financial Accounting Standards (SFAS) No. 115, "Accounting For Certain Investments in Debt and Equity Securities", which requires the company to classify each of its debt and equity securities into one of three categories: held to maturity, available for sale or trading. The company has concluded that its investments should be classified as held to maturity due to the existence of positive intent and ability to hold these securities to maturity. Accordingly, all investments have been measured at amortized cost in the statement of financial position. There was no effect on the company's consolidated financial statements from adoption of this statement.

Inventories:

Inventories are stated at cost, not in excess of market. The cost of domestic inventories ($26,571 and $26,500 at December 31, 1994 and 1993, respectively) has been determined by the last-in, first-out (LIFO) method. The excess of current cost over LIFO cost of inventories approximates $4,005 and $4,316 at December 31, 1994 and 1993, respectively. The cost of foreign inventories ($2,597 and $2,794 at December 31, 1994 and 1993, respectively) has been determined by the first-in, first-out (FIFO) method.

From time to time, the company enters into commodity futures and option contracts in order to fix the price, on a short-term basis, of certain future ingredient purchases which are integral to the company's manufacturing process and which may be subject to price volatility (primarily sugar and corn syrup). Gains or losses, if any, resulting from these contracts are considered as a component of the cost of the ingredients being hedged. Open contracts at December 31, 1994 and 1993 were not material.

Property, plant and equipment:

Depreciation is computed for financial reporting purposes by use of both the straight-line and accelerated methods based on useful lives of 5 to 35 years for both buildings and machinery and equipment. For income tax purposes the company uses accelerated methods on all properties.

Postretirement health care and life insurance benefits:

The company provides certain postretirement health care and life insurance benefits. The cost of these postretirement benefits is accrued during employees' working careers in accordance with SFAS No. 106, "Employers' Accounting for Postretirement Benefits other than Pensions."

Income taxes:

The company uses the liability method of computing deferred income taxes in accordance with SFAS No. 109 "Accounting For Income Taxes."

Excess of cost over acquired net tangible assets:

The excess of cost over the acquired net tangible assets of operating companies is amortized on a straight-line basis over a 40 year period. The company assesses the recoverability of its intangible assets using undiscounted future cash flows.

Foreign currency translation:

During 1992 management classified Mexico as a hyper-inflationary economy, as defined by SFAS No. 52, "Foreign Currency Translation." Under this classification, the dollar is used as the functional currency, and translation gains and losses are included in the determination of earnings. A translation loss of $124 related to the company's Mexican operations was charged to expense in 1992.

Effective January 1, 1993 management determined that the Mexican economy was no longer hyper-inflationary. Accordingly, the local currency is used as the functional currency and the net effect of translating the Mexican operation's financial statements is reported in a separate component of shareholders' equity.

NOTE 2—ACQUISITION:

On October 15, 1993, the company purchased certain tangible and intangible assets of a candy manufacturer (Cambridge Brands) for approximately $81,300. Funds for the acquisition were provided from $9,300 of the company's own funds and $72,000 in bank borrowings (Note 6). The acquisition was accounted for as a purchase and the net assets and the results of operations and cash flows of Cambridge Brands have been included in the company's consolidated financial statements from October 15, 1993.

The following unaudited pro forma information shows the results of the company's operations as though the purchase of Cambridge Brands had been consummated as of the beginning of each year:

	1993	1992
Net sales	$306,584	$303,576
Net earnings	36,592	32,763
Net earnings per common share	3.37	3.02

The pro forma results of operations are not necessarily indicative of the actual results of operations that would have occurred had the purchase actually been made at the beginning of periods presented or of future operations.

NOTE 3—ACCRUED LIABILITIES:

Accrued liabilities are comprised of the following:

	December 31,	
	1994	1993
Compensation and employee benefits	$ 5,512	$ 5,989
Commissions	736	856
Advertising and promotions	4,766	4,413
Workers' compensation	1,271	973
Other	4,761	5,688
	$17,046	$17,919

NOTE 4—INCOME TAXES:

The domestic and foreign components of pretax income are as follows:

	1994	1993	1992
Domestic	$58,439	$56,159	$48,450
Foreign	2,728	1,551	3,472
	$61,167	$57,710	$51,922

The provision for income taxes is comprised of the following:

	1994	1993	1992
Current:			
Federal	$18,096	$19,052	$17,820
Foreign	1,455	534	1,073
State	2,407	2,406	2,469
	21,958	21,992	21,362
Deferred:			
Federal	1,972	514	(1,318)
Foreign	(963)	(281)	(25)
State	269	43	(129)
	1,278	276	(1,472)
	$23,236	$22,268	$19,890

Deferred income taxes are comprised of the following:

	December 31,	
	1994	1993
Workers' compensation	$ 435	$ 331
Reserve for returns	438	445
Reserve for uncollectible accounts	174	230
Other accrued expenses	1,842	1,705
VEBA funding	(756)	(526)
Other, net	35	(91)
Net current deferred income tax asset	$ 2,168	$ 2,094

	December 31,	
	1994	1993
Depreciation	$ 7,229	$ 6,878
Post employment benefits	(1,709)	(1,536)
Deductible goodwill	2,071	1,342
Deferred compensation	(739)	(473)
DISC commissions	849	724
Other, net	15	(571)
Net long-term deferred income tax liability	$ 7,716	$ 6,364

The effective income tax rate differs from the statutory rate as follows:

	1994	1993	1992
U.S. statutory rate	35.0%	35.0%	34.0%
State income taxes, net	2.8	2.8	3.0
Amortization of excess of cost over acquired net tangible assets	0.7	0.7	0.8
Other, net	(0.5)	0.1	0.5
Effective income tax rate	38.0%	38.6%	38.3%

The company has not provided for U.S. federal or foreign withholding taxes on $2,701 of foreign subsidiaries' undistributed earnings as of December 31, 1994 because such earnings are considered to be permanently reinvested. When excess cash has accumulated in the company's foreign subsidiaries and it is advantageous for tax or foreign exchange reasons, subsidiary earnings may be remitted, and income taxes are provided on such amounts. It is not practicable to determine the amount of income taxes that would be payable upon remittance of the undistributed earnings.

NOTE 5—SHARE CAPITAL AND CAPITAL IN EXCESS OF PAR VALUE:

	Common Stock		Class B Common Stock		Capital in excess of par value
	Shares (000's)	Amount	Shares (000's)	Amount	
Balance at January 1, 1992	6,554	$4,552	3,378	$2,346	$ 64,200
Issuance of 3% stock dividend	197	136	100	69	21,962
Conversion of Class B common shares to common shares	83	58	(83)	(58)	—
Balance at December 31, 1992	6,834	4,746	3,395	2,357	86,162
Issuance of 3% stock dividend	204	142	101	70	24,946
Conversion of Class B common shares to common shares	31	21	(31)	(21)	—
Balance at December 31, 1993	7,069	4,909	3,465	2,406	111,108
Issuance of 3% stock dividend	211	147	103	71	21,889
Conversion of Class B common shares to common shares	26	18	(26)	(18)	—
Balance at December 31, 1994	7,306	$5,074	3,542	$2,459	$132,997

The Class B Common Stock has essentially the same rights as Common Stock, except that each share of Class B Common Stock has ten votes per share (compared to one vote per share of Common Stock), is not traded on any exchange, is restricted as to transfer and is convertible on a share-for-share basis, at any time and at no cost to the holders, into shares of Common Stock which are traded on the New York Stock Exchange.

Average shares outstanding and all per share amounts included in the financial statements and notes thereto have been adjusted retroactively to reflect the three percent stock dividend distributed in 1994.

NOTE 6—NOTES PAYABLE AND INDUSTRIAL DEVELOPMENT BONDS:

In October 1993, the company executed notes payable with three banks in the aggregate amount of $72,000 to provide funds for the acquisition of Cambridge Brands (Note 2). As of December 31, 1994 these notes have been repaid.

Additionally, in 1993, the company entered into two 3-year term notes aggregating $20,000 the proceeds of which were used to purchase the company's Chicago manufacturing facility and headquarters. These term notes bear interest payable monthly at 3.55% and mature entirely in 1996.

At December 31, 1994, the company had outstanding a three year interest rate swap agreement with a notional amount of $20,000. Under the agreement, the company exchanged a fixed rate of 4.24% for a variable rate adjusted monthly based upon 30 day LIBOR (6% at December 31, 1994). The company anticipates the counterparty to the swap agreement (a large financial institution) will fully perform on its obligations. The company accounts for the agreement using hedge accounting, and does not anticipate any circumstances, such as the early repayment of the underlying debt, which would cause a change in the accounting method used

During 1992, the company entered into an industrial development bond agreement with the City of Covington, Tennessee. The bond proceeds of $7.5 million are being used to finance the expansion of the company's existing facilities. Interest is payable at various times during the year based upon the interest calculation option (fixed, variable or floating) selected by the company. As of December 31, 1994 and 1993, interest was calculated under the floating option (4.1% and 3.4%, respectively) which requires monthly payments of interest. Principal on the bonds is due in its entirety in the year 2027.

At December 31, 1994 and 1993, unexpended bond proceeds of $162 and $1,061 were restricted for use on the capital expenditure projects discussed above. These funds, which are included as other assets in the accompanying consolidated balance sheet, are invested in short-term securities until expended.

In connection with the issuance of the bonds, the company entered into a letter of credit agreement with a bank for the amount of principal outstanding plus 48 days' accrued interest. The letter of credit, which expires in March 1996, carries an annual fee of 32 1/2 basis points on the outstanding principal amount of the bonds.

NOTE 7—EMPLOYEE BENEFIT PLANS:

Pension plans:

The company sponsors defined contribution pension plans covering certain nonunion employees with over one year of credited service. The company's policy is to fund pension costs accrued based on compensation levels. Total pension expense for 1994, 1993 and 1992 approximated $1,426, $1,202 and $1,075, respectively. The company also maintains certain profit sharing and savings-investment plans. Company contributions in 1994, 1993 and 1992 to these plans were $420, $321 and $291, respectively.

The company also contributes to multi-employer defined benefit pension plans for its union employees. Such contributions aggregated $352, $407 and $474 in 1994, 1993 and 1992, respectively. The relative position of each employer associated with the multi-employer plans with respect to the actuarial present value of benefits and net plan assets is not determinable by the company.

Postretirement health care and life insurance benefit plans:

The company provides certain postretirement health care and life insurance benefits for corporate office and management employees. Employees become eligible for these benefits if they meet minimum age and service requirements and if they agree to contribute a portion of the cost. The company has the right to modify and terminate these benefits and increase future participant contributions. The company does not fund postretirement health care and life insurance benefits in advance of payments for benefit claims.

The accrual for the accumulated postretirement benefit obligation at December 31, 1994 and 1993 consists of the following:

	December 31,	
	1994	1993
Retirees	$1,287	$1,285
Active employees	3,706	3,213
	$4,993	$4,498

Net periodic postretirement benefit cost for 1994, 1993 and 1992 included the following components:

	1994	1993	1992
Service cost—benefits attributed to service during the period	$318	$241	$246
Interest cost on the accumulated postretirement benefit obligation	291	259	288
Net periodic postretirement benefit cost	$609	$500	$534

For measurement purposes, a 13.5% annual rate of increase in the per capita cost of covered health care benefits was assumed for 1995; the rate was assumed to decrease gradually to 6.5% for 2002 and remain at that level thereafter. The health care cost trend rate assumption has a significant effect on the amounts reported. To illustrate, increasing the assumed health care cost trend rates by 1 percentage point in each year would increase the accumulated postretirement benefit obligation as of December 31, 1994 by approximately $485 and the aggregate of the service and interest cost components of net periodic postretirement benefit cost for the year then ended by approximately $116. The weighted-average discount rate used in determining the accumulated postretirement benefit obligation was 8% and 7% at December 31, 1994 and 1993, respectively.

NOTE 8—OTHER INCOME, NET:

Other income (expense) is comprised of the following:

	1994	1993	1992
Interest income	$1,288	$1,975	$2,376
Interest expense	(1,649)	(642)	(440)
Dividend income	1,509	1,992	1,624
Foreign exchange losses	(225)	(4)	(155)
Royalty income	149	634	289
Miscellaneous, net	107	238	295
	$1,179	$4,193	$3,989

NOTE 9—COMMITMENTS:

Future minimum rental commitments under non-cancelable operating leases are $2,395, $222, $42, $42 and $53 in the years 1995, 1996, 1997, 1998 and thereafter, respectively.

During 1993 and 1994, the company entered into operating leases for certain manufacturing equipment. These leases expire in 1998 but provide the company with the option to terminate the lease in 1996 and to purchase the equipment at its fair market value.

Rental expense aggregated $2,314, $1,015, and $1,243 in 1994, 1993 and 1992, respectively.

NOTE 10—DISCLOSURES ABOUT THE FAIR VALUE OF FINANCIAL INSTRUMENTS:

The following methods and assumptions were used to estimate the fair value of each class of financial instruments for which it is practicable to estimate that value.

Cash and cash equivalents and investments

The carrying amount approximates fair value of cash and cash equivalents because of the short maturity of those instruments. The fair values of investments are estimated based on quoted market prices.

Notes payable and industrial development bonds

The fair values of the company's notes payable and industrial development bonds are estimated based on the quoted market prices for the same or similar issues.

Interest rate swap agreement

The fair value of the company's interest rate swap agreement is calculated using a valuation model based on well recognized financial principles and current market information to provide a reasonable approximation of fair value.

Fair value

The estimated fair values of the company's financial instruments are as follows:

	1994		1993	
	Carrying Amount	Fair Value	Carrying Amount	Fair Value
Cash and cash equivalents	$16,509	$16,509	$ 1,986	$ 1,986
Investments held to maturity	45,861	47,073	54,217	56,272
Notes payable and industrial development bonds	27,500	27,500	50,101	50,101
Interest rate swap agreement	0	(1,214)	0	2,279

A summary of the aggregate fair value, gross unrealized holding gains, gross unrealized losses and amortized cost basis of the company's investments held to maturity by major security type is as follows:

December 31, 1994

	Amortized Cost	Fair Value	Unrealized Gains	Unrealized Losses
Unit investment trusts of preferred stocks	$ 7,836	$ 8,653	$ 849	($ 32)
Tax-free commercial paper	9,996	10,000	4	—
Municipal bonds	11,773	11,711	1	(63)
Unit investment trusts of municipal bonds	4,547	5,033	546	(60)
US gov't/agency obligations	9,901	9,872	—	(29)
Private export funding securities	1,808	1,804	—	(4)
	$45,861	$47,073	$ 1,400	($ 188)

December 31, 1993

	Amortized Cost	Fair Value	Unrealized Gains	Unrealized Losses
Unit investment trusts of preferred stocks	$11,250	$12,698	$ 1,482	($ 34)
Tax-free commercial paper	19,803	19,802	5	(6)
Municipal bonds	14,314	14,428	114	—
Unit investment trusts of municipal bonds	7,139	7,633	650	(156)
Private export funding securities	1,711	1,711	—	—
	$54,217	$56,272	$ 2,251	($ 196)

NOTE 11—GEOGRAPHIC AREA AND SALES INFORMATION:
Summary of sales, net earnings and assets by geographic area

1994

	United States	Mexico and Canada	Consolidated
Sales to unaffiliated customers	$268,582	$28,350	$296,932
Sales between geographic areas	1,382	2,204	
	$269,964	$30,554	
Net earnings	$ 36,139	$ 1,792	$ 37,931
Total assets	$297,981	$12,102	$310,083
Net assets	$229,066	$11,395	$240,461

1993

	United States	Mexico and Canada	Consolidated
Sales to unaffiliated customers	$234,460	$25,133	$259,593
Sales between geographic areas	2,186	3,219	
	$236,646	$28,352	
Net earnings	$ 34,144	$ 1,298	$ 35,442
Total assets	$288,506	$15,434	$303,940
Net assets	$199,862	$12,481	$212,343

1992

	United States	Mexico and Canada	Consolidated
Sales to unaffiliated customers	$225,001	$20,423	$245,424
Sales between geographic areas	806	1,649	
	$225,807	$22,072	
Net earnings	$ 29,478	$ 2,554	$ 32,032
Total assets	$211,099	$13,371	$224,470
Net assets	$171,838	$ 9,866	$181,704

Total assets are those assets associated with or used directly in the respective geographic area, excluding intercompany advances and investments.

Major customer

Revenues from a major customer aggregated approximately 16.8%, 13.6% and 12.5% of total net sales during the years ended December 31, 1994, 1993 and 1992, respectively.

Report of Independent Accountants

To the Board of Directors and Shareholders of Tootsie Roll Industries, Inc.

In our opinion, the accompanying consolidated statement of financial position and the related consolidated statement of earnings and of cash flows present fairly, in all material respects, the financial position of Tootsie Roll Industries, Inc. and its subsidiaries at December 31, 1994 and 1993, and the results of their operations and their cash flows for each of the three years in the period ended December 31, 1994, in conformity with generally accepted accounting principles. These financial statements are the responsibility of the Company's management; our responsibility is to express an opinion on these financial statements based on our audits. We conducted our audits of these statements in accordance with generally accepted auditing standards which require that we plan and perform the audit to obtain reasonable assurance about whether the financial statements are free of material misstatement. An audit includes examining, on a test basis, evidence supporting the amounts and disclosures in the financial statements, assessing the accounting principles used and significant estimates made by management, and evaluating the overall financial statement presentation. We believe that our audits provide a reasonable basis for the opinion expressed above.

Price Waterhouse LLP

Chicago, Illinois
February 15, 1995

Quarterly Financial Data

TOOTSIE ROLL INDUSTRIES, INC. AND SUBSIDIARIES

(Thousands of dollars except per share data)

1994	First	Second	Third	Fourth	Total
Net sales	$56,370	$62,891	$111,014	$66,657	$296,932
Gross margin	28,121	31,306	51,195	30,745	141,367
Net earnings	6,962	7,860	15,386	7,723	37,931
Net earnings per share	.64	.72	1.42	.72	3.50

1993					
Net sales	$50,017	$53,923	$93,239	$62,414	$259,593
Gross margin	25,281	27,232	45,318	27,784	125,615
Net earnings	6,696	7,345	14,380	7,021	35,442
Net earnings per share	.62	.68	1.32	.65	3.27

1992					
Net sales	$42,798	$51,494	$86,856	$64,276	$245,424
Gross margin	21,691	26,104	41,979	28,527	118,301
Net earnings	5,563	6,733	13,076	6,660	32,032
Net earnings per share	.51	.62	1.21	.61	2.95

Net earnings per share is based upon average outstanding shares as adjusted for 3% stock dividends issued during the second quarter of each year.

1994-1993 QUARTERLY SUMMARY OF TOOTSIE ROLL INDUSTRIES, INC. STOCK PRICE AND DIVIDENDS PER SHARE

STOCK PRICES*

	1994		1993	
	Hi	Lo	Hi	Lo
1st Qtr . . .	76-1/2	69-1/4	83-3/8	74
2nd Qtr . .	70	59-1/8	82-1/2	71-1/8
3rd Qtr . . .	63-3/4	59-1/2	74-1/4	65
4th Qtr . . .	63-3/4	54-1/8	79-1/4	69-1/4

*NYSE — Composite Quotations.

Estimated Number of shareholders at 12/31/94 9,500

DIVIDENDS*

	1994	1993
1st Qtr	$.0923	$.0707
2nd Qtr	$.1100	$.0923
3rd Qtr	$.1100	$.0923
4th Qtr	$.1100	$.0923

NOTE: In addition to the above cash dividends, a 3% stock dividend was issued on 4/22/94 and 4/22/93.

*Cash dividends are restated to reflect 3% stock dividends.

Five Year Summary of Earnings and Financial Highlights

TOOTSIE ROLL INDUSTRIES, INC. AND SUBSIDIARIES

(Thousands of dollars except per share, percentage and ratio figures)

(See Management's Comments starting on page 5)	1994	1993	1992	1991	1990
Sales and Earnings Date					
Net Sales	$296,932	$259,593	$245,424	$207,875	$194,299
Gross Margin	141,367	125,615	118,301	100,595	91,094
Interest Expense	1,649	642	440	196	527
Provision for Income Taxes	23,236	22,268	19,890	17,641	14,563
Earnings before cumulative effect of accounting changes	37,931	35,442	32,032	26,533	22,556
Cumulative effect of accounting changes (1)	—	—	—	(1,038)	—
Net Earnings	37,931	35,442	32,032	25,495	22,556
% of Sales	12.8%	13.7%	13.1%	12.3%	11.6%
% of Shareholders' Equity	15.8%	16.7%	17.6%	16.7%	17.4%
Per Common Share Data (2)					
Net Sales	$ 27.37	$ 23.93	$ 22.62	$ 19.16	$ 17.91
Earnings before cumulative effect of accounting changes	3.50	3.27	2.95	2.45	2.08
Cumulative effect of accounting changes (1)	—	—	—	(.10)	—
Net Earnings	3.50	3.27	2.95	2.35	2.08
Shareholders' Equity	22.17	19.57	16.75	14.08	11.97
Cash Dividends	.42	.35	.27	.23	.20
Stock Dividends	3%	3%	3%	3%	3%
Additional Financial Data					
Working Capital	$ 92,626	$ 61,052	$110,714	$ 80,569	$ 55,378
Current Ratio	4.5	2.2	5.9	4.8	3.5
Net Cash Provided by Operating Activities	40,495	33,397	35,623	35,826	26,685
Property, Plant & Equipment Additions (3)	8,179	52,492	10,956	3,985	5,155
Net Property, Plant & Equipment	85,648	86,699	40,257	34,019	32,099
Total Assets	310,083	303,940	224,470	184,427	159,702
Long Term Debt	27,500	27,500	7,500	—	—
Shareholders' Equity	240,461	212,343	181,704	152,759	129,845
Average Shares Outstanding (2)	10,848	10,848	10,848	10,848	10,848

(1) Reflects adoption of new accounting standards for income taxes and postretirement health care and life insurance benefits (see Notes 1, 4 and 7 to financial statements).
(2) Adjusted for stock dividends.
(3) 1993 includes $44,500 relating to the Cambridge Brands acquisition and the purchase of the Chicago office and plant facilities.

PART TWO

●···●

Materials for Analyzing
Liz Claiborne Corporation

INDUSTRY REPORTS
Value Line Industry Report: Apparel *51*
Moody's Industry Review: Apparel--Women's *52*
S&P's Industry Survey: Textiles, Apparel and Home
Furnishings *55*

COMPANY REPORTS
S&P's Stock Report: Liz Claiborne *81*
Value Line Report: Liz Claiborne *83*

Lackluster apparel sales thus far in 1995 have led retailers and manufacturers alike to take a cautious stance towards inventories for the upcoming holiday season. As it now stands business prospects appear unexciting for the balance of the year.

We expect business conditions to improve modestly in 1996. A conservative approach on the part of apparel makers is likely to lead to a recovery in profits.

In terms of probable year-ahead performance, the apparel industry is ranked to lag the broader market averages. Only a few companies are ranked favorably for Timeliness.

The Going Continues To Be Rough

Through the first six months of the year, a vast number of the apparel companies we cover have posted soft sales and lower earnings versus year-ago levels. This primarily reflects a competitive operating environment, with apparel retailers vying for business through the use of markdowns. This promotional stance has wreaked havoc on margins at both retail and producer levels. There are several reasons for the current down cycle in the apparel industry, in our opinion. For one, consumers are foregoing purchases of soft goods in favor of durable goods. Too, a vaguely defined fashion trend is keeping people from refurbishing their wardrobes.

Not surprisingly, most apparel companies are warier than ever about sales prospects over the next few months. This attitude is increasing the focus on operating conservatism, which should enable firms to strengthen their cost structures. For example, the manufacturers are trying to fend off margin erosion by keeping inventory levels relatively low. Also, they are maintaining lower balances on bank credit lines to keep interest expense in check. These typically represent an apparel company's biggest variable cost components. Assuming that retail conditions don't worsen, these initiatives may support more favorable earnings comparisons over the balance of the year.

INDUSTRY TIMELINESS: 82 (of 97)

"Discipline" Will Be The Watchword In 1996

Many apparel makers have a tendency to build up their inventories and widen their distribution channels rapidly when the retail climate suggests relative strength. Often, this aggressive bent backfires when the suggestion of a buoyant sales condition turns out to be illusory. As a result, the earnings stream of several apparel companies exhibits wide swings that accentuate the volatility of the industry as a whole.

However, we don't expect this to happen in the year ahead. The demand uncertainty outlined above is reason enough to keep operations on a conservative track. Though Value Line is calling for modest economic growth in 1996, many apparel makers may not subscribe to this forecast. Those that we have talked with are expecting demand conditions to remain challenging. In that light, we think nearly all of the companies in this group will continue to concentrate more on retrenchment efforts than expansion plans. Thus, inventories will probably be kept lean in order to reduce the risk of incurring widespread discounting, which is the largest items that contributes to reduced earnings results. Also, many companies are looking more at their own sourcing and manufacturing operations to see if cost savings could be effected.

If this scenario bears out, we think that, for the most part, earnings for the group may well show modest advances next year.

Investment Advice

Stocks in this group, in general, have turned in a lackluster performance over the past year, reflecting the weak consumer sentiment at retail. And based on recent price and earnings momentum, we think this industry will continue to lag the broader market averages in the year ahead. Only a handful of companies are favorably ranked for Timeliness. Given the cyclical nature of this industry and the tendency towards price volatility, we recommend that conservative investors shop among those issues that carry an average rank (3) for Safety and have a Financial Strength rating of B+ or higher.

Vik Malhotra

Composite Statistics: APPAREL INDUSTRY

1991	1992	1993	1994	1995	1996		98-00
13035	14999	15909	16085	17000	18000	Sales ($mill)	23655
13.5%	14.3%	13.4%	12.8%	13.0%	13.4%	Operating Margin	15.5%
398.9	434.8	479.4	515	565	610	Depreciation ($mill)	775
640.5	922.9	909.0	780	915	1050	Net Profit ($mill)	1605
40.0%	37.5%	36.5%	38.0%	39.0%	39.0%	Income Tax Rate	38.5%
4.9%	6.2%	5.7%	4.8%	5.4%	5.8%	Net Profit Margin	6.8%
3176.7	3655.6	4441.5	4415	4815	5200	Working Cap'l ($mill)	6855
2407.1	2667.0	2929.1	2785	2410	2450	Long-Term Debt ($mill)	2560
4477.1	5134.1	6068.4	6205	6950	7790	Net Worth ($mill)	10410
11.4%	13.4%	11.4%	10.0%	11.0%	11.5%	% Earned Total Cap'l	13.0%
14.3%	18.0%	15.0%	12.5%	13.0%	13.5%	% Earned Net Worth	15.5%
10.8%	15.1%	12.2%	10.0%	10.5%	11.0%	% Retained to Comm Eq	12.0%
26%	17%	20%	21%	20%	20%	% All Div'ds to Net Prof	18%
16.2	15.6	15.3	*Bold figures are*			Avg Ann'l P/E Ratio	12.0
1.03	.95	.90	*Value Line estimates*			Relative P/E Ratio	.90
1.5%	1.1%	1.3%				Avg Ann'l Div'd Yield	1.2%

Apparel
RELATIVE STRENGTH (Ratio of Industry to Value Line Comp.)
Index: June, 1967 = 100

MOODY'S INDUSTRY REVIEW
October 6, 1995
Volume: 14 No: 17

APPAREL—WOMEN'S

COMPARATIVE STATISTICS

COMPANY	FISCAL DATE	EXCH	SYMBOL	PRICE RANGE (12 MOS.) HIGH	PRICE RANGE (12 MOS.) LOW	RECENT PRICE	EARNINGS PER SHARE LATEST 12 MOS.	EARNINGS PER SHARE 1994	EARNINGS PER SHARE 1993	EARNINGS PER SHARE 1992	IND. CASH DIV.	1994 BOOK VALUE PER SH.	1994 STKHLDRS' EQUITY ($ MILL)	1994 LONG-TERM DEBT (%)
ALBA-WALDENSIAN, INC.	12/31	ASE	AWS	11½	8⅜	9	0.61	1.05	0.54	0.74	Nil	15.44	29.09	3.32
BISCAYNE APPAREL, INC.	12/31	ASE	BHA	2¾	1⅛	1¼	0.11	0.23	0.45	0.01	Nil	2.02	25.88	23.49
CACHE, INC.	12/31	NMS	CACH	8¼	3½	3⅞	0.38	0.53	0.42	0.13	Nil	1.81	16.43	18.18
CHAUS (BERNARD), INC.	6/30	NYS	CHS	6⅝	2⅞	5½	d2.61	d2.55	d0.60	0.19	Nil	...	d13.60	363.07
CLAIRE'S STORES, INC.	1/28	NYS	CLE	23	10¼	20½	1.22	1.15	1.15	0.71	0.120	5.88	122.15	2.40
CLOTHESTIME, INC. (THE)	1/28	NMS	CTME	4½	2½	2⅞	d0.93	d0.79	0.56	0.58	Nil	3.59	50.91	39.56
DEB SHOPS INC.	1/31	NMS	DEBS	6	2⅞	3⅝	d0.32	d0.21	0.33	0.46	0.200	6.80	87.38	2.28
DRESS BARN, INC. (THE)	7/31	NMS	DBRN	11⅛	8¾	10⅝	0.82	0.73	0.86	0.74	Nil	7.15	159.20	...
JACLYN, INC.	6/30	ASE	JLN	10⅛	3½	5	d0.87	0.59	d0.42	0.52	Nil	6.95	18.70	5.31
JONES APPAREL GROUP, INC.	12/31	NYS	JNY	36⅝	22⅝	35⅝	2.22	2.08	1.85	1.59	Nil	8.51	248.68	3.13
LIZ CLAIBORNE, INC.	12/31	NYS	LIZ	26	14⅜	25¼	1.11	1.06	1.54	2.61	0.450	12.77	982.98	0.12
MOVIE STAR, INC. (NY)	6/30	ASE	MSI	1⅜	⅜	⅝	0.06	d0.30	0.16	0.02	Nil	0.98	13.73	62.14
NANTUCKET INDUSTRIES INC.	2/25	ASE	NAN	6⅝	3½	4½	d1.15	d1.15	d3.81	0.15	Nil	1.83	5.47	64.53
OAK HILL SPORTSWEAR CORP.	12/31	NMS	OHSC	5⅛	1½	2½	0.25	0.11	0.08	d0.65	Nil	5.56	12.89	10.93
WARNACO GROUP, INC. (THE)	1/7	NYS	WAC	24½	14⅞	24	1.57	1.53	1.34	1.18	0.280	0.14	240.47	46.23
WOLF (HOWARD B.), INC.	5/31	ASE	HBW	7⅞	5⅝	6½	0.75	0.75	0.74	0.67	0.320	6.47	6.83	...
YES CLOTHING CO.	3/31	NAS	YSCO	10½	1	3⅛	d1.37	d1.22	d0.77	d0.26	Nil	0.40	1.54	29.97

† Indicates previous year's data. • Indicates subsequent year's data.
Ind. cash div. excludes stk. splits & stk. divs.

FINANCIAL DATA–LATEST ANNUAL RANKINGS

REVENUES ($ MILL.)

RANK	COMPANY	'94 AMT
1	Liz Claiborne, Inc.	2162.90
2	Warnaco Group, Inc. (The)	788.76
3	Jones Apparel Group, Inc.	633.26
4	Dress Barn, Inc. (The)	457.32
5	Clothestime, Inc. (The)	342.28
6	Claire's Stores Inc.	301.44
7	Chaus (Bernard), Inc.	206.33
8	DEB Shops Inc.	203.78
9	Cache, Inc.	104.71
10	Movie Star, Inc. (NY)	103.11
11	Oak Hill Sportswear Corp.	84.15
12	Jaclyn, Inc.	82.82
13	Biscayne Apparel, Inc.	72.35
14	Alba-Waldensian Inc.	56.51
15	Nantucket Industries	37.02
16	Yes Clothing Co.	29.01
17	Wolf (Howard B.) Inc.	14.44

NET INCOME ($ MILL.)

RANK	COMPANY	'94 AMT
1	Liz Claiborne, Inc.	82.85
2	Warnaco Group, Inc. (The)	63.33
3	Jones Apparel Group, Inc.	54.92
4	Claire's Stores Inc.	23.86
5	Dress Barn, Inc. (The)	16.15
6	Cache, Inc.	4.81
7	Biscayne Apparel, Inc.	2.05
8	Alba-Waldensian Inc.	1.95
9	Jaclyn, Inc.	1.59
10	Wolf (Howard B.) Inc.	0.79
11	Oak Hill Sportswear Corp.	0.23
12	DEB Shops Inc.	d2.72
13	Nantucket Industries	d3.15
14	Movie Star, Inc. (NY)	d4.19
15	Yes Clothing Co.	d4.65
16	Clothestime, Inc. (The)	d11.24
17	Chaus (Bernard), Inc.	d46.76

OPERATING PROFIT MARGIN (%)

RANK	COMPANY	'94 AMT
1	Jones Apparel Group, Inc.	13.87
2	Warnaco Group, Inc. (The)	12.58
3	Claire's Stores Inc.	12.47
4	Wolf (Howard B.) Inc.	7.73
5	Biscayne Apparel, Inc.	6.86
6	Alba-Waldensian Inc.	5.75
7	Liz Claiborne, Inc.	5.58
8	Cache, Inc.	5.40
9	Dress Barn, Inc. (The)	5.23
10	Jaclyn, Inc.	3.08
11	Oak Hill Sportswear Corp.	2.51
12	Movie Star, Inc. (NY)	d0.12
13	DEB Shops Inc.	d2.27
14	Clothestime, Inc. (The)	d4.04
15	Nantucket Industries	d5.27
16	Yes Clothing Co.	d14.37
17	Chaus (Bernard), Inc.	d20.77

RETURN ON CAPITAL (%)

RANK	COMPANY	'94 AMT
1	Cache, Inc.	23.97
2	Jones Apparel Group, Inc.	21.38
3	Claire's Stores Inc.	18.55
4	Warnaco Group, Inc. (The)	13.91
5	Wolf (Howard B.) Inc.	11.41
6	Dress Barn, Inc. (The)	10.03
7	Liz Claiborne, Inc.	8.40
8	Jaclyn, Inc.	7.33
9	Biscayne Apparel, Inc.	6.05
10	Alba-Waldensian Inc.	6.04
11	Oak Hill Sportswear Corp.	1.58
12	DEB Shops Inc.	d3.04
13	Movie Star, Inc. (NY)	d11.54
14	Clothestime, Inc. (The)	d11.94
15	Nantucket Industries	d20.42
16	Yes Clothing Co.	d212.23
17	Chaus (Bernard), Inc.	d903.48

Publication, Editorial and Executive Offices, 99 Church Street, New York, NY 10007

APPAREL—WOMEN'S (Cont'd.)

CASH & MARKETABLE SECURITIES ($ MILL.)

RANK	COMPANY	'94 AMT	RANK	COMPANY	'94 AMT	RANK	COMPANY	'94 AMT	RANK	COMPANY	'94 AMT
1	Liz Claiborne, Inc............	330.35	6	Jones Apparel Group, Inc.	21.13	10	Wolf (Howard B.) Inc.	1.38	15	Yes Clothing Co..............	0.23
2	Dress Barn, Inc. (The)	61.99				11	Movie Star, Inc. (NY)	0.92	16	Alba-Waldensian Inc........	0.10
3	DEB Shops Inc............	50.61	7	Jaclyn, Inc.	5.86	12	Cache, Inc.	0.81	17	Nantucket Industries........	0.03
4	Clothestime, Inc. (The)	48.51	8	Biscayne Apparel, Inc......	4.18	13	Chaus (Bernard), Inc.	0.47			
5	Claire's Stores Inc.	48.47	9	Warnaco Group, Inc. (The)	3.79	14	Oak Hill Sportswear Corp.	0.33			

CURRENT RATIO

RANK	COMPANY	'94 AMT	RANK	COMPANY	'94 AMT	RANK	COMPANY	'94 AMT	RANK	COMPANY	'94 AMT
1	DEB Shops Inc.	5.02	5	Liz Claiborne, Inc.............	3.37	10	Clothestime, Inc. (The)	1.88	14	Cache, Inc.	1.59
2	Jones Apparel Group, Inc.	4.80	5	Nantucket Industries..........	3.37	11	Biscayne Apparel, Inc......	1.85	15	Yes Clothing Co..............	1.44
			7	Claire's Stores Inc.	2.63	12	Oak Hill Sportswear Corp.	1.77	16	Warnaco Group, Inc. (The)	1.33
3	Alba-Waldensian Inc.........	4.59	8	Dress Barn, Inc. (The)	2.57						
4	Wolf (Howard B.) Inc.	4.08	9	Jaclyn, Inc.......................	2.45	13	Movie Star, Inc. (NY)	1.76	17	Chaus (Bernard), Inc.	1.08

ACCOUNTS RECEIVABLE TURNOVER

RANK	COMPANY	'94 AMT	RANK	COMPANY	'94 AMT	RANK	COMPANY	'94 AMT	RANK	COMPANY	'94 AMT
1	DEB Shops Inc.	199.46	6	Oak Hill Sportswear Corp.	8.56	10	Wolf (Howard B.) Inc.	7.09	14	Warnaco Group, Inc. (The)	5.73
2	Cache, Inc.	31.39				11	Jones Apparel Group, Inc.	6.93	15	Biscayne Apparel, Inc......	4.09
3	Clothestime, Inc. (The)	30.06	7	Chaus (Bernard), Inc.	8.54	12	Nantucket Industries........	6.19	16	Claire's Stores Inc.	...
4	Liz Claiborne, Inc.............	11.33	8	Movie Star, Inc. (NY)	7.63	13	Jaclyn, Inc.......................	6.13	16	Dress Barn, Inc. (The)	...
5	Yes Clothing Co..............	11.01	9	Alba-Waldensian Inc.........	7.24						

INVENTORY TURNOVER

RANK	COMPANY	'94 AMT	RANK	COMPANY	'94 AMT	RANK	COMPANY	'94 AMT	RANK	COMPANY	'94 AMT
1	Yes Clothing Co..............	9.39	6	Claire's Stores Inc.	5.92	11	Biscayne Apparel, Inc......	3.33	16	Warnaco Group, Inc. (The)	2.17
2	Clothestime, Inc. (The)	8.67	7	DEB Shops Inc.	5.28	12	Liz Claiborne, Inc.............	3.26			
3	Cache, Inc.	7.41	8	Chaus (Bernard), Inc.	5.22	13	Alba-Waldensian Inc.........	2.69	17	Movie Star, Inc. (NY)	1.81
4	Jaclyn, Inc.......................	6.74	9	Jones Apparel Group, Inc.	3.92	14	Nantucket Industries........	2.68			
5	Oak Hill Sportswear Corp.	5.97	10	Dress Barn, Inc. (The)	3.82	15	Wolf (Howard B.) Inc.	2.52			

PRICE-EARNINGS RATIO

RANK	COMPANY	'94 AMT	RANK	COMPANY	'94 AMT	RANK	COMPANY	'94 AMT	RANK	COMPANY	'94 AMT
1	Wolf (Howard B.) Inc.	8.67	5	Biscayne Apparel, Inc......	11.94	9	Jones Apparel Group, Inc.	16.05	12	Clothestime, Inc. (The)	...
2	Cache, Inc.	10.20	6	Dress Barn, Inc. (The)	12.65	10	Claire's Stores Inc.	16.80	12	DEB Shops Inc.	...
3	Oak Hill Sportswear Corp.	10.25	7	Alba-Waldensian Inc.........	14.75	11	Liz Claiborne, Inc.............	22.75	12	Jaclyn, Inc.......................	...
			8	Warnaco Group, Inc. (The)	15.29	12	Chaus (Bernard), Inc.	...	12	Nantucket Industries........	...
4	Movie Star, Inc. (NY)	11.47							12	Yes Clothing Co..............	...

YIELD (%)

RANK	COMPANY	'94 AMT	RANK	COMPANY	'94 AMT	RANK	COMPANY	'94 AMT	RANK	COMPANY	'94 AMT
1	Jaclyn, Inc.......................	10.00	6	Alba-Waldensian Inc........	...	6	Dress Barn, Inc. (The)	...	6	Oak Hill Sportswear Corp.	...
2	DEB Shops Inc.	5.52	6	Biscayne Apparel, Inc......	...	6	Jones Apparel Group, Inc.	...	6	Warnaco Group, Inc. (The)	...
3	Wolf (Howard B.) Inc.	4.92	6	Cache, Inc.	...	6	Movie Star, Inc. (NY)	...			
4	Liz Claiborne, Inc.............	1.78	6	Chaus (Bernard), Inc.	...	6	Nantucket Industries........	...	6	Yes Clothing Co..............	...
5	Claire's Stores Inc.	0.59	6	Clothestime, Inc. (The)	...						

12-MONTH PRICE SCORE

RANK	COMPANY	'94 AMT	RANK	COMPANY	'94 AMT	RANK	COMPANY	'94 AMT	RANK	COMPANY	'94 AMT
1	Claire's Stores Inc.	126.55	4	Chaus (Bernard), Inc.	106.63	9	Nantucket Industries........	83.23	14	Oak Hill Sportswear Corp.	66.72
2	Jones Apparel Group, Inc.	112.44	5	Liz Claiborne, Inc.............	106.01	10	Alba-Waldensian Inc........	80.58			
			6	Dress Barn, Inc. (The)	91.54	11	Jaclyn, Inc.......................	80.33	15	Biscayne Apparel, Inc......	64.89
3	Warnaco Group, Inc. (The)	110.14	7	Clothestime, Inc. (The)	88.07	12	DEB Shops Inc.	79.21	16	Cache, Inc.	64.87
			8	Wolf (Howard B.) Inc.	86.24	13	Movie Star, Inc. (NY)	67.00	17	Yes Clothing Co..............	64.65

7-YEAR PRICE SCORE

RANK	COMPANY	'94 AMT	RANK	COMPANY	'94 AMT	RANK	COMPANY	'94 AMT	RANK	COMPANY	'94 AMT
1	Wolf (Howard B.) Inc.	103.80	6	Dress Barn, Inc. (The)	68.00	10	Jaclyn, Inc.......................	49.20	14	Jones Apparel Group, Inc.	...
2	Alba-Waldensian Inc.........	99.00	7	Nantucket Industries........	62.60	11	Movie Star, Inc. (NY)	40.80			
3	Claire's Stores Inc.	96.70	8	Liz Claiborne, Inc.............	56.60	12	Clothestime, Inc. (The)	39.50	14	Warnaco Group, Inc. (The)	...
4	Chaus (Bernard), Inc.	84.20	8	Oak Hill Sportswear Corp.	56.60	13	DEB Shops Inc.	37.40			
5	Cache, Inc.	68.20				14	Biscayne Apparel, Inc......	...	14	Yes Clothing Co..............	...

APPAREL—WOMEN'S (Cont'd.)

COMPOSITE STOCK PRICE MOVEMENTS

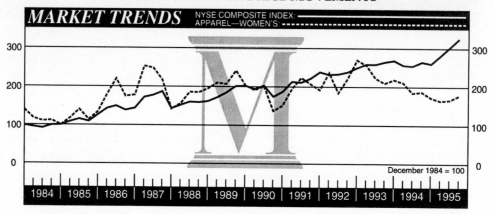

Moody's Industry Review (ISSN 1047-3114) is published every two weeks on Friday by Moody's Investors Service, 99 Church St., New York, N.Y. 10007. Subscription rate $495 per annum. Second-class postage paid at New York, N.Y. and additional mailing offices. POSTMASTER: Send address changes to Moody's Industry Review, 99 Church St., New York, NY 10007.
Reproduction of material appearing in Moody's Industry Review permitted only on written permission from Moody's Investors Service.

SEPTEMBER 28, 1995 (Vol. 163, No. 39, Sec. 1)   Replaces Basic Analysis dated February 3, 1994

STANDARD & POOR'S

industry surveys

Overview 75

Demographics & Consumer Attitudes 76

Textiles 82

Textile Industry Fundamentals 88

Apparel 93

Apparel Fundamentals 95

Home Furnishings 102

Furniture Fundamentals 106

Major Appliances 109

Appliance Fundamentals 113

Personal-Care & Household
Cleaning Products 116

Personal-Care & Household
Cleaning Products Fundamentals 118

Composite Industry Data 121

Comparative Company Analysis 123

textiles, apparel
& home furnishings
includes appliances, personal-care &
household cleaning products
BASIC ANALYSIS

Consumer spending remains flat

More than a year ago, we stated that the go-go 1980s were over and that the free-spending mind-set that characterized that era was gone. We still maintain that opinion. Consumers continue to be frugal: owning expensive cars and wearing designer clothes are *passé,* while shopping at Wal-Mart, getting a "good deal", and being comfortable remain *au courant.*

We attribute the transformation of the 1980s consumer into the 1990s consumer to several factors. Most importantly, the bulk of the population is older. Many who were single in the 1980s are now married, and many of these married consumers have children to support, mortgages to pay, and jobs to worry about. Time has also become more precious, and leisure activities have become more important. Many of the 1980s shoppers no longer consider shopping at the mall a leisure-time activity; instead, they prefer being at home or pursuing family-oriented activities.

Today's consumers could also be described as more intelligent. They don't appear to fall for fashion styles the way they did in the 1980s. They also are more willing to shop for the best price, and tend to wait until a store has a major promotion sale before making purchases. Consumers are also more discerning when it comes to quality *vis-à-vis* price: why buy a $250 jacket when one can buy a similar-looking jacket (although of somewhat lesser quality) for $89?

We also feel that the uncertain economy has stalled consumer spending. The 1990–91 recession wreaked havoc with consumers, and we believe the mind-set that was created during that period still remains with most. During that recession, a long series of highly publicized lay-offs began; even now, four years since the end of the most recent recession, many major companies have continued to restructure and/or consolidate, laying off employees in the process. Challenger, Gray & Christmas Inc., an outplacement firm in Chicago, reported that U.S. companies announced in August 1995 that they had plans to cut 32,262 jobs, up from July's announced cutbacks of 23,283. (These layoff programs typically take place over a period of several years; furthermore, the planned cutbacks announced in any given month are added to the totals of previous months.) Compared with 1994, the trend appears to be accelerating. A special problem with the most recent layoffs is that many workers are having difficulty finding new jobs with pay and benefits at least equal to their old ones.

At the same time, personal income is not growing as fast as it did in the 1980s, even though inflation is under control. Many wealth-wishing consumers of the 1980s now realize that their standard of living is often below that of their parents (when their parents were their age). Saving for retirement is also becoming a more important issue. Many of today's consumers realize that future Social Security payments, along with retirement benefits (if they have any), may not provide enough funds to last through their old age. As consumers try to save more, they have become more value-oriented and price conscious.

This new 1990s consumer affects all industries covered in this Survey. Growth in the textile industry over the past year has been limited by mediocre demand for home textiles. And, despite efforts by fashion designers to stimulate demand, clothing sales have also been slack, resulting in weak demand for apparel fabrics. We do not expect any significant pick-up in demand for textiles or apparel in the near future.

The outlook for furniture and appliances is slightly better. These industries are closely tied to interest rate levels, and we feel that as interest rate levels decline (as they typically do going into an election year), the housing market should pick up. A stronger housing market means higher demand for furniture and appliances. There is a down side, however. Both industries, which are very competitive, are finding that consumers are being very selective when it comes to buying furniture and appliances: they won't pay higher prices for a product unless they perceive that they're getting additional value or more features commensurate with the higher prices. The high-end furniture business, for example, had been predicted to be a big growth area in the 1990s, but consumers have confounded all expectations by opting for less expensive furniture instead. One reason is that consumers often cannot understand the higher price *vis-à-vis* the higher quality offered. The same trends are in evidence in the appliance sector.

We expect the personal and household goods industry will continue to grow, although at a very slow rate, given the maturity of the U.S. market. This industry will most likely remain as competitive as it has been over the past several years, as manufacturers vie for shelf space. Penetration into less saturated, overseas markets should provide the leading personal and household goods manufacturers with steady growth in the future. ∎

Elizabeth Vandeventer
Textiles, Apparel & Home Furnishings Analyst

DISPOSABLE PERSONAL INCOME & RETAIL SALES
(Seasonally Adjusted)

Sources: Dept. of Commerce; Bureau of Economic Analysis; *Business Conditions Digest.*

Consumers: who are they and what are they doing?

In this section, we will briefly examine some important demographic and consumer trends taking shape in the United States. According to the Census Bureau, as of 1992 (latest available) the population could be divided into five segments:

● **Senior citizens**—Those born earlier than the mid-1920s, aged 68 and older. As of 1992, this segment of the population consisted of 27.2 million individuals, or about 10.6% of the total U.S. population.

● **The Eisenhower generation**—Those born during the mid-1920s, Depression, or World War II (1925–1945); also known as war babies, pre-boomers, Depression babies, or the silent generation, aged 47–67. As of 1992, this segment of the population consisted of 48.2 million individuals, or about 18.8% of the total. Parents consist of senior citizens.

● **The baby boomers**—Those born in the 18 years after World War II (1946–1964), aged 28–46. As of 1992, this segment of the population consisted of 77.1 million individuals, or about 30.1% of the total. Parents include Eisenhowers mainly, but also senior citizens.

● **Generation X**—Those born in the 12 years following the baby boomers (1965–1977); also known as the baby busters, grunge kids, or slackers, aged 15–27. As of 1992, this segment of the population consisted of 47.7 million individuals, or 18.6% of the total. Parents include boomers mainly, but also Eisenhowers.

● **The baby boomlet**—Those born after the baby busters (1978–1992), aged 0–14. For comparative purposes, we assume that all babies born between 1992 and 1995 are also baby boomlets. As of 1992, this segment of the population consisted of 55.8 million individuals, or 21.8% of the total. Parents mainly include late boomers, but also some Generation Xers.

Demographics: a dynamic area

One of the most important factors to remember when studying demographics is that these statistics are dynamic.

In the year 2025, *American Demographics* magazine expects that the Eisenhower generation, which will then be more than 80 years old, will make up only 4.0% of the population (versus 18.8% in 1992). Baby boomers will make up 19.4% (30.1%) of the population and will be aged 61–79. Generation Xers, aged 49–60 in 2025, will make up 13.6% (18.6%) of the whole, while boomlets, aged 30–48, will make up about 23.9% (21.8%). The largest cohort in 2025 will be a new one—the post-boomlets—aged under 30. This cohort is expected to make up about 38.9% of the entire population in 2025.

The implications of these dynamics are somewhat unclear; however, it appears that there will be a big job market opening up for boomlets as boomers retire. The big question is whether there will ever be a plethora of jobs available for Generation Xers, since boomers are not likely to retire at early ages due to lack of money; and for post-boomlets, since boomlets will probably control the majority of jobs as post-boomlets enter into their working years.

In the short term, these demographics favor manufacturers of children's items as well as products for the home. According to *American Demographics*, the number of household formations was 98,872 in 1995; this number is expected to rise to 117,696 in 2010, an increase of 19% in total and an average annual increase of 1.3%. Family households, the largest segment of all households, are expected to increase about 16% over this period. These demographics also favor medical care and financial service companies.

Who's who, and what do they do?

We will begin our review of demographics and consumer attitudes with a look at the largest demographic group, the baby boomers, and then move on to the way that these boomers live and work. We will also examine some of the attitudes that affect these boomers' needs for goods and services—both now and in the future. These attitudes are not exclusive to just the boomers, and many can also be applied to the Eisenhower generation. We will then move on to reviews of Eisenhowers and Generation Xers.

Baby boomlets currently make up the second largest demographic cohort. Although this group has substantial influence in determining or influencing what parents or grandparents buy, we do not feel boomlets have developed strong enough spending habits and generational attitudes to discuss at this time. We have opted to pass on a discussion on senior citizens as well, since this generation's annual expenditures fall about 36% below the nation's median in consumer spending and are concentrated on healthcare and housing.

THE BOOMERS

● **The baby boomers are aging.** According to the Department of Commerce, the number of people between 35 and 54 years of age will increase from 25.3% of the U.S. population in 1990 to 30.1% by the year 2000. Other segments of the population are expected to decline as a percentage of the total population, with the exception of individuals aged 54 and older. This segment of the population will grow slightly, from 21.2% in 1990 to 22% by the year 2000.

● **The baby boomers are growing wealthier.** The baby boomers are entering their peak earning years. The median

*U.S. population projections

Age group	1995		2000		2005	
	Number (thous.)	% of total	Number (thous.)	% of total	Number (thous.)	% of total
Under 5 yrs.	19,553	7.4	18,908	6.9	18,959	6.6
5 to 14 yrs.	38,120	14.5	39,982	14.5	40,086	14.0
15 to 19 yrs.	18,024	6.9	19,758	7.2	20,982	7.3
20 to 24 yrs.	17,885	6.8	18,161	6.6	19,845	6.9
25 to 29 yrs.	18,994	7.2	17,836	6.5	18,072	6.3
30 to 34 yrs.	21,850	8.3	19,580	7.1	18,423	6.4
35 to 39 yrs.	22,267	8.5	22,168	8.1	19,894	6.9
40 to 44 yrs.	20,233	7.7	22,494	8.2	22,390	7.8
45 to 49 yrs.	17,440	6.6	19,824	7.2	22,041	7.7
50 to 54 yrs.	13,642	5.2	17,230	6.3	19,569	6.8
55 to 64 yrs.	21,153	8.1	23,988	8.7	29,647	10.4
65 yrs. & over	33,594	12.8	34,886	12.7	36,414	12.7
All Ages	262,755	100.0	274,815	100.0	286,322	100.0

*Includes Armed Forces abroad.
  Source: Department of Commerce, Population Series P-25.

income for those aged 35 to 44 is $40,869; for the group between the ages of 45 and 54, median income is $46,412. In contrast, the median income for individuals in the 25- to 34-year-old age group is $31,392; for people aged 55 to 64, the median is $37,791.

In addition, inheritances will boost the wealth of many consumers in the 1990s. By and large, the baby boomers are the children of a generation that lived through the Great Depression. This generation has a higher savings rate than any other. The parents of many baby boomers own homes that have appreciated substantially in value since the time the houses were originally purchased. While it is probably true that this group—basically the Eisenhower generation—is going to live longer than previous generations, the grim but certain fact is that they won't live forever. Thus, the boomers may experience a rush of inherited wealth on top of what they will make on their own.

● **Baby boomers will continue to earn more.** The baby boomers have had more formal education than any other generation in history. As of 1988, 30.7% of all persons over age 25 had a college degree, versus only 12.1% in 1970. Another 17% of the population had at least some college education, versus 10.2% in 1970. In the seven years that have elapsed since this data was collected, we suspect that an even greater proportion of the population is now college educated or has had some college education. In general, the level of one's education has a direct relationship to one's potential earning power.

Living and working

● **Married couples are on the rise.** The number of married couples, who now make up about 55% of all households, for a total of 51.3 million households, will also increase in the 1990s. (As a percentage of total households, however, the number of married couples will decrease.) According to *American Demographics* magazine, married couples and their families spend about 70% of all consumer dollars. *American Demographics* reports that the biggest spenders are married couples with children under 18 years of age. Although this group currently makes up only 27% of all households, the number of married couples with children under 18 is expected to grow to 39% by 2000, thanks to the current baby boomlet. According to the U.S. Department of Commerce, the number of births through 2000 should range from 3.5 million to 3.8 million annually.

"There is nothing like a child to change a couple's spending priorities, and baby boom parents have been making a lot of changes since the mid-1980s," says Margaret K. Ambry of *American Demographics*. According to Ms. Ambry, spending patterns change as children arrive and grow up, meaning that children born to baby boomers during the 1980s and early 1990s will demand the lion's share of household spending for the remainder of the decade. As these children grow, the portion of the family budget devoted to them will certainly expand.

● **Household formations will increase in the 1990s.** According to the U.S. Bureau of the Census, there were approximately 93.3 million households in America in 1990. This number is expected to swell to 106.0 million by 2000. Fueling this growth is the increasing number of single people living alone and the rising number of households headed by single persons.

● **There are more homeowners than renters.** According to the U.S. Bureau of the Census, 70% of all people

U.S. households and home ownership

Year	Households (Millions)	Percent owner occupied
E2000	106.0	71.0
1990	93.3	64.0
1980	80.8	64.4
1970	63.4	62.9
1960	52.8	61.9
1950	43.6	55.0
1940	34.9	43.6

E–Estimated.
Source: Home Improvement Research Institute.

U.S. home ownership by age

Age group	Percent of total households owning homes	Age group	Percent of total households owning homes
Under 25 yrs.	17	45 to 49 yrs.	74
25 to 29 yrs.	35	50 to 54 yrs.	77
30 to 34 yrs.	53	55 to 59 yrs.	79
35 to 39 yrs.	63	55 to 64 yrs.	80
40 to 44 yrs.	70	65 yrs. & over	76
Total	64		

Source: Home Improvement Research Institute.

between the ages 40 and 44 own their homes. The proportion increases with each successive age group: 74% of those aged 45 to 49 own a home; 77% of those in the 50- to 54-year-old age group; 79% of those aged 55 to 59; and 80% of individuals between 60 and 64 years of age own their homes. These statistics indicate that older individuals and couples tend to own homes, rather than rent them. With the bulk of the population moving into the over-40 group, the U.S. Bureau of the Census estimates that the percentage of all households occupied by owners rather than renters will increase to 70% by 2000 (74.2 million households), from 64% (59.7 million) in 1993.

● **Women are a big presence in the work force.** In 1970, 43.3% of all adult females were in the work force; by 1990, that figure was 57.5%. What is especially interesting is the growing proportion of women in their child-bearing years (defined here as those aged 16 to 44) who are in the work force. In 1970, 53.1% of women aged 16 to 24 were employed, as were 45.0% of 25- to 34-year-olds, and 51.1% of 35- to 44-year-olds. By 1990, the percentages for all groups had risen dramatically: 16–24, 63.1%; 25–34, 73.6%; 35–44, 76.5%. These figures point to the likelihood of a growing number of very busy, working mothers. They also indicate that, in many households, both mom and dad are working, which boosts the family's earning power.

Changing consumer attitudes

● **Cocooning.** Aging baby boomers are seeking more comfortable lifestyles. Indeed, some have accused this generation of founding the "couch potato" syndrome. Name-calling aside, there is clearly an upward trend in the demand for comfortable clothes, shoes, and home products. As consumers marry and have children, or just set up a house, many have participated in the process known as "cocooning," *i.e.*, spending more time at home. Videotape rental outlets, restaurants, and other stores that offer free delivery have helped make staying in for the evening an attractive option. Spending all that time at home has meant that having a pleasing and comfortable environment is becoming increasingly important.

58

● **Easy shopping.** A recent study conducted by MasterCard International found that consumers want a more satisfying shopping experience: one that is quick, convenient, and doesn't completely drain their pockets. Given the demands placed on their time, energy, and money, many consumers feel that they deserve nothing less. The proliferation of shopping outlets—from sprawling warehouse clubs to specialty boutiques—has made people increasingly choosy about where they go for what they want.

Confusion and frustration are common complaints shoppers have about their experiences at retail stores. One reason is the dizzying array of indistinguishable products. Another is the futility of looking for something that will probably be out of stock. As a result, according to the MasterCard study, consumers are moving toward a "male" pattern of shopping. Men tend to avoid haphazard or confusing shopping environments. They shun department stores and boutiques and prefer organized environments such as grocery stores or hardware outlets.

As shopping becomes less of a leisure activity, retailers must make it as painless as possible. For manufacturers of home furnishings and apparel, this means working closely with retailers to make sure the right merchandise is always in stock, that salespeople are well trained and knowledgeable, and that the merchandise itself is displayed in an attractive and inviting manner.

● **Vigilance.** The election of Bill Clinton to the office of President was a clear indication that voters wanted to take charge and bring about dramatic changes in their government. As consumers, these voters have also taken charge. A recent study by Kurt Salmon Associates found that 95% of those interviewed had doubts about the credibility of pricing policies at traditional department and specialty stores. In response, consumers are flocking to mass merchandisers and discount stores in search of quality and better value. (This trend can partially be attributed to the 1990–91 recession.) In fact, many agree that today's shoppers are more knowledgeable than ever before about the quality and price of the goods and services they buy.

● **"Ego-nomics."** Consumers are increasingly seeking out items that express their individuality. Purchases are sometimes made because they are "ego-nomical" rather than merely economical. This trend can be observed in both durable and non-durable spending. Consumers are increasingly ordering custom upholstered furniture and custom-made draperies rather than purchasing off-the-shelf merchandise.

The remodeling market has been so strong lately due in large part to consumers who want to tailor their homes to their particular needs and desires. One of the top complaints consumers have voiced over the past few years is that stores all carry the same merchandise, and that this has partly ruined the shopping experience. In order to survive, successful retailers and manufacturers must offer unique, exclusive merchandise and ensure the continuing availability of fresh, new selections.

● **Small indulgences.** Many boomers are willing to pay more for small luxuries that will enhance the quality of their life—an expensive scarf, pricey costume jewelry, hand cream or bubble bath, high-priced cookware, coordinated bed linens, or state-of-the art, high-tech appliances. Barbara Caplan, vice president at Yankelovich Partners, a consumer demographic consulting firm, believes that shoppers are still being careful, but they're starting to buy things that bring pleasure. Now and then they want items that are just plain frivolous.

● **Environmental consciousness.** Consumers are becoming more environmentally conscious. This trend is evident in consumers' growing enthusiasm for products manufactured from recycled materials and in the popularity of cosmetics and other health and beauty products that have not been tested on animals.

● **Well-being.** Consumers are becoming increasingly concerned about health, exercise, and a general sense of well-being. Aging Americans want to live longer and feel healthier and are willing to sacrifice time and money to achieve these goals. People are buying more vitamins than ever, going to spas for vacations, becoming less and less tolerant of smokers, and trying to eschew fatty foods and alcohol in favor of exercise and bottled water.

THE EISENHOWERS

● **The Eisenhower generation is wealthier than any other demographic group.** While smaller in number and less intensively studied and catered to by marketers than baby boomers, many members of the Eisenhower generation are at the top of their careers and earning power. The majority of today's corporate leaders belong in this demographic group.

According to a Census Bureau Survey of Income and Program Participation Survey in 1991, the net worth of those aged between 45 and 54 was $58,300 in 1991, and for those aged between 55 and 64, $83,000. This compared with a national median of $36,600. These numbers, which do not include equity in pension plans, life insurance policies, home furnishings, and jewelry, most likely underestimate the true wealth of many mature householders. Given most of the Eisenhower generation's capital appreciation in their homes, and with their pension plans mostly intact, this may be the last American generation with reasonably bright prospects for retirement.

● **Marketers are paying attention.** Recently, more and more attention has been focused on this age cohort. According to Jeff Ostroff, author of *Successful Marketing to the 50+ Consumer*, the Eisenhower generation provides a glimpse of what baby boomers will be like when they hit their 50s. Mr. Ostroff claims that companies that target the Eisenhower generation now will be much better prepared for marketing to mature consumers in the 21st century.

Living and working

● **Eisenhowers' responsibilities to children are mostly filled.** Members of the Eisenhower generation are often referred to as empty nesters, since their children have mostly moved out of the house, or have at least become more financially independent. As a result, many in this age bracket have more free time and fewer financial burdens—not to mention questions about what to do with all those empty bedrooms.

● **They're rethinking living spaces.** According to the Home Research Institute, 77%–80% of those aged between 50 and 64 own their own homes, higher than the national average. However, as children leave, many Eisenhowers are moving into smaller homes. Others are converting empty bedrooms into studies or hobby rooms.

● **Leisure-time activities are becoming more important.** Many in this generation are still working. According to the U.S. Department of Labor, the unemployment rate for civilian labor force participants aged 50–64 remains only two percentage points below the national average. But with few or no children at home and more money, Eisenhowers are pursuing leisure-time activities. These may include traveling to faraway places, taking long road trips in recreational vehicles, doing volunteer work, and attending lectures on investing and other personal growth topics. This generation is also returning to the hobbies of their youth, including photography, wood working, gardening, and painting.

● **Grandparenting comes to the fore.** Many Eisenhowers are now grandparents, which translates into all the joys of being with children—without the work. For retailers, this means that grandparents tend to be big buyers of toys and children's clothing. Many grandparents are also buying the necessities for their grandchildren, including baby furniture, car seats, and strollers.

● **They're buying more expensive cars.** Vern Parker, a writer at *The Washington Times*, says that while Eisenhowers don't buy as many cars as the baby boomers, the cars cost a lot more. Mr. Parker estimates that 17% of those aged between 45 and 59 were expected to buy a new car in 1995, compared with 23% for those aged between 30 and 44. However, the Bureau of the Census estimates that those aged between 45 to 54 tend to spend about 17.6% more on a car than do those aged between 35–44. (For more details on this topic, see the adjoining table entitled "Annual Household Expenditures, by Age of Householder—1990".)

Eisenhowers' attitudes

● **The work ethic.** The Eisenhowers are a mix between senior citizens and baby boomers. Most in this generation possess the work ethic of their parents, including self-discipline and thrift. For example, according to one study, 61% of pre-retirees in this age bracket actively save for retirement, compared with only 38% of all baby boomers.

● **Enjoying life.** On the other hand, Eisenhowers also share in many of the same attitudes as baby boomers, including enjoying life and not saving simply to give it to children and grandchildren. No wonder Eisenhowers are spending so much on travel and other leisure-time activities, as well as on cars. Like the baby boomers, Eisenhowers try to be interested in health and exercise; currently, many magazines cater to these interests. Life expectancy for Eisenhowers is also longer than for their parent's generation. This implies that Eisenhowers may continue to work longer than their parents—either with the company where they have been employed for many years, or after retirement, on a part-time basis, at home or away from home.

GENERATION X

Generation Xers, as the media has dubbed this particular age group, are difficult to describe. Unlike the baby boomers and the Eisenhowers, marketers find it hard to uniformly identify what Generation Xers need, want, or would buy. For one, this generation is the most ethnically diverse group of young adults ever in the United States. Secondly, this generation has not been shaped by any grand defining event or era, such as the Vietnam War, women's rights, or the big money-making Reagan years. Not surprisingly, this generation also has difficulty in describing itself; despises being labeled as the lost generation, Generation X, or baby busters; and prefers being referred to simply as a group of independent spirits.

Living and Working

● **The job outlook is bleak.** One of the most important influences affecting Generation X is the lack of meaningful jobs following college. In the 1980s, college graduates hoped for—and often got—high-paying jobs that offered big promotions. Today, in contrast, once-hopeful college graduates complain that there are no decent jobs—because they have all been filled by the baby boomers. This dearth of white-collar jobs is exacerbated by an ongoing corporate trend to improve results by reducing their work forces. The targets of these reductions typically include the most recent hirees, middle managers, and those who are near retirement age.

Results from a recent study taken by the Bureau of Labor Statistics confirm this point. According to this government agency, nearly one-third of college graduates from the classes of 1990 through 2005 will take jobs whose content will not require a college degree, up sharply from 19% in 1980.

● **Wages are lower, causing a decline in living standards.** According to the Bureau of Labor Statistics, between 1983 and 1992, the median weekly earnings of young men aged 16–24 who were full-time workers fell 9%, from $314 per week to $285 per week. Over the same period, earnings of young women in the same age group slipped 4%, from $277 to $267 per week. The earnings of men aged 25 and older also declined, but only by 6%. However, wage rates for women 25 and older increased 6%.

These less-than-uplifting statistics are due in part to the loss of high-paying manufacturing jobs as a result of automation, foreign competition, and a shifting of jobs to countries with lower labor costs. Although service industries are creating many new jobs, they typically pay minimal wages and benefits. The implication of this trend is that Generation Xers are experiencing and expect to continue to experience a decline in their living standards, *vis-à-vis* that of their parents and even their own childhoods.

● **Generation Xers are living at home longer.** The Census Bureau's Current Population Survey discovered that Generation Xers are living longer with their parents than the previous age cohort did in the early 1980s. The survey found that the proportion of women in their 20s living with Mom and Dad rose from 17% in 1977 to 24% in 1993. Approximately 35% of all young men in their 20s lived with their parents in 1993, up from 30% in 1977. This trend has its roots in several developments. First, Generation Xers are marrying at a much later age than previous generations. Second, and probably more important, the high cost of housing, low wage scales, and declining living standards have forced this age cohort to continue living with their parents.

● **Generation Xers aren't scrambling for degrees—but they still go to college.** According to *American Demographics* magazine, 24% of adults aged 25–29 had bachelor's degrees as of March 1993, not much different from the 22% with such degrees in 1982. However, the percentage of 18- to 24-year-olds enrolled in college or having completed one or more years of college was 54% in October 1992, up from 43% a decade earlier, according to the Current Population Survey. The need for technical skills and educational credentials to earn decent wages probably explains this increased college participation by Generation Xers. But, as mentioned previously, full degrees are not required for most of the jobs available to Generation Xers.

- **Generation Xers are more likely to come from broken marriages or single parent families than previous generations.** According to Census Bureau statistics, the percentage of children born to single parents doubled between 1965 and 1977, the years when the Generation Xers were born. At the same time, the number of divorces that occurred between 1965 and 1977 was considerably higher than when the boomers were being born. These factors may have affected the mental stability of many Generation Xers. One study found that 26% of all children born in the late 1960s had received some type of psychological treatment by the time they reached adulthood. This implies that many Generation Xers are not embarrassed to seek psychological treatment, and will continue to seek treatment in years ahead as they deem necessary.

Generation Xers' attitudes

- **Frustration and disillusionment.** Not surprisingly, given the lack of employment prospects and lower wage scales, Generation Xers feel some resentment towards the baby boomers. Many Generation Xers believe that most of the good jobs have been taken by the baby boomers, who will go to extreme lengths to protect those jobs, including de-emphasizing career development for younger employees.

Many Generation Xers also blame some of the current financial problems in the U.S. on the baby boomer generation. They believe baby boomers' propensity to spend rather than save will have severe implications as the boomers reach their retirement years. Many Generation Xers believe that by the time they are ready to retire, there will be no money left in Social Security.

For many, the stock market crash in 1987 inaugurated this feeling of frustration and disillusionment, as many college-aged Generation Xers realized that the era of making big bucks was ending. Optimism for a better life was replaced with uncertainty and a feeling that the United States had no place for their generation.

While feeling disillusioned and frustrated, Generation Xers also possess a sharp sense of reality and awareness. Unlike older age cohorts, Generation Xers want more from life than to be a dispensable, unappreciated employee at a typical American company.

- **Increased political apathy.** Generation Xers are fed up with bureaucracy—many think that the baby boomers have expanded and exploited the system in order to justify their existence. Many Generation Xers have also been particularly disappointed with President Clinton. They voted for him, hoping that he would do what he promised and not get caught up in "politics-as-usual". Unfortunately, President Clinton has been unable to deliver on much of what he promised prior to his election; instead, he has become enmeshed in Washington's bureaucracy and the "Potomac two-step". Many Generation Xers now believe that the whole idea of having two parties—the Republicans and Democrats—is a complete waste of time. Generation Xers are well aware of the problems facing the United States, and they simply don't understand why people in power won't do what needs to be done in order to make real and lasting changes. As a result, many Generation Xers now feel that there is nothing they can do to improve conditions in the U.S.

- **Non-materialistic.** Most likely stemming from their resentment of what they perceive as the spendthrift, status-seeking boomer generation (as well as their own lack of income), the Generation Xers, as a whole, are not a con-sumption-oriented group. Nor are Generation Xers as label, brand name, or trend-oriented as the boomers; this age cohort instead seeks individuality. This makes selling products to this generation difficult indeed for marketers. However, there are some niche markets that are benefiting from Generation X. These include technological and visually-oriented products, such as computer and video games, VCRs and televisions, films, comic and self-help books, and *Nike* athletic footwear.

- **Technology-oriented.** Having grown up with computers, video games, and VCRs, Generation Xers tend to be more familiar with technology than the baby boomers. As a result, one major source of frustration for this generation is that some organizations run by baby boomers can't seem to keep up with technological advances. One author has suggested that the baby boom generation's less-than-enthusiastic response to technology is another way in which the boomers are protecting their jobs from being automated into obsolecence. By downplaying technology, the boomers can also protect their positions from younger, more computer literate competitors.

- **More visually oriented.** In a survey performed by the National Endowment for the Arts, young adults are increasingly interested in the visual arts. According to this survey, the percentage of adults aged 18 to 24 who had visited a museum in the last 12 months was 29% in 1992 (versus 23% in 1982); would like to attend museums more often, 42% (32%); and watched a liberal arts program in the last 12 months, 26% (18%). On the down side, Generation Xers don't read as much as young adults did in the early 1980s. The percentage of 18- to 24-year-olds who read any novels, short stories, poetry, or plays in the previous 12 months fell to 53% in 1992 from 60% in 1982, according the Current Population Survey by the Census Bureau.

- **Less physical.** The Current Population Survey performed by the Census Bureau also found that the proportion of 18- to 24-year-olds who engaged in active sports in the last 12 months declined to 59% in 1992, from 66% in 1982. Those who went hiking, canoeing, or took part in other outdoor activities fell to 43% in 1992, from 51% 10 years earlier. These figures for the Generation Xers are in contrast to the results for all adults surveyed: the proportion of adults who exercised regularly increased to 60% in 1992, from 51% in 1982.

This is not to say, however, that Generation Xers are lazy. Many are simply spending more time on other activities, such as attending college classes or starting up their own businesses.

- **More entrepreneurial.** As a result of a less-than-welcoming work environment and a strong desire to remain independent and control their own destinies, many of the Generation Xers are opting to become entrepreneurs. A poll conducted by Opinion Research Corp. found that 54% of those aged 18 to 34 were extremely or very interested in starting their own businesses, compared with 36% of those 35 to 64. Meanwhile, a study performed at Marquette University found that nearly 10% of Americans aged 25 to 34 are actively working on starting a business—about three times greater than for any other age group.

Having grown up with computers and related technological equipment, many of these entrepreneurs have found niches in the technology field. However, Generation X's creativity goes beyond technology. Many in this age cohort have also established successful businesses in food services, apparel manufacturing, and the like. As entrepreneurs, the Generation Xers can be independent and not waste time in corporate politics and/or bureaucracy. Although starting one's own business is risky, many Generation Xers consider that working for a corporation—with its ongoing work force reductions—is equally risky. Running one's own business also means not having to have a college degree—typically a requirement to land a decent job in a corporation. ■

Apparel sales continue to be disappointing

The back-to-school period, a time when retailers and apparel makers hope that demand will be strong and stimulate further demand, "simply didn't happen," according to management of The Limited. Volume had been lackluster for most of 1995, and industry pundits had hoped sales would pick up. Most agree that hot, sunny summer weather kept shoppers away from stores.

The depressed state of the apparel industry follows a disappointing 1994, when consumer expenditures on clothes barely increased from 1993's level. Those in the industry had optimistically predicted that sales in 1994 would rise about 5%, breaking a four-year trend of disappointing results. In 1994, however, the holiday season—a time of year when retailers and apparel makers conduct most of their annual sales and generate most of the year's earnings—was terrible. The poor results generated during this time also signaled that perhaps the old indicators of predicting apparel sales, such as pent-up demand, have become *passé*, and that forecasters should pay more attention to consumer attitudes.

We attribute recent weak apparel sales to many factors. For one, the weather has discouraged consumers from going shopping. The 1994 holiday season was very warm, which kept shoppers out of stores. This warm weather has continued through most of 1995, exacerbated by little rain in the summer, and stamped out a lot of desire to spend the day in the mall. We think other reasons suppressing apparel sales include a general disinterest in clothes, higher sales of electronic hard goods, a lack of any compelling fashion style, the same merchandise in all stores, too many stores, and changing demographics.

About the only way retailers can get customers to spend anything at all on apparel is to use promotions, which have now become a way of life for both retailers and consumers. Today's consumer typically will only buy merchandise that has been marked down anywhere from 30% to 40% or more; if the price isn't right, consumers are willing to wait it out until retailers mark a product down in order to move inventories. In December 1994, for example, only 20% of all department store merchandise was sold at its full price. A recent study performed by BKG America, a market research company, found that promotional pricing typically brings in a whopping 45% of a store's customers.

As a result of this heavy promotional environment and cost-conscious consumers, apparel prices are falling. Apparel prices declined 1.9% in 1994 from 1993's level, according to the U.S. Department of Labor. Prices of women's apparel (which accounts for 50% of all apparel sold) sagged the most: down 4.4%, year to year, in 1994, the largest decline since 1952. According to NPD Group Inc., a market research firm based in Port Washington, N.Y., the average price of a dress fell to $35.78 in 1994, from $39.20 in 1991; the average price for a woman's blazer was $37 in 1994, down from $41 a year earlier. Prices for men's clothing fell 1.2%. The major culprit behind this deflation was that retailers stocked too much inventory and demand was weaker than expected.

The outlook's not too rosy

The big question is what is going to happen in the remainder of 1995 and in 1996. Some believe that the apparel industry is long overdue for a cyclical swing in its favor. The rationale is that the general economic slowdown should steer consumers away from high-ticket hard goods and bring some improvement to the slow-moving soft goods industry. Other analysts question how long people can wear the same clothes. They believe that sooner or later consumers will have to start buying more apparel to replace old, worn-out clothes.

While the above arguments have merit, we believe that changing demographics and consumer attitudes are likely to have the biggest effect on apparel sales for the foreseeable future—more than any other factor and no matter what the economy does or what fashion designers create. Today's consumers seem to prefer spending their money on services (like vacations or piano lessons) and their homes, and we see no compelling reason why this trend will change anytime soon. This is not to say, however, that all players in the apparel industry will suffer. As in all industries, there will always be some companies that can quickly adapt to the changing marketplace and find success, while others will be forced out of business.

Consumers are not likely to change their buying habits in the near future, either, which will force retailers to continue to drive sales through promotions. However, after the bad experience retailers suffered through in late 1994 with their inventory accumulation, we expect retailers will be more conservative on inventories in 1995. This should help reduce markdowns. Retailers are also trying to differentiate themselves more this year—carrying apparel items that cannot be found in other stores. This could also help in reducing markdowns in that a consumer will be unable to "shop" various stores for the best price.

Margins are being squeezed

As a result of this very difficult retail environment, apparel manufacturers are having trouble maintaining their margins. Wholesale prices for all apparel were up only 0.4% in 1994, largely due to a 1.1% increase in men's and boy's apparel. Women's apparel prices, however, did not increase, reflecting competitive pressures from imports and from retailers who want to hold the line on prices to attract customers.

With an ongoing promotional retail environment, coupled with higher apparel sales at discount stores, the need for apparel makers to be competitive on price is likely to continue in the remainder of 1995 and into 1996. In order

Consumer spending for apparel & shoes
(In millions of dollars)

Year	Footwear	Apparel Women's & girls'	Infants	Men's & boys'	Military	Total	Total apparel & shoes
1994	34,088	123,208	11,011	71,111	337	205,667	239,755
1993	33,014	119,300	10,663	65,559	310	195,832	228,846
1992	32,687	114,836	10,265	62,710	214	188,025	220,712
1991	31,224	105,903	9,466	59,572	177	175,118	206,342
1990	31,459	102,332	9,148	58,731	151	170,362	201,821
1989	30,135	98,516	8,807	56,529	157	164,009	194,144
1988	27,416	91,993	8,223	53,139	151	153,506	180,922
1987	25,782	86,047	7,692	49,750	146	143,635	169,417
1986	24,279	80,685	7,213	46,241	144	134,283	158,562
1985	22,781	74,650	6,673	43,526	133	124,982	147,763

Source: Bureau of Economic Analysis.

to keep their margins from being eroded, apparel manufacturers are likely to keep the price pressures in check by trimming costs. According to Carl Priestland, an economist at the American Apparel Manufacturers Association, apparel makers can trim costs by offering fewer fabric colors, changing fabric blends, or dropping a few styles from a line.

Major manufacturers had mixed results in '94

Given these difficulties, it comes as no surprise that the results of major apparel manufacturers were disappointing overall in 1994. For leading women's apparel maker Liz Claiborne, sales were flat for the year ending December 1994 and earnings (excluding one-time charges) fell significantly, as operations were hurt by the promotional retail environment. Leslie Fay, another leading women's apparel maker, continues to operate in Chapter 11 bankruptcy.

Leading casual apparel manufacturers—including Oxford Industries, Phillips-Van Heusen, Kellwood Corp. and Fruit of the Loom—also reported disappointing results. Both Oxford and Phillips-Van Heusen saw their margins erode as a result of higher-than-expected costs associated with rolling out their wrinkle-free men's apparel products. Kellwood Corp. reported lower-than-expected earnings mainly due to acquisition expenses. Fruit of the Loom's earnings were hurt by a less profitable product mix, reflecting acquisitions, pricing pressures, and higher raw material costs.

On the bright side, VF Corp. and Russell Corp., both makers of casual apparel, and Hartmarx, a men's apparel maker, saw improved sales and earnings in 1994. These companies benefited mainly from higher volume and increased market share.

Results through the first half of 1995 were similar to those reported in 1994. Only a few companies, including VF Corp., reported higher sales and earnings, while results for the remainder were either flat or down. ■

Making it ready to wear

The U.S. apparel industry is large, with sales at the wholesale level amounting to $78.4 billion in 1994. Apparel retail sales (comprising domestic wholesale sales, the value of apparel imports at entry, and retail markups of apparel) approximated $211 billion in 1994, which was equal to about 4.3% of disposable personal income. Production includes the manufacture of men's, boys', women's, girls', children's, and infants' apparel and apparel accessories (excluding footwear). Apparel is made by cutting and sewing woven and knit textile fabrics or by knitting from yarn.

At retail, apparel is typically priced within four categories: popular, moderate, upper moderate, and upper (*e.g.*, designer or high-priced ready-to-wear). A new women's apparel category, called bridgewear, was introduced several years ago; it is priced between upper moderate and upper.

INDUSTRY STRUCTURE

The domestic apparel market can be broken into two tiers. The first tier consists of national brands, which account for about 30% of all U.S. wholesale sales of apparel and are produced by about 20 different companies, all of which are sizable firms. The second tier comprises niche brands and store or private label goods and accounts for about 70% of all apparel distributed. This huge market is served by thousands of small- to medium-size firms.

● **National brands.** The 20 or so manufacturers of national brands include publicly traded companies, divisions of publicly-traded companies, and privately-held companies. A list of these firms includes makers of basic and casual apparel, such as VF Corp., Fruit of the Loom Inc., the apparel division of Sara Lee Corp., and the privately-held Levi Strauss; women's apparel makers, including Liz Claiborne Inc.; men's apparel makers, such as Phillips-Van Heusen Corp. and Hartmarx Corp.; and children's apparel makers, including Oshkosh B'Gosh Inc. Counted in this category is any apparel manufactured overseas directly by a U.S.-based apparel manufacturer.

Leading brand names include *Lee, Wrangler, Healthtex, Champion, Fruit of the Loom, Liz Claiborne, Bass, Vanity Fair, Izod, Hanes, Leslie Fay, Oshkosh B'Gosh, Arrow, Hart Schaffner & Marx,* and *Hickey-Freeman,* to name just a few.

Most companies produce more than one brand. VF Corp., for example, manufactures more than 25 brands. And, in many cases, these companies produce private or store brand labels as well.

● **Small brands and private labels.** According to the U.S. Bureau of the Census, approximately 23,048 establishments were engaged in the manufacture of apparel in 1992 (the most recent count taken), which shows how fragmented this tier of the business is. These small firms, which tend to be privately held, consist of manufacturers, jobbers, and contractors.

Manufacturers perform the entire range of production, from designing to finishing. *Jobbers* design their own garments, acquire the necessary fabric and related materials, and arrange for the sale of the finished garment; however, they contract out most production operations (*i.e.*, sewing and finishing), with the exception of cutting. *Contractors* receive already-cut garment bundles from jobbers and process them into finished garments.

Manufacturers can easily expand and contract output by employing jobbers and contractors. By doing this, manufacturers can reduce capital investment needed when business is expanding and minimize the costs associated with unused capacity when business is contracting. Typically, these smaller manufacturers are under-capitalized, lack broad-based global sourcing, and—something that is becoming more and more important—lack the systems technology that the major retailers demand.

EMPLOYMENT AND PRODUCTIVITY

The number of employees in the apparel manufacturing industry has dwindled since peaking at 1.438 million in 1973. In that year, apparel industry employees accounted for 1.9% of all non-agriculture employees in the United States. By 1994, the number of employees manufacturing apparel in the U.S. had dwindled to 969,000 (0.8% of all non-agriculture employees). During this period, the apparel market was flooded with cheaper imports, forcing many garment workers to seek work in other industries.

Like other industries in the U.S., however, domestic apparel making has become more productive. This, too, has

Total retail trade
(In millions of dollars)

Category	1985	1986	1987	R1988	R1989	R1990	R1991	R1992	R1993	1994	Percent change 1993–94	*10 yr. growth rate
Retail trade, total	1,375,027	1,449,636	1,541,299	1,656,202	1,758,971	1,844,611	1,855,937	1,951,589	2,074,499	2,236,966	7.83	5.68
Durable goods stores, total	498,125	540,688	575,863	629,154	657,154	668,835	649,974	703,604	777,539	880,426	13.23	6.84
Nondurable goods stores, total	876,902	911,948	965,436	1,027,048	1,101,817	1,175,776	1,205,963	1,247,985	1,296,960	1,356,540	4.59	5.00
General merchandise group	158,636	169,397	181,970	192,521	206,306	215,514	226,730	246,420	264,617	282,541	6.77	6.52
Department stores	126,412	134,486	144,017	151,523	160,524	165,808	172,922	186,423	200,494	218,089	8.78	6.11
Variety stores	8,459	7,447	7,134	7,458	7,936	8,306	8,341	9,516	9,044	7,891	-12.75	-0.97
Apparel group	70,195	75,626	79,322	85,307	92,341	95,819	97,441	104,212	107,184	109,603	2.26	5.47
Men's and boy's wear group	8,458	8,646	9,017	9,826	10,507	10,450	10,435	10,197	10,291	12,157	18.13	4.01
Women's apparel, accessory stores	26,149	28,600	29,208	30,567	32,231	32,812	32,865	35,750	36,820	34,867	-5.30	3.91
Family & other apparel stores	17,827	19,336	21,472	23,902	26,375	28,398	30,521	33,222	34,892	37,054	6.20	8.46
Shoe stores	13,054	13,947	14,594	15,444	17,290	18,043	17,504	18,122	18,206	18,345	0.76	4.07
Furniture & appliance group	68,287	75,714	78,072	85,390	91,301	91,545	91,676	96,947	105,728	119,626	13.15	6.89

R–Revised. *Calculated by S&P.
Source: Department of Commerce.

Largest U.S. apparel makers			
Company	Sales* (Mil $)	Company	Sales* (Mil $)
1. VF Corp.	4,972	6. Russell Corp.	1,098
2. Liz Claiborne	2,163	7. Warnaco	789
3. Fruit of the Loom	2,298	8. Hartmarx	718
4. Kellwood	1,365	9. Jones Apparel Group	633
5. Phillips-Van Heusen	1,255		

*Latest fiscal year
Source: Company reports.

contributed to the decline in the number of employees. In 1973, each employee in the domestic apparel industry represented $7,094 in wholesale apparel sales, while in 1994 each employee in the domestic apparel industry represented $75,757. These figures are not adjusted for inflation, so they somewhat overstate the productivity gains, but the increase is substantial nonetheless.

The production of apparel is labor-intensive, and manufacturers seek to provide low wages in order to offer competitive prices. As a result, apparel is one of the nation's largest employers of women and minorities. People from small towns with few alternatives, the under-educated, and immigrants are widely employed in the industry, providing a low wage, exploitable work force. In fact, "underground" or illegal and unregulated apparel operations, account for up to 35% of all domestic apparel production, according to some estimates.

Most apparel organizations employ very few people. Based on the number of establishments manufacturing apparel in 1992 (latest available) and the number of employees in the apparel industry at the end of 1994, the average firm employs about 41 people. In fact, the Bureau of the Census reported that in 1992 only 8,564 establishments had more than 20 employees. Because of the small size of the typical garment firm and the large size of the national apparel market, apparel firms tend to be specialized, producing a single generic product or a small number of similar products.

INDUSTRY UNIONIZATION

Historically, the apparel industry has had two unions: The International Ladies Garment Workers Union (ILGWU), which was founded in 1900, and the Amalgamated Clothing Workers of America (ACWA), which was founded in 1914 and merged with the Textile Workers Union of America in 1976 to form the Amalgamated Clothing and Textile Workers Union (ACTWU). In late February 1995, the executive boards of the ILGWU and the ACTWU announced that the two unions were joining forces to create the Union of Needletrades, Industrial & Textile Employees, or UNITE. Following the merger, UNITE is expected to have about 355,000 active members: 200,000 from ACTWU and 155,000 from ILGWU. The new union will also have about 228,000 retired members.

Executives from both unions agree that the merger is necessary in order to protect employees in the apparel industry from the reemergence of sweatshops and to counter the union-busting tactics of many employers in recent years. The merger should also create a financially stronger union, one with more governmental representation, and one that will be more willing to work with manufacturers to compete with imports.

MANUFACTURING

Given the nature and structure of the domestic apparel manufacturing industry, capital requirements are minimal. The basic equipment used in apparel firms is the sewing machine, which has remained fundamentally the same for 100 years or more. The sewing machine is a mechanized piece of equipment that doesn't cost very much and is easily adaptable to the ever-changing styles and fabrics of the apparel industry.

The unchanging nature of the machinery notwithstanding, technology does have a place in apparel manufacturing. While sewing accounts for the largest portion of the labor costs associated with producing an apparel item, industry pundits believe some 70%–80% of the time spent "sewing" is

U.S. production of apparel

Category	Unit shipments (thousands of dozens)				Value (millions of dollars)			
	1991	1992	1993	1994	1991	1992	1993	1994
Men's and boys' apparel								
Suits	792	836	851	986	1,106.5	1,093.5	1,105.5	1,095.5
Coats	*	4,432	4,912	5,346	*	2,026.3	2,149.7	2,092.1
Tops	93,666	110,505	112,346	*	5,936.6	6,917.0	7,054.8	*
Bottoms	48,357	52,355	52,448	54,582	6,675.9	7,162.1	7,479.9	8,384.3
Underwear and nightwear	98,888	110,646	110,618	102,547	1,664.6	1,714.5	1,797.3	1,815.7
Other garments	6,347	6,313	8,119	8,586	812.3	869.9	1,147.0	1,250.4
Women's and girls' apparel								
Dresses	13,443	13,158	14,626	16,425	4,529.9	4,226.2	4,578.2	4,782.4
Coats	*	3,872	4,889	*	*	1,836.3	2,106.4	*
Tops	40,939	41,156	53,168	55,954	4,165.0	4,028.1	5,219.5	5,295.5
Bottoms	39,239	43,390	*	49,465	5,338.0	5,778.4	*	6,440.0
Underwear and nightwear	95,531	99,361	97,687	108,216	3,518.1	3,652.9	3,664.6	3,925.6
Other garments	11,660	11,648	12,825	*	1,644.5	1,640.8	1,956.8	*
Infants' apparel	14,927	14,168	13,063	12,957	690.8	713.6	720.5	701.0
Coats and jackets	*	*	57	36	*	*	10.4	9.2
Dresses	524	520	519	524	66.2	64.6	69.9	65.2
Knit shirts	1,278	1,464	1,423	1,499	64.9	73.3	67.4	71.3
Sets	947	984	1,175	1,125	69	64.2	76.1	83.2
Pants and shorts	828	1,112	1,130	1,076	49.1	56.7	51.0	45.3
Play clothing	2,441	2,798	2,661	2,442	189.7	199.4	203.9	165.9
Underwear	5,935	4,642	2,966	2,734	82.3	75.4	56.4	54.4
Nightwear	2,903	2,545	3,078	3,429	161.6	169.4	182.0	199.5

*Data withheld to avoid disclosing figures for individual companies
Source: Department of Commerce.

really being used for materials handling, an area that could be more automated.

Making patterns and cutting fabrics using computer-controlled systems can speed up the manufacturing process by anywhere from two to 20 days. In addition, efficient cutting tools minimize fabric waste, which can vary from 8% to 25% of the total amount used. Since fabric accounts for one-third to one-half of a garment's cost, this waste represents a major loss. Where production volumes are sufficiently large, more advanced technologies are being used. Some of the larger apparel manufacturing plants now have automatic sewing machines and conveyor systems for handling in-process goods.

To make the design process easier and quicker, large companies are using computers with special software. Designers can electronically sketch a garment's design, color, and texture onto a computer screen. The flexibility and speed of these systems allows an infinite number of designs to be created and multiple possibilities to be reviewed in minutes.

BARRIERS TO ENTRY AND COMPETITION

Given that the apparel manufacturing industry is characterized by simple technologies, low fixed assets per employee, and the ability to quickly expand or reduce output by using contractors, the barriers to entry are relatively low. On the other hand, however, the mortality rate of apparel firms is high. Firms making dresses, for example, compete with those making skirts, blouses, sweaters, etc. Such competition results in a high rate of turnover in the business each year.

WHOLESALE PRICE AND PROFIT MARGINS

The intense competition that characterizes the apparel manufacturing industry is reflected in a slower rise in apparel prices *vis-à-vis* overall price inflation. Between 1988 and 1994, the wholesale price of all apparel increased 10.1%, with women's wear prices rising 7.5%, men's wear 13%, and children's clothing 11%. For all commodities, wholesale prices increased 15% during this period. Competition in this industry is also demonstrated by its low profit margins. According to Internal Revenue Service data, after-tax profits for apparel firms typically range between 1% and 2%, substantially below those for all manufacturing.

OVERSEAS MANUFACTURING & U.S. OUTSOURCING

In 1994, approximately 44% of all apparel sold in the U.S. was made outside the U.S., and we suspect that this percent-age has continued to increase in 1995. (This figure excludes imported fabric and yarn that went into apparel that was produced domestically.) Much of the clothing made overseas has been contracted out by U.S.-based apparel companies. The main reason that domestic companies have increased manufacturing overseas is to compete with lower priced imports.

Companies can establish overseas production in three ways: 1) buy or build a plant, 2) establish agents in the foreign country who have their own locally-owned factories, or 3) have the apparel manufactured by locally-owned factories. Typically, U.S.-based apparel companies establish overseas production in all of the above ways.

There is no straight formula as to where a domestic apparel producer manufactures. Kellwood Corp., for example, made 46% of its apparel overseas during its fiscal year ended April 30, 1995, up from 39% in fiscal 1990. Approximately 69% of its products were made by outside contractors in fiscal 1995, compared with 49% in fiscal 1990. The remainder was produced in Kellwood-owned plants located in the U.S. and throughout the world.

Apparel companies can achieve several goals by stepping up their use of overseas manufacturing and/or their use of outside domestic contractors. Overseas sourcing allows manufacturers to compete price-wise with less expensive imports. Domestic sourcing allows companies to respond quickly to fashion changes and to retailers' needs for automatic inventory replenishment.

Import penetration is low for those apparel products that have a low labor content and are subject to automation. Basic men's wear, where styles change slowly and domestic production is highly automated, tends to be made in the U.S. The production of fleecewear and jeans are relatively simple to automate as well and, as a result, these products tend to be made in the United States. High-fashion goods also tend to have low import penetration: their extremely short selling life complicates dealings with foreign contractors, who may need several months to deliver products. In addition, these high-ticket items are aimed at consumers who are comparatively insensitive to price.

In contrast, foreign penetration is highest in seasonal products, particularly private label products. Market uncertainty and difficulty in training personnel to sew new products has led to low domestic productivity in the seasonal products. Furthermore, low-wage foreign producers have a competitive advantage over U.S. firms in selling these labor-intensive product lines. Nonetheless, the domestic manufacture of seasonal goods is not completely dead: it is in this area that new production systems, mostly in the form of quick response technologies and strategies, can have their greatest impact.

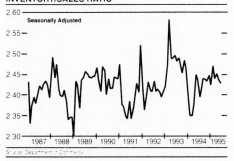

DEPARTMENT, APPAREL & ACCESSORY STORES — INVENTORY/SALES RATIO

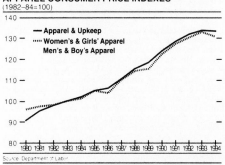

APPAREL CONSUMER PRICE INDEXES
(1982–84=100)

— Apparel & Upkeep
····· Women's & Girls' Apparel
—— Men's & Boy's Apparel

PRODUCTION, SALES & INVENTORIES OF APPAREL PRODUCTS
(In billions of dollars)

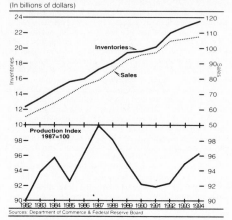

Sources: Department of Commerce & Federal Reserve Board

MARKET SEGMENTS

Domestic markets for apparel can be divided roughly into three categories, each of which presents different problems in production and sales:

● **Fashion products**, with an average 10-week product life, make up about 35% of the market;

● **Seasonal products**, with a 20-week product life, make up about 45% of the market;

● **Basic products**, sold throughout the year, make about 20% of the market.

Generally, markets for men's and children's clothing are less subject to change from year to year and are therefore more suited to large-scale production. Women's garments tend to dominate seasonal sales, which are more difficult to predict.

WHAT DRIVES APPAREL SALES

There are three major factors that drive apparel sales: developments in the economy as a whole, consumer attitudes and demographic trends, and fashion. Each of these affects apparel sales in different ways.

● **The economy.** Consumers tend to spend more on apparel when the economy is strong than when it is weak. From 1983 through 1990, for example, the U.S. economy was growing and disposable personal income was rising at a healthy average annual rate of 7.2%. Apparel expenditures increased at a strong 6.8% annual rate during this period. In the 1990s, however, growth in disposable personal income has slowed and so have apparel expenditures. From 1990 through 1994, personal disposable income rose by 4.9% a year, on average, and apparel expenditures increased at an average annual rate of just 4.7%.

● **Consumer attitudes and demographic trends.** Changes in the population as a whole can affect what kinds of apparel people want to buy. During the 1980s, many consumers tended buy clothing that they perceived would

give them a certain image and/or would associate them with a certain designer. The look, not the cost, was the force driving apparel purchases. Today, however, many consumers are value- and price-conscious. The severe markdowns on apparel that were common in the recession of 1990–91 have made consumers suspicious of "list" prices; they are more likely to buy apparel only if they perceive they are getting a discount or "sale" price.

Casual dressing has become more popular as well, for several reasons. For one, the bulk of the population is getting older; many people now prefer a more casual lifestyle than was the case in the go-go 1980s. And more recently, the trend of dressing down at work has reduced the need dressy, expensive garments. The result has been increased demand for moderately-priced casual clothing.

In the 1980s, a time when many women entered or returned to the work force, demand for moderately expensive to expensive clothing appropriate for work was strong. The go-go money-making 1980s also led to strong sales of men's suits. All this has changed in the 1990s, and the kind of apparel produced reflects the shift. The number of men's suits produced in 1994, for example, was down 14% from 1988, while the number of tops increased 19% and bottoms were up 15%. On the women's wear side, the number of dresses manufactured in 1994 was 3.7% below the number made in 1988.

● **Fashion.** Historically, the main impetus driving women's clothing sales has been new fashion trends—the miniskirt, for example. But fashion's ability to spur women to buy clothes has faded. So far in the 1990s, women's clothing designers have failed to introduce a trend-setting style that has gained wide appeal. What has happened instead is that fashion designers are promoting all sorts of styles—long skirts, short skirts, tailored suits, dresses reminiscent of the 1940s, grunge wear, shirt dresses, conservative chic suits, and dresses that echo the early 1960s style popularized by Babe Paley and Jackie Kennedy. While there always are consumers who immediately pick up on the latest fad, their numbers are usually small. Instead, most women today tend to wear what is comfortable and what they want, not what some designer dictates.

MAJOR MARKET TRENDS

At the consumer level

Consumers have a markdown mentality. Shoppers have come to expect promotional pricing and other kinds of sales gimmicks. When the last recession hit in late 1990, many retailers could not generate enough cash to pay even the interest (much less the principal) owed on funds that banks had loaned them during the leveraged buyout frenzy of the mid- to late 1980s. Desperate to raise cash, retailers slashed prices to boost volume. As a result, most consumers are now unwilling to purchase an item unless it appears to be a bargain—either marked down or "value-priced," in retailing parlance.

Consumers are buying less apparel. Today, consumers spend only 4.3% of their disposable income on apparel, compared with 4.5% in the 1980s. This may not sound like a lot less, but it represents an annual loss of $11 billion in retail apparel sales.

Consumers have changed where they shop. In the 1990s, a combination of more casual lifestyles and certain other factors—fears of potential unemployment and slower growth in disposable personal income—have caused many consumers to shift from the more expensive apparel items found at department stores to basic apparel items (jeans, T-shirts, and fleecewear) and moderately priced sportswear found at mass merchandisers and discounters.

Discounters fast becoming consumers' sole shopping destination. This shift is evident in market share data. Discount stores accounted for 31% of all apparel sales in 1993 (latest available), up from 27% in 1987, according to the American Apparel Manufacturers Association. This translates into an annual growth rate of 7.7%, considerably higher than the 5.3% annual growth in overall apparel expenditures during that period. Department stores saw their share of apparel sales decline to 23% in 1993, from 26.3% in 1987.

At the retail level

The number of retailers is shrinking. The retail scene is consolidating across the board—from discounters to department stores—and has come mainly at the expense of specialty stores, such as The Limited. According to Management Horizons, a division of Price Waterhouse and a well-known consulting firm specializing in retailing, more than half of the retailers operating today will be out of business by the end of this decade.

Retailers are getting bigger. The department store segment, for example, has become so concentrated that 77% of the sales generated by the top 10 department stores come from just four companies—Sears Roebuck & Co., J.C. Penney Co. Inc., Federated Department Stores Inc. (including Macy's), and May Department Stores Inc. The December 1994 acquisition of Macy's by Federated Department Stores illustrates the scope of retail industry consolidation. Combined, the two department store chains will have sales of about $14 billion, which considerably expands the buying clout of the combined company.

Consolidation has given retailers greater leverage over suppliers. The on-going consolidation trend has reduced the number of retail entities, but the surviving retailers are larger and more powerful. Many retailers, including Wal-Mart Stores Inc. and Kmart Corp., now dwarf the companies that supply them. They want to do business only with large, well-financed suppliers who can assure them of consistent delivery, information flow, and quality. In addition, retailers' growth has changed the balance of power that prevailed in soft goods in the past, when manufacturers set prices and dictated product lines.

There are fewer stores for apparel makers to sell clothes to. The consolidation of retail companies usually results in the closing of numerous redundant stores. This is bad news for apparel makers, because fewer stores means that less merchandise needs to be carried.

Retailers are reducing the number of vendors with whom they do business. Here, again, the Macy's/Federated merger illustrates how the changing retail scene affects apparel makers. Prior to merging with Macy's, about 65% of all of Federated's merchandise had been supplied by a core list of vendors (some of whom also supplied Macy's). After the merger, supplier lists of Federated and Macy's were combined and revamped; as a result, some suppliers were eliminated. Those suppliers that remained have met different fates: some have been given additional orders, others have seen orders remain stable, and yet others have seen orders decrease. We believe that some of those supplier

eliminations and order decreases resulted from the closing of redundant stores after the merger.

Retail consolidation tends to benefit larger apparel suppliers, at the expense of smaller companies. Retailers' demands—that an apparel maker have electronic data interchange technology, for example—can involve investment that is out of reach for small, undercapitalized companies. Although these demands make it difficult for new and/or smaller apparel manufacturers, there will always be opportunities for them to do business with retailers who seek some differentiation.

Discounters continue to expand. For Wal-Mart, the country's leading retailer (as well as discounter), sales growth has significantly outpaced that of any other domestic retailer. From $6.4 billion in the fiscal year ended January 31, 1985, Wal-Mart's sales exploded to $82.5 billion in the fiscal year ended January 31, 1995 and are expected to hit $100 billion in fiscal 1996.

Moderately priced brand names are becoming more important. Brand names, both manufacturer and private label, are becoming more important. Retailers are reshuffling their store's brand-name/private label mix. As consumers change where they shop, leading mass merchandisers and discounters are paying more attention to their apparel offerings. In the past, these retailers were the destination of choice for basic apparel. This is quickly changing, however, as mass merchandisers and discounters are stepping up their apparel assortments to include more fashion-forward merchandise that is moderately priced.

Discounters are offering more kinds of apparel. Wal-Mart is being particularly aggressive in expanding its brand-name apparel offerings. In early 1995, this retailing mammoth launched a moderately-priced line of women's casual apparel called the *Kathie Lee Collection*, named after the well-known television personality, Kathie Lee Gifford. The initial test results of this new line were very successful, and the manufacturer of this private line—Halmode Apparel, which is a division of Kellwood Corp.—expects that sales will exceed Kmart's *Jacqueline Smith* line. (The *Jacqueline Smith* line has annual sales of around $300 million and is the biggest selling brand name private label.) Wal-Mart also added the *Catalina* label for sportswear and activewear in the spring of 1995. This established label has been repositioned for the mass market by its owner, Authentic Fitness.

MAJOR INDUSTRY TRENDS

In today's tough competitive climate and in the face of increasingly demanding retailers, it is difficult—but not impossible—for apparel manufacturers to generate real growth. Strategies vary, but what they basically come down to is expanding product offerings through acquisitions, new brand creation, licensing, and brand-name extension into new apparel categories; seeking wider and deeper distribution; and becoming more merchandise- and technology-oriented. None of these strategies is mutually exclusive.

Expanding product offerings

●**Acquisitions.** Acquisition has been—and always will be—the fastest way to increase market share. Apparel manufacturers make acquisitions for one or more reasons: to acquire a new product or product category; to increase market share in one product category; to increase the kinds of apparel products they can offer to a particular retailer; and to deepen distribution (*i.e.*, the manufacturer will have certain brands for department stores and other brands specifically for the mass market). Historically, acquisitions have been the most popular form of growth among apparel makers.

● **New brand creation.** Creating new brands as a vehicle of growth is more difficult than other ways, since it takes significant resources (*e.g.*, capital, highly experienced personnel, and solid relationships with retailers) to launch a totally new brand. The most successful roll-out of a new brand in recent years is VF Corp.'s *Rider* denim apparel line. In 1993, VF Corp. pulled its well-known *Lee* brand of denim apparel out of mass merchandisers and repositioned it as a more upscale product to be distributed to moderate and upper-moderate department stores. VF Corp. then began distributing its new *Rider* brand to the mass market. By 1994, the company says the new brand had been established with the consumer, and *Rider* began experiencing double-digit increases in retail sell-throughs.

● **Licensing.** Licensing is a growth vehicle that benefits two parties: the apparel manufacturer and the apparel designer. The apparel manufacturer typically has its own brands, but may also produce private label products. The apparel designer has no manufacturing operations. Tommy Hilfiger Corp., a well-known designer of men's clothing, is a good example of a company that licenses its name. Oxford Industries Inc., a leading producer of private label and branded apparel, produces *Tommy Hilfiger* dress shirts under a license, while Hartmarx Corp., a leading producer of mainly brand-name apparel, produces *Tommy Hilfiger* tailored suits. Other familiar designers that license their names include Oscar de la Renta, Gloria Vanderbilt, and Bill Blass.

● **Brand-name extension.** Many apparel companies find that extending their existing brands into other apparel categories is a successful way to generate growth. VF Corp., for example has successfully transferred its *Lee* label, which is generally associated with denim products, to fleecewear.

Wider and deeper distribution

● **Diversifying retail distribution.** One growth strategy taken by some apparel companies is diversifying distribution to include discounters, mass merchandisers, and department stores. Liz Claiborne Inc. expanded its distribution to include mass merchandisers and moderate department stores by acquiring the *Russ*, *Crazy Horse*, and *Villager* names from Russ Togs in 1992. Prior to owning these trademarks, Liz Claiborne distributed its merchandise only to upscale department stores and specialty stores. Jones Apparel Group Inc. has also expanded distribution from upscale department stores to the mass market by acquiring the *Evan Picone* trademark from Crystal Brands Inc. This approach is not without peril, however. When upscale manufacturers decide to enter the mass market, it is imperative that they introduce a separate brand so as not to upset their "upstairs" accounts and to avoid tarnishing their upscale brands.

Other companies that are actively diversifying their distribution base include Kellwood Corp. and VF Corp. In late 1994, Kellwood Corp., a manufacturer of moderately priced apparel, acquired David Dart, a leading domestic designer of more expensive bridge sportswear, in order to broaden its distribution from the mass market into more upscale department stores. VF Corp., meanwhile, offers more than 25 brands to all distribution outlets. In lingerie, for example, VF Corp.'s *Vanity Fair* line can be found in department stores, while its *Vassarette* line can be found in the mass market.

● **Apparel manufacturers/retailers.** Over the past several years, many apparel manufacturers have opened their own retail outlets as a vehicle for growth. Liz Claiborne Inc. began the trend in the 1980s when it opened its Liz Claiborne and First Issue stores. Other apparel manufacturers subsequently followed suit by opening their own specialty stores (though not to the extent that Liz Claiborne did). For Liz Claiborne Inc., however, results have been mixed. Although the company continues to expand the number of Liz Claiborne stores (there are more than 20 of them), it announced in late 1994 that it would close all 56 First Issue stores.

This is not to say, however, that apparel manufacturers cannot succeed at retailing. Companies such as The Limited Inc., Gap Inc., AnnTaylor Inc., and Talbot's Inc. are all known mainly as retailers. But what most don't know is that these companies could also be classified as apparel manufacturers—even though, like Liz Claiborne Inc., they don't own any manufacturing facilities. What these companies do is design most of their own apparel and have it made to their exact specifications through outside sourcing, either in the U.S. or overseas. The only difference between these retailers and Liz Claiborne is that the retailers have apparel made solely for their own stores, while Liz Claiborne has apparel made for its own stores as well as for stores it doesn't operate.

While operating specialty stores has not been a major trend among apparel manufacturers, operating outlet stores has. Top players in the outlet store arena range from mass market manufacturers to the most prestigious designer labels. Phillips-Van Heusen Corp. has enjoyed unprecedented success by opening outlet stores. The company, which originally entered this market to keep overruns away from discounters, operated 872 outlet stores at the end of its most recent fiscal year, January 31, 1995, and currently derives most of its revenues from them. Its outlet stores include Geoffrey Beene, Van Heusen, Bass, Windsor Shirt, and Cape Isle Knitters. Most other leading apparel manufacturers, including VF Corp. and Liz Claiborne Inc., also operate outlet stores.

Apparel manufacturers like operating outlet stores for several reasons. For one, they can sell extra or second-quality merchandise—including irregulars, overruns, and odd lots—that are generally associated with the outlet format. When manufacturers have such merchandise to get rid of, they prefer using outlet stores rather than off-price retailers because doing so minimizes the risk that their brand names will be tarnished—something that can occur when too much merchandise is sold at off-price. In addition, outlet stores tend to be located in remote areas, far from conventional department and specialty stores. This decreases the chance that the manufacturer's regular retail customer will lose sales to the outlet stores.

Equally important to apparel manufacturers, however, are the incremental sales and profits that can be derived from operating outlet stores. Sales growth at outlet stores has far outpaced that of the retail industry over the past few years. One important reason for this trend is that value-conscious consumers think they can get a better deal shopping at outlet centers versus more conventional stores. More often than not, this is true. Because overhead expenses are so low, outlet stores often sell apparel and accessories for as little as half the price charged by department and specialty stores. And today's outlet stores frequently carry first-quality merchandise from current inventory.

● **International markets offer growth.** Many domestic apparel companies are targeting international markets as a vehicle for growth. Many of these markets are huge and largely untapped. International expansion can take several forms: increasing exports; increasing the number of overseas

Quick response: automated efficiency

The goal of quick response is to maintain lean inventories and avoid overstocking, insuring that retailers have the merchandise customers want to buy, when they want to buy it. Electronic data interchange (EDI) is vital to this effort.

An EDI system employs interconnected computer terminals throughout the entire manufacturing and sales system. Electronic point-of-sale scanners read bar codes, which allows the EDI system to record which merchandise has been sold, its price, and even such details as an item's color or size. The information is relayed to the manufacturer, giving the manufacturer an up-to-the-minute report on a given retail store's sales. By giving a manufacturer detailed information about consumer purchasing trends, the manufacturer can tailor production to consumer demand. The data recorded by bar code scanners in an EDI system are also used for automatic reordering (what the industry calls

"flow," "automatic replenishment," or "just-in-time"), enabling a manufacturer to quickly restock a retailer's shelves, using no more than a computer for communication.

In addition to providing for "automatic replenishment," distribution and shipping information processing is more efficient in an EDI system. For example, once a shipment is ready to go, a labeling document is be processed and a bill is automatically generated and transmitted electronically to the retailer. Ultimately, EDI will also support electronic funds transfer, enabling retailers to pay bills electronically.

Unlike more fashion-oriented apparel, the nature of basic apparel lends itself to EDI and "automatic replenishment." Basics are relatively simple to produce, require short lead times, and are typically manufactured in highly-automated factories. Retailers favor EDI systems and "automatic replenishment" because they help restrain inventory costs and avoid product obsolescence. ∎

distributors with which the company does business; acquiring foreign companies; starting up a manufacturing plant overseas; and increasing the number of stores overseas.

Apparel companies are following the lead of Nike and Reebok, which have built their brand-name basic products into major international franchises. Leading U.S. manufacturers of basic apparel—VF Corp., Sara Lee Corp.'s apparel division, Levi Strauss, Russell Corp., and Fruit of the Loom Inc.—already have plants in Europe and are recognized names there. Companies in the fashion apparel business are entering overseas markets as well: Liz Claiborne Inc., for example, has entered European, Latin American, and Asian markets. Makers of moderately priced apparel have now entered the arena. Kellwood Corp. recently announced that it plans to derive 5% of its revenues from overseas markets (primarily Asia); currently, the company's international sales account for barely 1% of revenues.

Becoming more merchandise- and technology-oriented

Domestic apparel companies can plan for growth all they want, but unless they have strong relationships with their customers—the retailers—they might as well close their doors. Today's retailer has become a savvy money manager, and as such, is focused on keeping costs down. One major cost-cutting area has been inventories. Historically, stocking inventories has been one of retailing's highest costs; retailers seeking to reduce their expenses are forcing manufacturers to carry inventories for them.

While the term "quick response" (see boxed item above) has been around the industry for a long time, only recently has this process become necessary for survival among today's apparel manufacturers. This approach to inventory management is based on replenishing core and fashion merchandise at the retail level as it sells out. Retailers also prefer buying as close to the selling season as possible. To do this, they depend on electronic data interchange (EDI) programs for both basic and fashion merchandise. This means that apparel manufacturers must be able to give retailers what they want, when they want it, or risk losing the business. At the same time, the vendor must be able to advise the retailer and

to manufacture the product at a profit. Only a few apparel manufacturers have the resources to satisfy all of these requirements.

VF Corp. exemplifies a basic apparel manufacturer who can handle what these demanding retailers want. Over the past few years, VF Corp. has invested between $125 million and $150 million on technological systems and processes. The company's "Market Response System" links its suppliers, customers, plants, and distribution centers. For all of its larger retailers and some of the smaller ones, VF Corp. can now generate orders based on point-of-sale data. If a particular product that a retailer needs is not in stock, VF can have the product cut, sewn, finished, sent to the warehouse, and be on the truck to the retailer—all in a matter of days. Unlike most other manufacturers. VF ships 50% of its orders directly to stores. The key to VF Corp.'s ability to "automatically replenish" shelves is reduced turnaround time: what used to take two weeks to manufacture, now takes only a day or so.

While quick response and other technologies have proven successful with basic goods, which are subject to automation and can be competitively made in the U.S., these strategies have been more difficult to implement with seasonal and fashion items. Because of the higher content of labor in seasonal and fashion items, these apparel products tend to be made offshore, mainly in the Caribbean or Southeast Asia.

However, apparel companies involved in seasonal and fashion items are making strides in improving the manufacturing process. Traditionally, the amount of time that elapsed between the design of these garments to their delivery in the store was six to nine months. Cygne Designs Inc., a leading private label apparel manufacturer that counts AnnTaylor Inc. and The Limited among its major customers, has cut this time to 45–60 days. The company has achieved this by working with the retailer to create the design, sending the design via computer to its offices overseas, cutting the garments themselves, having the garment sewn by an outside contractor, and air freighting the garment back into the United States. Cygne is also unique in that it does not manufacture anything unless the garments have already been sold. ∎

COMPOSITE INDUSTRY DATA
*Per share data based on Standard & Poor's group stock price indexes

HOUSEHOLD FURNISHINGS & APPLIANCES
The companies used for this series are:
Armstrong World (from 1989); Bassett Furniture; Fedders Corp. (through 1993); Maytag; Mohasco (from 1988); Roper (from 1988); Rubbermaid (through 1988); Whirlpool; White Consolidated Inds.; Zenith Electronics.

TEXTILES
The companies used for this series are: Cluett Peabody; Hartmarx; Liz Claiborne; Oshkosh B'Gosh ; Russell Corp.; Springs Industries (from 1993); V.F. Corp.

Household Furnishings & Appliances

1987	1988	1989	1990	1991	1992	1993	1994	
713.26	758.15	989.54	1025.00	1008.02	1052.25	1030.87	1121.90	Sales
70.51	75.82	107.62	102.39	100.63	103.14	105.28	127.21	Operating Income
9.89	10.00	10.88	9.99	9.98	9.80	10.21	11.34	Profit Margin%
18.42	19.40	33.57	37.72	39.32	42.83	38.53	38.56	Depreciation
21.70	18.12	22.09	17.77	15.09	11.74	15.43	25.68	Taxes
47.27	49.64	67.56	54.53	55.14	44.34	56.19	74.07	Cash Flow
28.84	30.24	33.98	16.82	15.83	1.50	18.03	35.85	Earnings
12.24	13.42	16.64	17.80	13.57	13.12	13.52	14.04	Dividends
4.04	3.99	3.43	1.64	1.57	0.14	1.75	3.20	Earnings as a % of Sales
42.44	44.38	48.97		85.72		74.99	39.16	Dividends as % of Earnings
580.52	478.58	550.04	482.26	434.21	539.85	671.78	708.46	Price (1941–43=10) —High
349.18	378.94	426.05	261.26	284.74	387.43	467.37	504.18	—Low
20.13	15.83	16.19	28.67	27.43		37.26	19.76	Price-Earnings Ratios —High
12.11	12.53	12.54	15.53	17.99		25.92	14.06	—Low
3.51	3.54	3.91	6.81	4.77	3.39	2.89	2.78	Dividend Yield % —High
2.11	2.80	3.03	3.69	3.13	2.43	2.01	1.98	—Low
198.84	219.01	264.66	266.57	268.25	231.04	147.26	156.01	Book Value
14.50	13.81	12.84	6.31	5.90	0.65	13.84	22.98	Return on Book Value %
104.47	124.69	150.68	110.44	82.74	54.69	63.12	95.04	†Working Capital
34.28	27.44	42.07	46.67	43.11	40.58	38.71	49.50	Capital Expenditures

Textiles

	1987	1988	1989	1990	1991	1992	1993	1994
Sales	171.69	176.69	205.39	223.00	243.42	275.59	306.50	335.30
Operating Income	28.00	25.83	31.99	31.30	32.18	37.25	35.81	40.33
Profit Margin%	6.31	14.62	15.58	14.04	13.22	13.52	11.68	12.03
Depreciation	4.64	5.08	6.18	7.00	7.10	7.65	9.40	10.74
Taxes	9.76	7.45	9.39	7.18	8.60	10.40	8.73	9.42
Cash Flow	17.39	17.38	21.31	17.74	21.12	18.58	23.21	26.12
Earnings	12.75	12.30	15.14	10.74	14.02	10.93	13.81	15.38
Dividends	3.09	3.35	3.78	3.85	3.98	3.94	4.58	4.77
Earnings as a % of Sales	7.43	6.96	7.37	4.82	5.76	3.97	4.51	4.59
Dividends as % of Earnings	24.24	27.24	24.97	35.85	28.39	36.05	33.16	31.01
Price —High	254.27	166.49	212.94	209.17	265.35	290.04	289.20	218.90
—Low	122.32	140.63	153.19	127.98	162.81	235.13	181.03	192.48
Price-Earnings Ratios —High	19.94	13.54	14.06	19.48	18.93	26.54	20.94	14.23
—Low	9.59	11.43	10.12	11.92	11.61	21.51	13.11	12.52
Dividend Yield % —High	2.53	2.38	2.47	3.01	2.44	1.68	2.53	2.48
—Low	1.22	2.01	1.78	1.84	1.50	1.36	1.58	2.18
Book Value	50.08	59.03	61.48	65.48	76.47	98.47	114.63	123.06
Return on Book Value %	25.46	20.84	24.63	16.16	18.33	11.10	12.19	12.50
†Working Capital	41.79	46.22	61.22	59.1	63.68	71.59	75.24	69.52
Capital Expenditures	6.96	9.3	9.96	9.86	9.66	12.46	14.19	10.30

*NOTE: Per share data are expressed in terms of the S&P Stock Price Index, I.E. stock prices 1984=100. Each of the items shown is first computed on a true per share basis for each company. Totals for each company are then reconstructed using the same number of shares outstanding as was used to compute our stock price index as of December 31. This is done because the shares used on reconstructed totals is them related to the base period value used to compute the stock price index. As a double check, we relates the various items to he dividends as these are the most stable series. So, for example, if total sales amount to fifteen times the total dividend payments, then with per share dividends at 3.50 the indicated per share sales will be (15x3.50) 52.50 in terms of the S&P Stock Index. For comparability between the various groups, all data are on a calendar year basis, corporate data being posted in the year in which most months fall. Fiscal years ending June 30th are posted in the calendar year in which the fiscal year ends. † Current assets less current liabilities, without allowance for long-term debt. R—Revised. cr.—credit. d—deficit. NA—Not available.

COMPARATIVE COMPANY ANALYSIS — Textiles - Apparel - Home Furnishings

		Operating Revenues — Million $							Compound Growth Rate (%)			Index Basis (1984 = 100)				
Company	Yr. End	1984	1989	1990	1991	1992	1993	1994	1-Yr.	5-Yr.	10-Yr.	1990	1991	1992	1993	1994
TEXTILES																
DIXIE YARNS INC	DEC	283.2	570.8	556.2	492.0	469.8	594.6A,C	688.5A	15.8	3.8	9.3	196	174	166	210	243
FAB INDUSTRIES INC	NOV	114.8	162.2	167.9	185.6	189.3	189.6	189.8	0.1	2.8	5.1	146	162	165	165	165
FIELDCREST CANNON	DEC	572.8	1362.4	1242.1	1212.4	1217.3	1000.1A,C	1063.7	6.4	4.8	6.4	217	212	213	175	186
GUILFORD MILLS INC	SEP	360.6C	619.7	544.1	528.8	614.9	654.4	703.7	7.5	2.6	6.9	151	147	171	182	195
SPRINGS INDUSTRIES -CL A	DEC	945.0	1909.3A	1878.0	1890.4A	1975.7A	2022.8C	2068.9	2.3	1.6	8.2	199	200	209	214	219
TEXFI INDUSTRIES	OCT	119.7	233.9A	274.5	322.3	328.9C	311.2D	282.9	-9.1	3.9	9.0	229	269	275	260	236
APPAREL MANUFACTURERS & MARKETERS																
BEEBA'S CREATIONS INC	AUG	33.9	128.6	158.0	132.3	117.3	116.2	119.3	2.7	-1.5	13.4	466	390	346	342	352
CHAUS (BERNARD) INC	JUN	NA	268.0	291.1	232.4	254.2	235.8	206.3	-12.5	-5.1	NA	NA	**	**	**	**
CRYSTAL BRANDS	DEC	NA	857.2D	868.5	826.9	589.0D	444.3D	NA	NA	NA	NA	NA	**	**	**	**
FARAH INC	OCT	250.8A	239.0	139.6	151.2	152.0	180.1	242.8	34.8	0.3	-0.3	56	60	61	72	97
FRUIT OF THE LOOM INC -CL A	DEC	NA	1320.9	1426.8	1628.1	1855.1	1884.4	2297.8	21.9	11.7	NA	NA	**	**	**	**
GARAN INC	SEP	176.9	136.7	145.3	146.3	170.4	189.6	173.0	-8.7	4.8	-0.2	82	83	96	107	98
HAGGAR CORP	SEP	NA	NA	NA	NA	380.8	394.1	491.2	24.7	NA	NA	NA	**	**	**	**
HAMPTON INDUSTRIES	DEC	162.9	181.8	166.9	162.2	203.7	196.4	172.0	-12.4	-1.1	0.6	102	100	125	121	106
HARTMARX CORP	NOV	1070.8	1297.0	1295.8	1215.3	1063.9	732.0	717.7	-2.0	-11.2	-3.9	121	114	98	68	67
JONES APPAREL GROUP INC	DEC	NA	NA	289.3	334.1	438.1	546.1A	641.7	17.5	NA	NA	NA	**	**	**	**
KELLWOOD CO	APR	588.5	779.9A	808.0A	914.9	1077.7A	1203.1A	1364.8A	13.4	11.8	8.8	137	155	183	204	232
LIZ CLAIBORNE INC	DEC	391.3	1410.7	1728.9	2007.2	2194.3	2204.3	2162.9	-1.9	8.9	18.6	442	513	561	563	553
MUNSINGWEAR INC	DEC	192.6	111.8D	39.0D	36.6D	59.8	41.3	NA	1.6	-17.8	NA	42	40	43	45	45
OAK HILL SPORTWEAR CORP	DEC	95.3	117.8	118.2	91.2	86.4	83.9	84.2	0.3	-6.5	-1.2	124	96	91	88	88
OSHKOSH B'GOSH INC -CL A	DEC	137.4	315.1	323.4	365.2	346.2	340.2	363.4	6.8	2.9	10.2	235	266	252	248	264
OXFORD INDUSTRIES INC	MAY	558.7	550.4	505.8	527.7	572.9	624.6	657.0	5.2	3.6	1.6	91	94	103	112	118
PHILLIPS-VAN HEUSEN	JAN	590.8G	732.9	806.3A	904.1	1042.6	1152.4	1255.5	8.9	11.4	7.8	136	153	176	195	213
RUSSELL CORP	JAN	353.0	688.0	713.8	804.6	899.1	930.8	1098.3A	18.0	9.8	12.0	202	228	255	264	311
SALANT CORP	DEC	198.8	469.6	411.7	398.5	380.2D	407.2C	419.3D	3.0	-2.2	7.8	207	200	191	205	211
SIGNAL APPAREL CO	DEC	82.5	90.6	76.8	90.1A	172.2	131.0	95.8A	-26.9	1.1	1.5	93	109	209	159	116
STAGE II APPAREL CORP	DEC	NA	101.2F	83.2F	67.8F	76.8F	67.6A,F	66.0F	-2.2	-8.2	NA	NA	**	**	**	**
TULTEX CORP	DEC	286.3	334.0F	355.1F	315.2F	503.9A,F	533.6F	565.4F	6.0	11.1	7.0	124	110	176	186	198
UNITED MERCHANTS &MFRS	JUN	563.2	499.5	350.3	216.0	206.7	193.7	98.3D	-49.3	-27.8	-16.0	62	38	37	34	17
VF CORP	DEC	1167.4A	2532.7	2612.6	2952.4	3824.4A	4320.4	4971.7A	15.1	14.4	15.6	224	253	328	370	426
WARNACO GROUP INC -CL A	DEC	561.4A	516.4D	545.2D	559.3D	625.1	703.8	788.8	12.1	8.8	3.5	97	100	111	125	141
SHOE PRODUCERS																
BARRY (R G)	DEC	120.2	122.8	108.9	102.8	101.8	101.2	116.7	15.4	-1.0	-0.3	91	86	85	84	97
L A GEAR INC	NOV	NA	617.1	902.2	618.1D	430.2	398.4	416.0	4.4	-7.6	NA	NA	**	**	**	**
NIKE INC -CL B	MAY	946.4A	2235.2	3003.6A	3405.2	3931.0	3789.7	NA	NA	NA	NA	317	360	415	400	**
REEBOK INTERNATIONAL LTD	DEC	66.0	1822.1A	2159.2	2734.5A,C	3022.6	2893.9	3280.4	13.4	12.5	47.8	3270	4142	4578	4383	4969
STRIDE RITE CORP	NOV	289.5	454.4D	515.8	574.4	585.9	582.9	523.3	-10.1	2.9	6.1	178	198	202	201	181
SUAVE SHOE CORP	SEP	96.4	86.7	62.1D	53.0	58.0	31.0	27.6	-10.9	-20.5	-11.8	64	55	60	32	29
WOLVERINE WORLD WIDE	DEC	378.6	323.6	322.2	313.8C	293.1D	333.1	378.5D	13.6	3.2	-0.0	85	83	77	88	100
SHOE PRODUCERS & RETAILERS																
BROWN GROUP INC	JAN	1571.7	1820.5	1763.8	1727.8	1791.2	1597.8D	1464.6D	-8.3	-4.3	-0.7	112	110	114	102	93
EDISON BROTHERS STORES	JAN	1064.7A	1073.5A	1253.6A	1385.3	1508.8	1452.8A	1476.4A	0.9	6.6	3.4	119	131	143	139	140
GENESCO INC	JAN	606.3	492.2	476.3	471.7D	539.9A	572.9	462.9D	-19.2	-1.2	-2.7	79	78	89	95	76
INTERCO INC	DEC	2625.7	1656.1D	1439.2D	1471.7D	1265.8H	1656.8	1072.7D	-35.3	-8.3	-8.6	55	56	48	63	41
MELVILLE CORP	DEC	4423.5	7554.0	8686.8A	9886.2	10432.8	10435.4	11285.5	8.1	8.4	9.8	196	224	236	236	255
FURNITURE & BEDDING																
BASSETT FURNITURE INDS	NOV	398.1A	459.9	435.7	401.6	473.4	503.8	510.6	1.3	2.1	2.5	109	101	119	127	128
LA-Z-BOY CHAIR CO	APR	282.7	592.3	608.0	619.5	684.1	804.9	850.3A	5.6	7.5	11.6	215	219	242	285	301
LADD FURNITURE INC	DEC	192.7A	453.0A	511.9	429.1	496.7A	521.2	591.6A	13.5	5.5	11.9	266	223	258	270	307
(cont'd)																

Data by Standard & Poor's Compustat, A Division of The McGraw-Hill Companies

Company	Yr. End	Million $							Compound Growth Rate (%)			Index Basis (1984 = 100)				
		1984	1989	1990	1991	1992	1993	1994	1-Yr.	5-Yr.	10-Yr.	1990	1991	1992	1993	1994
APPAREL MANUFACTURERS & MARKETERS																
BEEBA'S CREATIONS INC	AUG	1.1	4.1	-3.4	2.7	5.5	1.3	-3.4	NM	NM	NM	-313	253	504	122	-316
CHAUS (BERNARD) INC	JUN	NA	-3.3	1.5	-12.0	3.5	-11.0	-46.8	NM	NM	NA	NA	*	*	*	*
CRYSTAL BRANDS	DEC	NA	27.4	28.9	-32.2	-30.0	-118.3	NA	NA	NA	NA	NA	*	*	*	*
FARAH INC	OCT	15.6	-11.6	-6.6	-5.5	-9.6	0.1	10.8	NM	NM	-3.6	-42	-35	-62	1	69
* FRUIT OF THE LOOM INC -CL A	DEC	NA	72.0	77.1	111.0	188.5	212.8	60.3	-71.7	-3.5	NA	NA	*	*	*	*
GARAN INC	SEP	11.9	8.5	10.0	10.2	15.3	16.8	9.4	-44.5	1.8	-2.4	84	85	129	141	79
HAGGAR CORP	SEP	NA	NA	NA	NA	12.4	15.0	25.7	71.1	NA	NA	NA	*	*	*	*
HAMPTON INDUSTRIES	DEC	4.4	3.6	-0.5	-0.6	1.4	-2.4	1.0	NM	-22.4	-13.8	-11	-14	33	-55	23
HARTMARX CORP	NOV	41.7	17.4	-61.5	-38.4	-220.2	6.2	20.0	221.7	2.8	-7.1	-147	-92	-528	15	48
JONES APPAREL GROUP INC	DEC	NA	NA	27.5	34.1	41.3	48.4	54.9	13.6	NA	NA	NA	*	*	*	*
KELLWOOD CO	†APR	15.5	14.0	12.4	22.8	28.7	35.6	11.1	-68.8	-4.6	-3.3	80	147	185	230	72
LIZ CLAIBORNE INC	DEC	41.9	164.6	205.8	222.7	218.8	125.3	82.8	-33.9	-12.8	7.0	491	531	522	299	198
MUNSINGWEAR INC	DEC	0.1	-10.8	-13.4	-6.6	1.2	-0.3	-0.4	NM	NM	NM	NM	NM	1306	-360	-434
OAK HILL SPORTSWEAR CORP	DEC	1.0	0.1	-3.6	0.5	-1.3	0.2	0.2	42.2	12.2	-13.4	-372	48	-140	17	24
OSHKOSH B'GOSH INC -CL A	DEC	12.9	37.6	29.6	23.6	15.7	4.5	7.0	55.6	-28.5	-5.8	230	183	122	35	55
OXFORD INDUSTRIES INC	†MAY	7.1	7.9	5.5	12.5	14.8	19.2	10.6	-44.9	5.9	4.0	78	176	207	269	148
PHILLIPS-VAN HEUSEN	†JAN	15.3	24.2	26.4	31.1	37.9	43.3	30.0	-30.6	4.4	7.0	172	204	248	283	196
RUSSELL CORP	DEC	27.9	64.7	67.9	56.8	82.2	49.1	78.8	60.5	4.0	10.9	243	204	295	176	282
SALANT CORP	DEC	-19.0	-9.4	-43.9	-19.1	7.3	7.2	3.5	-51.5	NM	NM	NM	NM	NM	NM	NM
SIGNAL APPAREL CO	DEC	-0.6	-0.9	-6.1	-31.9	-20.5	-33.9	-53.3	NM	NM	NM	NM	NM	NM	NM	NM
STAGE II APPAREL CORP	DEC	NA	3.1	-1.2	0.9	2.2	0.8	-0.9	NM	NM	NA	NA	*	*	*	*
TULTEX CORP	DEC	9.7	5.0	23.1	7.1	17.2	5.9	9.0	5.6	12.2	-0.8	241	73	177	61	92
UNITED MERCHANTS &MFRS	†JUN	11.0	-26.2	-137.1	-56.9	-33.0	-25.2	-23.2	NM	NM	NM	-1243	-516	-299	-229	-211
VF CORP	DEC	124.7	176.0	81.1	161.3	237.0	246.4	274.5	11.4	9.3	8.2	65	129	190	198	220
WARNACO GROUP INC -CL A	DEC	20.5	-7.9	-7.9	-19.5	47.6	53.3	63.3	18.9	NM	12.0	-38	-95	232	260	309
SHOE PRODUCERS																
BARRY (R G)	DEC	0.1	3.7	-7.0	-1.3	3.0	3.8	3.8	0.3	0.4	38.8	-4892	-878	2112	2638	2647
L A GEAR INC	NOV	NA	55.1	31.3	-45.0	-71.9	-32.5	-22.2	NM	NM	NA	NA	*	*	*	*
* NIKE INC -CL B	†MAY	10.3	243.0	287.0	329.2	365.0	298.8	254.5	-14.8	7.8	45.1	2795	3206	3854	2909	3636
* REEBOK INTERNATIONAL LTD	DEC	6.1	175.0	176.6	234.7	114.8	223.4	254.5	13.9	7.8	13.8	2874	3820	1868	1135	4141
* STRIDE RITE CORP	NOV	5.4	46.2	55.5	66.0	61.5	60.3	19.8	-67.2	-15.6	13.8	1025	1217	1135	1113	365
SUAVE SHOE CORP	SEP	-0.3	0.4	2.8	-4.3	1.3	-4.3	-8.2	NM	NM	NM	NM	NM	NM	NM	NM
WOLVERINE WORLD WIDE	DEC	2.1	7.3	-5.7	3.3	4.6	11.5	18.1	57.1	19.9	23.8	-268	152	216	538	845
SHOE PRODUCERS & RETAILERS																
BROWN GROUP INC	†JAN	54.1	30.8	31.8	15.7	4.7	-6.7	33.6	NM	1.7	-4.7	59	29	9	-12	62
EDISON BROTHERS STORES	†JAN	32.9	61.2	59.0	60.8	71.1	22.1	20.5	-7.2	-19.6	-4.6	179	185	216	67	62
GENESCO INC	†JAN	11.0	18.9	1.3	0.5	9.7	-51.8	-18.5	NM	NM	NM	12	4	88	-469	-168
INTERCO INC	DEC	72.2	-50.9	-151.4	-48.6	157.7	45.4	27.9	-38.4	NM	-9.1	-210	-67	219	63	39
* MELVILLE CORP	DEC	190.4	398.1	385.3	346.7	156.0	331.8	307.5	-7.3	-5.0	4.9	202	182	82	174	162
FURNITURE & BEDDING																
BASSETT FURNITURE INDS	NOV	30.9	19.0	5.1	19.8	27.5	25.9	25.0	-3.5	5.7	-2.1	17	64	89	84	81
LA-Z-BOY CHAIR CO	†APR	21.4	28.3	23.4	25.1	27.3	34.7	36.3	4.6	5.1	5.4	109	118	128	163	170
LADD FURNITURE INC	DEC	14.8	16.7	0.5	-12.7	5.2	3.8	4.3	12.0	-23.8	-11.6	3	-86	35	26	29
LEGGETT & PLATT INC	DEC	19.4	45.9	29.4	39.4	62.5	85.9	115.4	34.3	20.2	19.5	152	203	322	443	596
* MASCO CORP	DEC	115.9	220.9	138.8	44.9	183.1	221.1	193.7	-12.4	-2.6	5.3	120	39	158	191	167
FLOOR COVERINGS																
ARMSTRONG WORLD INDS INC	DEC	92.2	153.7	143.2	60.6	-61.6	63.5	210.4	231.3	6.5	8.6	155	66	-67	69	228
SHAW INDUSTRIES INC	DEC	22.9	47.6	65.4	33.1	58.0	100.6	132.5	31.7	22.7	19.2	286	144	253	439	579
MISCELLANEOUS HOUSEHOLD GOODS																
NEWELL COMPANIES	DEC	14.2	85.4	101.4	112.2	163.3	165.3	195.6	18.3	18.0	30.0	715	792	1152	1167	1380
* PREMARK INTERNATIONAL INC	DEC	NA	78.4	52.0	102.3	144.6	172.5	225.5	30.7	23.5	NA	NA	*	*	*	*
* RUBBERMAID INC	DEC	46.9	116.4	143.5	162.7	166.9	211.4	228.1	7.9	14.4	17.1	306	347	356	451	487
THOMAS INDUSTRIES INC	DEC	15.9	20.6	11.7	3.8	-2.0	3.8	10.5	177.1	-12.6	-4.0	74	24	-13	24	67

Data by Standard & Poor's Compustat. A Division of The McGraw-Hill Companies

Net Income

Company	Yr. End	Million $ 1984	1989	1990	1991	1992	1993	1994	Comp. Growth 1-Yr.	5-Yr.	10-Yr.	Index 1990	1991	1992	1993	1994
HOUSEHOLD APPLIANCES																
* BLACK & DECKER CORP	DEC	95.4	30.0	51.1	53.0	-73.3	95.2	127.4	33.8	33.5	2.9	54	56	-77	100	134
* FEDDERS CORP	AUG	22.1	-15.6	-37.0	-24.9	-1	19.2		NM	-2.8	14.7	-319	-760	-511	-36	394
* GENERAL ELECTRIC CO	DEC	2280.0	3939.0	4303.0	4435.0	4305.0	4424.0	5915.0	33.7	8.5	10.0	189	195	189	194	259
* MAYTAG CORP	DEC	63.1	131.5	98.9	79.0	-8.4	51.3	151.1	194.8	2.8	9.1	157	125	-13	81	239
NATIONAL PRESTO INDS INC	DEC	16.2	28.7	29.1	36.7	25.9	18.7	21.5	15.0	-5.7	2.9	180	227	160	115	133
* WHIRLPOOL CORP	DEC	189.6	187.2	72.0	170.0	205.0	231.0	158.0	-31.6	-3.3	-1.8	38	90	108	122	83
* ZENITH ELECTRONICS CORP	DEC	63.6	-17.0	-52.3	-51.6	-105.9	-97.0	-14.2	NM	NM	NM	-82	-81	-167	-153	-22
COSMETICS & TOILETRIES																
* ALBERTO-CULVER CO -CL B	SEP	4.5	29.4	35.0	30.1	38.6	41.3	44.1	6.8	8.4	25.6	774	665	853	912	974
* AVON PRODUCTS	DEC	181.7	152.4	195.3	210.7	175.0	249.6	264.8	6.1	11.7	3.8	107	116	96	137	146
CARTER-WALLACE INC	†MAR	20.7	50.3	51.8	45.7	47.2	26.6	-56.3	NM	NM	NM	250	221	228	128	-272
* GILLETTE CO	DEC	159.3	284.7	367.9	427.4	513.4	426.9	698.3	63.6	19.7	15.9	231	268	322	268	438
HELENE CURTIS INDS	†FEB	2.7	16.8	6.5	19.2	22.1	14.3	19.2	34.1	2.6	21.7	241	714	820	530	711
* INTL FLAVORS & FRAGRANCES	DEC	69.2	138.6	156.7	168.7	176.7	202.5	226.0	11.6	10.3	12.6	226	244	255	292	326
SOAPS & DETERGENTS																
* CHURCH & DWIGHT INC	DEC	11.2	8.6	23.2	26.5	29.5	29.5	6.1	-79.3	-6.7	-5.9	207	236	263	263	55
* CLOROX CO/DE	JUN	79.7	145.6	153.6	52.7	117.8	167.9	180.0	7.2	4.3	8.5	193	66	148	211	226
* COLGATE-PALMOLIVE CO	DEC	53.6	280.0	321.0	124.9	477.0	548.1	580.2	5.9	15.7	26.9	599	233	890	1023	1083
* DIAL CORP/DE	DEC	125.0	108.7	116.4	10.9	28.0	110.3	140.3	27.2	5.2	1.2	93	9	22	88	112
* PROCTER & GAMBLE CO	JUN	890.0	1206.0	1602.0	1773.0	1872.0	269.0	2211.0	721.9	12.9	9.5	180	199	210	30	248
* UNILEVER PLC -AMER SHRS	DEC	242.0	594.1	700.0	649.4	608.9	606.0	775.7	28.0	5.5	12.4	289	268	252	250	321
* UNILEVER N V -NY SHARES	DEC	342.0	1106.7	1440.0	1549.7	1677.6	1343.1	1608.8	19.8	7.8	16.7	421	453	491	393	470

Note: Data as originally reported.   * Company included in the Standard & Poor's 500.   † Of the following calendar year.

Return on Revenues (%) / Return on Assets (%) / Return on Equity (%)

Company	Yr. End	ROR 1990	1991	1992	1993	1994	ROA 1990	1991	1992	1993	1994	ROE 1990	1991	1992	1993	1994
TEXTILES																
DIXIE YARNS INC	DEC	1.2	NM	1.2	0.8	NM	1.9	NM	1.6	1.1	NM	3.8	NM	3.9	2.9	NM
FAB INDUSTRIES INC	NOV	6.5	8.3	8.9	9.0	8.0	8.8	11.7	12.1	11.5	9.4	11.3	14.9	15.5	14.6	11.9
FIELDCREST CANNON	DEC	NM	0.3	1.7	1.5	1.7	NM	0.4	2.3	1.9	4.0	NM	1.3	7.7	6.1	12.4
GUILFORD MILLS INC	SEP	NM	2.6	4.0	4.4	3.6	NM	3.5	6.3	6.3	4.7	NM	7.7	12.9	13.5	10.8
* SPRINGS INDUSTRIES -CL A	DEC	NM	1.4	2.3	2.3	3.0	NM	2.2	3.6	3.7	4.8	NM	4.8	7.7	8.4	11.0
TEXFI INDUSTRIES	OCT	1.2	NM	4.0	NM	NM	2.3	NM	9.0	NM	NM	0.2	NM	46.8	NM	NM
APPAREL MANUFACTURERS & MARKETERS																
BEEBA'S CREATIONS INC	AUG	NM	2.1	4.7	1.1	NM	NM	5.2	11.0	2.4	NM	NM	7.8	18.8	5.3	NM
CHAUS (BERNARD) INC	JUN	0.5	NM	1.4	NM	NM	1.9	NM	4.2	NM	NM	3.0	NM	8.7	NM	NM
CRYSTAL BRANDS	DEC	3.3	NM	NM	NM	NA	4.2	NM	NM	0.1	NA	11.5	NM	NM	NM	NA
FARAH INC	OCT	NM	NM	NM	0.1	4.5	NM	NM	NM	8.5	7.8	NM	NM	NM	0.3	16.7
* FRUIT OF THE LOOM INC -CL A	DEC	5.4	6.8	10.2	11.3	2.6	3.8	5.2	8.6	8.5	2.0	20.7	20.1	24.4	22.4	5.6
GARAN INC	SEP	6.9	7.0	9.0	8.9	5.4	10.6	10.0	14.1	14.4	7.8	14.7	13.8	18.9	18.8	10.0
HAGGAR CORP	SEP	NM	NA	3.3	3.8	2.7	NA	NA	NA	8.0	11.1	NA	NA	NA	13.3	17.6
HAMPTON INDUSTRIES	DEC	NM	NM	0.7	0.6	0.8	NM	NM	1.4	NM	5.0	NM	NM	NM	NM	1.9
HARTMARX CORP	NOV	NM	NM	NM	0.9	2.6	NM	NM	NM	1.4	NM	NM	NM	NM	6.9	16.9
JONES APPAREL GROUP INC	DEC	9.5	10.2	9.4	8.9	8.6	NA	31.4	26.4	21.4	18.8	NA	56.0	37.4	29.9	25.1
* KELLWOOD CO	†APR	1.5	2.5	2.7	3.0	0.8	2.6	4.5	4.9	5.6	1.6	6.3	9.9	10.6	12.1	3.6
* LIZ CLAIBORNE INC	DEC	11.9	11.1	10.0	5.7	3.8	22.5	20.6	17.8	9.9	6.6	31.1	27.5	22.9	12.7	8.4
* MUNSINGWEAR INC	DEC	NM	NM	3.1	NM	8.0	NM	NM	5.6	NM	NM	NM	NM	8.0	NM	NM
OAK HILL SPORTWEAR CORP	DEC	NM	0.5	NM	0.2	0.3	NM	1.4	NM	0.6	0.9	NM	3.4	NM	1.3	1.8

(cont'd)

Data by Standard & Poor's Compustat, A Division of The McGraw-Hill Companies

Company	Yr. End	ROR 1990	ROR 1991	ROR 1992	ROR 1993	ROR 1994	ROA 1990	ROA 1991	ROA 1992	ROA 1993	ROA 1994	ROE 1990	ROE 1991	ROE 1992	ROE 1993	ROE 1994
APPAREL MANUFACTURERS & MARKETERS (cont'd)																
OSHKOSH B GOSH INC -CL A	DEC	9.1	6.5	4.5	1.3	1.9	16.8	11.7	7.1	2.0	3.2	21.1	14.8	9.2	2.6	4.3
OXFORD INDUSTRIES INC	†MAY	1.6	2.4	2.6	3.1	1.6	2.8	6.5	7.1	8.4	3.9	5.4	12.0	13.2	15.8	8.1
PHILLIPS-VAN HEUSEN	†JAN	3.3	3.4	3.1	3.8	3.6	7.4	8.3	8.3	8.1	5.2	33.6	24.1	15.3	18.9	11.5
RUSSELL CORP	DEC	9.5	7.1	5.6	5.3	7.2	9.0	7.0	9.2	8.0	7.6	15.7	31.2	15.3	8.5	13.0
SALANT CORP	DEC	NM	NM	1.9	1.8	0.8	NM	NM	2.8	2.9	1.3	NM	NM	NM	NM	4.7
SIGNAL APPAREL CO	DEC	NM	NM	NM	NM	NM	NM	NM	NM	NM	NM	NM	NM	NM	NM	NM
STAGE II APPAREL CORP	DEC	6.6	1.3	2.9	1.2	1.6	7.9	2.7	6.7	2.5	1.9	16.8	3.8	9.1	3.2	5.2
TULTEX CORP	DEC	NM	2.2	3.4	1.1	NM	NM	2.4	4.7	1.3	NM	NM	4.8	10.4	2.9	NM
UNITED MERCHANTS & MFRS	JUN	NM	NM	NM	NM	NM	NM	NM	NM	NM	NM	NM	NM	NM	NM	NM
VF CORP	DEC	3.1	5.5	6.2	5.7	5.5	4.3	8.1	9.8	8.8	8.8	9.4	17.8	22.2	18.0	16.5
WARNACO GROUP INC -CL A	DEC	NM	NM	7.6	7.6	8.0	NM	NM	8.1	8.1	8.6	NM	NM	66.8	36.1	31.7
SHOE PRODUCERS																
BARRY (R G)	DEC	NM	NM	3.0	3.8	3.3	NM	NM	6.0	7.1	5.7	NM	NM	12.0	12.9	10.5
L A GEAR INC	NOV	3.5	NM	NM	NM	NM	9.9	NM	NM	NM	NM	16.8	NM	NM	NM	NM
* NIKE INC -CL B	†MAY	9.6	9.7	9.3	7.7	NA	20.5	18.4	18.0	13.1	NA	31.6	27.8	24.5	17.6	NA
* REEBOK INTERNATIONAL LTD	DEC	8.2	8.6	3.8	7.7	7.8	13.7	16.6	8.3	16.3	16.7	19.2	25.8	13.8	26.5	27.7
* STRIDE RITE CORP	NOV	10.8	11.5	10.5	10.4	3.8	21.5	22.1	17.2	15.2	4.9	31.9	31.3	24.0	21.0	6.7
SUAVE SHOE CORP	SEP	4.5	NM	2.2	NM	NM	7.4	NM	4.6	NM	NM	13.0	NM	7.3	NM	NM
WOLVERINE WORLD WIDE	DEC	NM	1.0	1.6	3.5	4.8	NM	1.6	2.2	5.6	8.3	NM	3.0	4.4	10.8	14.7
SHOE PRODUCERS & RETAILERS																
BROWN GROUP INC	†JAN	1.8	0.9	0.3	NM	2.3	4.4	2.2	0.6	NM	4.8	9.4	4.8	1.5	NM	13.9
EDISON BROTHERS STORES	†JAN	4.7	4.4	4.7	1.5	1.4	9.3	8.1	8.7	2.6	2.3	20.1	16.7	17.7	5.3	5.1
GENESCO INC	†JAN	0.3	0.1	1.8	NM	2.6	0.5	0.2	3.5	3.8	2.7	0.7	0.1	6.5	NM	NM
INTERCO INC	DEC	2.7	NM	12.5	2.5	2.7	4.7	5.9	13.0	10.9	2.7	NM	NM	6.5	14.4	9.1
* MELVILLE CORP	DEC	4.4	3.5	1.5	3.2	2.7	11.5	9.0	3.8	7.8	6.8	21.4	16.9	6.8	14.7	12.6
FURNITURE & BEDDING																
* BASSETT FURNITURE INDS	NOV	1.2	4.9	5.8	5.1	4.9	1.8	7.1	9.0	8.0	7.4	2.0	7.9	10.4	9.2	8.6
LA-Z-BOY CHAIR CO	†APR	3.8	4.1	4.0	4.3	4.3	6.4	6.8	7.0	8.0	7.8	10.5	10.6	10.7	12.5	11.8
LADD FURNITURE INC	DEC	0.1	NM	1.0	0.6	0.7	0.1	NM	1.7	1.2	1.2	0.4	NM	4.0	2.6	2.9
LEGGETT & PLATT INC	DEC	2.7	3.6	5.3	5.6	6.2	4.7	5.9	9.4	10.9	11.4	10.1	12.4	16.5	18.3	20.2
* MASCO CORP	DEC	4.3	1.4	5.2	5.7	4.3	3.8	1.2	4.7	5.5	4.6	7.6	2.5	9.9	11.4	9.4
FLOOR COVERINGS																
* ARMSTRONG WORLD INDS INC	DEC	5.7	2.5	NM	2.5	7.6	6.9	2.8	NM	3.2	10.1	13.3	4.7	NM	9.1	31.3
SHAW INDUSTRIES INC	DEC	4.4	2.1	3.3	4.3	5.0	9.8	4.1	6.1	8.5	8.9	31.1	15.0	17.6	17.9	19.2
MISCELLANEOUS HOUSEHOLD GOODS																
* NEWELL COMPANIES	DEC	9.5	10.0	11.2	10.1	9.4	11.6	11.7	12.5	9.4	8.8	21.1	20.1	22.3	18.0	18.6
* PREMARK INTERNATIONAL INC	DEC	1.9	3.6	0.2	5.6	6.5	2.7	5.0	0.2	8.5	10.1	6.7	12.8	0.6	22.7	25.3
* RUBBERMAID INC	DEC	9.4	9.8	9.2	10.8	10.5	14.1	13.8	13.0	14.9	14.2	21.0	19.7	17.8	20.0	18.9
THOMAS INDUSTRIES INC	DEC	2.5	0.9	NM	0.8	2.3	3.6	1.2	NM	1.3	3.5	8.3	2.7	NM	3.0	8.1
HOUSEHOLD APPLIANCES																
* BLACK & DECKER CORP	DEC	1.1	1.1	NM	2.0	2.4	0.8	0.9	NM	1.8	2.4	6.2	5.5	NM	9.2	12.1
FEDDERS CORP	AUG	NM	NM	NM	NM	8.3	NM	NM	NM	NM	21.1	NM	NM	NM	NM	52.2
* GENERAL ELECTRIC CO	DEC	7.5	7.5	7.7	7.4	10.0	3.1	2.8	2.4	2.1	2.7	20.2	20.5	19.1	18.0	22.9
* MAYTAG CORP	DEC	3.2	2.1	NM	NM	4.5	3.9	3.1	NM	NM	6.1	10.1	7.8	NM	NM	9.1
NATIONAL PRESTO INDS INC	DEC	22.9	22.7	20.2	15.7	16.8	12.0	14.4	9.8	6.9	7.5	14.6	17.6	12.0	8.4	9.1
WHIRLPOOL CORP	DEC	2.5	2.5	2.8	3.1	2.0	1.3	2.8	3.3	3.8	2.5	5.1	11.6	13.2	14.2	9.4
ZENITH ELECTRONICS CORP	DEC	NM	NM	NM	NM	NM	NM	NM	NM	NM	NM	NM	NM	NM	NM	NM
COSMETICS & TOILETRIES																
ALBERTO-CULVER CO -CL B	SEP	4.4	3.4	3.5	3.6	3.6	8.8	6.0	6.5	6.9	7.3	17.9	12.5	14.4	14.1	14.1
* AVON PRODUCTS	DEC	5.7	5.9	4.2	6.2	6.2	9.4	11.1	10.1	13.5	13.5	54.4	61.4	62.3	79.9	NM
CARTER-WALLACE INC	†MAR	8.1	6.7	7.2	4.0	NM	9.6	8.0	8.0	4.3	4.3	14.2	11.6	10.7	6.5	NM
* GILLETTE CO	DEC	8.5	9.1	9.9	7.9	11.5	10.8	11.3	12.7	9.2	13.2	NM	58.8	39.2	29.2	40.8
HELENE CURTIS INDS	†FEB	0.8	1.9	1.5	1.2	1.5	4.4	3.9	3.9	2.4	3.0	4.4	12.2	12.5	7.4	9.1
* INTL FLAVORS & FRAGRANCES	DEC	16.3	16.6	15.7	17.0	17.2	14.9	14.4	14.2	16.2	17.2	18.8	18.2	18.2	21.7	23.8

Data by Standard & Poor's Compustat. A Division of The McGraw-Hill Companies

Return on Revenues (%) · Return on Assets (%) · Return on Equity (%)

Company	Yr. End	ROR 1990	ROR 1991	ROR 1992	ROR 1993	ROR 1994	ROA 1990	ROA 1991	ROA 1992	ROA 1993	ROA 1994	ROE 1990	ROE 1991	ROE 1992	ROE 1993	ROE 1994
SOAPS & DETERGENTS																
CHURCH & DWIGHT INC	DEC	5.4	5.4	5.7	5.8	1.2	9.3	10.6	11.6	10.8	2.1	20.2	20.5	19.8	18.0	3.8
* CLOROX CO/DE	JUN	10.4	3.2	6.9	10.3	9.8	13.1	3.9	7.3	10.3	10.8	19.2	6.6	14.7	19.8	20.1
* COLGATE-PALMOLIVE CO	DEC	5.6	2.1	6.8	7.7	7.6	8.3	2.9	9.8	9.3	9.7	24.5	6.5	20.5	23.7	30.6
* DIAL CORP/DE	DEC	3.3	0.3	0.8	3.7	4.0	2.2	0.2	0.8	3.4	4.0	11.0	0.2	4.0	2.1	27.2
* PROCTER & GAMBLE CO	JUN	6.7	6.6	6.4	0.9	7.3	9.2	9.1	8.4	1.1	8.8	22.7	22.4	21.4		26.4
UNILEVER PLC -AMER SHRS	DEC	4.7	4.6	4.6	4.8	5.8	8.7	7.5	7.6	7.8	9.2	30.0	24.6	23.5	23.8	27.4
* UNILEVER N V -NY SHARES	DEC	5.2	5.2	5.5	4.6	5.0	9.8	9.4	10.0	8.0	8.9	56.9	47.6	41.8	31.4	34.3

Note: Data as originally reported.
* Company included in the Standard & Poor's 500. † Of the following calendar year.

Current Ratio · Debt / Capital Ratio (%) · Debt as % of Net Working Capital

Company	Yr. End	CR 1990	CR 1991	CR 1992	CR 1993	CR 1994	D/C 1990	D/C 1991	D/C 1992	D/C 1993	D/C 1994	DNWC 1990	DNWC 1991	DNWC 1992	DNWC 1993	DNWC 1994
TEXTILES																
DIXIE YARNS INC	DEC	3.2	3.7	2.9	2.5	2.4	40.1	50.3	50.9	43.0	44.0	129.6	155.1	197.7	205.3	204.4
FAB INDUSTRIES INC	NOV	5.2	4.5	4.6	4.8	3.6	0.9	0.7	0.7	0.6	0.5	1.2	1.0	1.2	0.8	1.1
FIELDCREST CANNON	DEC	2.8	1.4	2.7	2.7	3.1	59.7	47.5	52.0	56.3	53.7	140.8	183.4	119.2	112.3	112.5
GUILFORD MILLS INC	SEP	2.6	2.6	2.6	2.6	2.4	32.1	28.8	25.5	38.2	38.4	66.8	64.7	54.9	97.0	107.5
* SPRINGS INDUSTRIES -CL A	DEC	2.5	2.2	2.2	2.3	2.5	30.1	31.9	30.5	33.9	30.2	73.0	87.3	83.4	82.9	71.1
TEXFI INDUSTRIES	OCT	1.9	1.3	1.4	1.4	1.3	54.9	69.7	63.3	76.1	76.8	174.7	384.7	420.1	470.2	576.3
APPAREL MANUFACTURERS & MARKETERS																
BEEBA'S CREATIONS INC	AUG	2.4	4.4	2.4	2.6	3.4	0.0	0.0	0.0	0.0	0.0	0.0	0.0	0.0	0.0	0.0
CHAUS (BERNARD) INC	JUN	4.8	3.8	2.8	2.0	1.1	22.3	39.6	25.5	30.8	363.1	24.5	43.1	28.5	36.0	562.2
CRYSTAL BRANDS	OCT	2.1	1.8	3.1	0.5	NA	46.9	49.9	70.2	NM	NA	124.5	148.9	170.6	NM	NA
FARAH INC	DEC	2.1	2.1	2.1	1.5	2.2	10.6	10.2	10.2	2.6	5.7	13.1	12.6	10.1	3.6	7.7
* FRUIT OF THE LOOM INC -CL A	DEC	1.3	1.8	1.7	3.8	3.2	70.8	54.1	46.9	52.1	55.2	756.5	283.6	244.0	172.5	193.4
GARAN INC	SEP	4.4	4.0	4.6	4.8	5.8	8.1	6.7	5.0	4.2	3.6	10.4	8.2	6.4	5.2	4.4
HAGGAR CORP	SEP	NA	NA	3.0	2.7	2.6	NA	NA	23.2	3.9	8.7	NA	NA	29.0	4.9	11.5
HAMPTON INDUSTRIES	DEC	5.6	4.0	2.2	4.8	4.1	29.5	26.9	27.2	29.1	24.0	43.3	41.2	42.4	42.5	34.6
HARTMARX CORP	NOV	2.4	1.7	2.2	3.8	3.2	43.7	26.9	77.9	65.6	56.6	67.7	45.6	105.0	83.3	77.5
JONES APPAREL GROUP INC	DEC	1.7	3.1	3.7	4.0	4.8	11.4	5.8	3.4	4.8	3.1	14.6	6.6	3.9	6.0	3.9
KELLWOOD CO	†APR	2.2	2.5	1.9	2.7	3.4	35.5	28.4	25.3	31.2	29.5	67.4	50.5	52.1	58.3	61.1
LIZ CLAIBORNE INC	DEC	3.5	4.1	4.1	2.9	3.4	2.0	0.2	0.1	0.1	0.2	2.5	0.2	0.2	0.1	0.2
MUNSINGWEAR INC	DEC	0.2	2.2	2.5	2.9	1.5	NM	4.1	1.2	9.9	0.2	NM	10.4	4.1	18.4	0.6
OAK HILL SPORTWEAR CORP	DEC	1.5	1.7	1.7	1.9	1.8	13.9	12.9	2.0	11.9	10.9	22.1	19.4	19.9	17.5	15.9
OSHKOSH B'GOSH INC -CL A	DEC	4.5	4.2	4.2	3.8	3.6	2.2	1.4	0.7	0.4	0.3	3.5	2.2	1.2	0.7	0.5
OXFORD INDUSTRIES INC	†MAY	2.7	2.5	2.3	2.1	2.1	20.9	17.1	13.0	8.6	25.6	28.1	22.4	17.1	11.3	32.7
PHILLIPS-VAN HEUSEN	DEC	3.1	2.9	3.6	3.8	3.8	50.9	43.4	44.6	40.8	38.1	72.1	61.2	57.6	54.9	53.8
RUSSELL CORP	DEC	3.9	4.6	3.6	3.2	2.2	27.2	24.5	22.9	20.4	17.5	76.6	70.6	65.0	58.8	46.5
SALANT CORP	DEC	5.1	3.9	3.5	3.2	2.2	NM	NM	NM	58.6	60.5	0.0	0.0	0.0	109.0	114.2
SIGNAL APPAREL CO	DEC	2.3	2.3	3.0	2.4	1.3	43.6	65.3	76.6	36.1	98.1	68.3	158.4	157.9	105.4	375.7
STAGE II APPAREL CORP	DEC	2.5	2.6	2.5	2.4	1.1	0.0	1.3	0.9	0.0	3.8	0.0	2.1	1.9	0.0	52.9
TULTEX CORP	DEC	2.3	1.9	2.0	6.4	1.7	30.7	24.9	38.6	54.4	29.1	90.7	73.4	95.5	94.8	67.6
UNITED MERCHANTS &MFRS	JUN	2.3	2.1	0.7	0.3	2.9	182.0	NM	114.4	NM	166.7	325.0	NM	NM	NM	286.8
* VF CORP	DEC	1.4	2.5	1.7	1.5	1.3	39.7	36.7	38.7	24.5	22.1	123.8	104.1	112.6	62.8	80.9
WARNACO GROUP INC -CL A	DEC						107.3	90.8	67.1	60.7	46.2	588.6	250.4	196.3	201.3	197.9
SHOE PRODUCERS																
BARRY (R G)	DEC	2.6	3.0	3.4	3.3	3.3	36.1	35.5	29.9	23.6	28.6	58.1	57.4	45.6	35.0	42.1
L A GEAR INC	NOV	2.1	3.3	3.7	3.8	4.2	0.0	0.0	0.0	25.4	28.1	0.0	0.0	0.0	30.9	33.8
* NIKE INC -CL B	†MAY	2.0	3.3	3.6	3.2	NA	2.8	4.9	0.9	0.7	NA	4.6	7.2	1.3	1.0	3.8
* REEBOK INTERNATIONAL LTD	DEC	3.5	2.4	2.8	2.8	2.6	9.5	16.9	12.1	13.5	11.5	14.4	28.3	17.2	18.4	15.8
* STRIDE RITE CORP	NOV	3.5	3.9	3.5	3.4	3.5	2.5	1.6	1.2	0.8	0.6	3.0	1.9	1.4	1.0	0.7
(cont d)																

Data by Standard & Poor's Compustat. A Division of The McGraw-Hill Companies

Price-Earnings Ratio (High-Low) · Dividend Payout Ratio (%) · Yield (High % - Low %)

Company	Yr End	P/E 1990	P/E 1991	P/E 1992	P/E 1993	P/E 1994	Div 1990	Div 1991	Div 1992	Div 1993	Div 1994	Yld 1990	Yld 1991	Yld 1992	Yld 1993	Yld 1994
TEXTILES																
DIXIE YARNS INC	DEC	23-11	NM-NM	22-13	41-21	NM-NM	96	NM	31	49	NM	4.2-8.6	2.8-5.6	1.4-2.3	1.2-2.3	1.8-3.0
FAB INDUSTRIES INC	NOV	11-9	15-6	14-9	13-11	15-12	24	16	19	18	46	2.3-2.6	1.1-2.6	0.0-0.0	1.4-1.7	3.1-3.7
FIELDCREST CANNON	DEC	NM-NM	NM-20	12-7	23-15	11-7	NM	0	0	0	0	2.1-8.7	0.0-0.0	0.0-0.0	0.0-0.0	0.0-0.0
GUILFORD MILLS INC	SEP	NM-NM	60-20	18-10	15-9	11-10	NM	52	31	28	33	2.1-5.8	2.4-4.7	3.2-3.2	2.1-3.2	2.5-3.2
* SPRINGS INDUSTRIES -CL A	DEC	NM-NM	22-11	18-12	19-13	12-8	NM	78	48	45	34	3.0-7.1	3.3-5.6	2.7-3.9	2.4-3.6	2.9-4.1
TEXFI INDUSTRIES	OCT	NM-NM	NM-NM	6-3	NM-NM	NM-NM	0	NM	0	NM	NM	0.0-0.0	0.0-0.0	0.0-0.0	0.0-0.0	0.0-0.0
APPAREL MANUFACTURERS & MARKETERS																
BEEBA'S CREATIONS INC	AUG	NM-NM	20-5	8-5	25-14	NM-NM	NM	11	45	59	NM	1.9-8.4	0.6-2.1	5.6-9.2	2.4-4.3	2.2-5.3
CHAUS (BERNARD) INC	JUN	69-23	NM-NM	53-15	NM-NM	NM-NM	0	NM	0	NM	NM	0.6-1.5	0.7-1.6	0.3-2.0	1.0-2.4	0.0-0.0
CRYSTAL BRANDS	DEC	10-4	NM-NM	NM-NM	NM-NM	NA-NA	6	NM	NM	NM	NA	0.7-1.6	0.0-0.0	0.0-0.0	0.0-0.0	0.0-0.0
FARAH INC	OCT	NM-NM	NM-NM	NM-NM	19-8	19-6	0	NM	NM	NM	0	0.0-0.0	0.0-0.0	0.0-0.0	0.0-0.0	0.0-0.0
* FRUIT OF THE LOOM INC -CL A	DEC	12-5	18-5	20-11	18-8	42-29	0	0	0	0	0	0.0-0.0	0.0-0.0	0.0-0.0	0.0-0.0	0.0-0.0
GARAN INC	SEP	8-5	10-6	12-6	11-8	18-8	39	49	39	54	98	4.7-8.2	5.0-8.2	3.1-6.3	5.0-6.3	5.5-11.6
HAGGAR CORP	SEP	NA-NA	NA-NA	13-11	14-8	14-7	NA	NA	0	5	7	NA-NA	NA-NA	0.0-0.0	0.4-0.6	0.5-1.0
HAMPTON INDUSTRIES	DEC	NM-NM	NM-NM	45-19	41-26	32-22	NM	NM	0	NM	0	0.0-0.0	0.0-0.0	0.0-0.0	0.0-0.0	0.0-0.0
HARTMARX CORP	NOV	NM-NM	NM-NM	NM-NM	22-10	12-8	NM	NM	0	0	0	4.5-16.4	NA-NA	0.0-0.0	0.0-0.0	0.0-0.0
JONES APPAREL GROUP INC	DEC	NA-NA	22-10	26-14	—	17-11	0	0	0	0	0	NA-NA	0.0-0.0	0.0-0.0	0.0-0.0	0.0-0.0
KELLWOOD CO	†APR	22-5	14-5	16-10	16-9	51-36	75	42	38	32	113	3.5-15.2	3.0-8.5	2.4-3.7	2.0-3.5	2.2-3.1
LIZ CLAIBORNE INC	DEC	15-9	19-11	18-8	28-12	25-15	10	12	15	28	42	0.7-1.2	0.6-1.2	1.0-2.2	1.0-2.4	1.7-2.9
MUNSINGWEAR INC	DEC	NM-NM	NM-NM	19-8	NM-NM	NM-NM	NM	NM	0	NM	NM	0.0-0.0	0.0-0.0	0.0-0.0	0.0-0.0	0.0-0.0
OAK HILL SPORTSWEAR CORP	DEC	NM-NM	25-10	NM-NM	63-19	49-32	NM	0	0	0	0	0.0-0.0	0.0-0.0	0.0-0.0	0.0-0.0	0.0-0.0
OSHKOSH B'GOSH INC -CL A	DEC	21-8	26-14	28-18	73-44	44-25	24	32	48	165	76	1.1-2.9	1.2-2.3	1.7-2.7	2.3-4.8	1.7-3.1
OXFORD INDUSTRIES INC	†MAY	21-10	13-6	16-8	16-9	28-18	81	39	37	31	62	3.8-7.7	3.0-8.0	2.3-4.4	2.7-4.6	2.2-3.5
PHILLIPS-VAN HEUSEN	JAN	12-5	18-6	21-14	23-16	13-9	15	12	11	9	14	1.2-2.7	0.7-2.0	0.8-1.2	0.4-0.6	0.4-1.1
RUSSELL CORP	DEC	19-10	26-14	20-14	31-22	23-18	19	23	17	33	21	1.0-2.0	0.7-1.6	0.8-1.9	1.1-1.5	1.3-1.8
SALANT CORP	DEC	NM-NM	NM-NM	5-1	11-6	41-19	NM	NM	0	NM	NM	0.0-0.0	0.0-0.0	0.0-0.0	0.0-0.0	0.0-0.0
SIGNAL APPAREL CO	DEC	NM-NM	NM-NM	NM-NM	NM-NM	NM-NM	NM	NM	0	NM	NM	0.0-0.0	0.0-0.0	0.0-0.0	0.0-0.0	0.0-0.0
STAGE II APPAREL CORP	DEC	NM-NM	20-5	15-6	39-20	NM-NM	NM	0	5	60	NM	1.2-5.5	0.0-0.0	0.9-3.1	1.5-3.0	2.2-4.4
TULTEX CORP	DEC	12-8	36-24	19-12	66-41	27-14	42	123	36	125	17	3.6-5.5	3.4-5.1	1.9-3.1	1.9-3.1	0.6-1.2
UNITED MERCHANTS &MFRS	JUN	NM-NM	NM-NM	NM-NM	NM-NM	NM-NM	74	37	28	32	NM	2.9-8.6	2.5-5.8	1.9-2.9	2.2-3.1	0.0-0.0
* VF CORP	DEC	25-9	15-6	14-10	15-10	13-11	NA	NA	37	0	31	NA-NA	2.6-3.8	1.9-2.9	2.2-3.1	2.4-2.9
WARNACO GROUP INC -CL A	DEC	NA-NA	24-10	17-10	15-10	13-9	NA	NA	0	0	0	NA	NA	0.0-0.0	0.0-0.0	0.0-0.0
SHOE PRODUCERS																
BARRY (R G)	DEC	NM-NM	NM-NM	11-4	16-6	34-14	NM	NM	0	0	0	0.0-0.0	0.0-0.0	0.0-0.0	0.0-0.0	0.0-0.0
L A GEAR INC	NOV	32-6	NM-NM	NM-NM	NM-NM	NM-NM	0	NM	NM	NM	NA	0.0-0.0	0.0-0.0	0.0-0.0	0.0-0.0	0.0-0.0
* NIKE INC -CL B	†MAY	13-6	18-8	19-12	23-11	NA-NA	19	15	13	20	10	1.0-2.0	0.8-1.7	0.8-1.3	0.9-1.9	1.2-1.9
* REEBOK INTERNATIONAL LTD	DEC	13-9	15-5	29-17	19-10	13-9	19	13	24	12	10	1.3-3.7	0.8-2.8	0.8-1.4	0.8-1.3	0.7-1.1
* STRIDE RITE CORP	NOV	14-9	24-10	27-14	20-8	47-26	7	20	26	29	95	1.3-2.1	0.8-1.9	1.0-1.9	1.5-2.9	2.0-3.6
SUAVE SHOE CORP	SEP	9-4	NM-NM	14-6	NM-NM	NM-NM	7	NM	0	0	0	0.7-1.8	1.2-5.0	1.1-2.1	0.5-1.2	0.6-0.9
WOLVERINE WORLD WIDE	DEC	NM-NM	26-16	22-11	20-8	16-11	NM	32	23	10	10	1.3-2.6	1.2-2.1	1.1-2.1	0.5-1.2	0.6-1.2
SHOE PRODUCERS & RETAILERS																
* BROWN GROUP INC	†JAN	16-11	31-24	NM-78	20-16	20-16	86	174	593	NM	84	5.3-8.1	5.6-7.4	5.5-7.6	4.5-5.6	4.1-5.2
EDISON BROTHERS STORES	†JAN	18-8	16-8	25-13	49-26	35-18	37	37	35	123	133	2.1-5.9	2.4-4.9	2.4-3.7	2.5-4.8	3.9-7.3
GENESCO INC	JAN	NM-NM	NM-NM	3-0	18-11	NM-NM	0	NM	NM	NM	NM	0.0-0.0	0.0-0.0	0.0-0.0	0.0-0.0	0.0-0.0
INTERCO INC	DEC	NM-NM	NM-NM	—	18-13	29-11	NM	NM	NM	NM	0	NM-NM	0.0-0.0	0.0-0.0	0.0-0.0	0.0-0.0
* MELVILLE CORP	DEC	16-9	17-12	41-32	—	15-11	40	45	110	51	55	2.5-4.3	2.6-3.8	2.7-3.5	2.8-3.9	3.7-5.2
FURNITURE & BEDDING																
* BASSETT FURNITURE INDS	NOV	58-43	15-11	18-10	25-15	21-14	192	39	33	44	46	3.3-4.4	2.5-3.2	1.8-3.3	1.8-2.9	2.1-3.2
LA-Z-BOY CHAIR CO	APR	17-10	18-11	18-12	18-13	20-13	43	42	40	34	34	2.5-4.5	2.3-4.2	2.1-3.4	1.6-2.5	1.7-2.7
LADD FURNITURE INC	DEC	NM-NM	17-12	50-26	87-44	62-26	933	71	71	71	63	2.2-6.6	2.9-6.6	1.3-2.6	1.6-2.6	1.0-2.5
LEGGETT & PLATT INC	DEC	23-12	88-57	22-11	24-16	18-12	50	39	28	26	22	2.2-4.2	2.2-3.4	1.3-2.8	1.7-2.6	1.6-2.9
* MASCO CORP	DEC	29-16	—	25-18	27-18	33-17	59	190	50	45	71	2.0-3.8	2.0-3.4	2.7-3.5	2.2-2.8	2.2-4.1
FLOOR COVERINGS																
* ARMSTRONG WORLD INDS INC	DEC	12-6	31-21	NM-18	42-22	11-7	36	107	NM	91	24	2.9-6.3	3.5-5.2	3.2-4.9	2.2-4.2	2.2-3.5
SHAW INDUSTRIES INC	DEC	16-7	33-17	37-18	36-20	27-14	21	43	30	23	22	1.3-3.1	1.3-2.6	0.8-1.6	0.6-1.2	0.8-1.6

Data by Standard & Poor's Compustat, A Division of The McGraw-Hill Companies

Company	Yr. End	P/E 90	P/E 91	P/E 92	P/E 93	P/E 94	Pay 90	Pay 91	Pay 92	Pay 93	Pay 94	Yld 90	Yld 91	Yld 92	Yld 93	Yld 94
MISCELLANEOUS HOUSEHOLD GOODS																
* NEWELL COMPANIES	DEC	21-11	25-13	25-16	20-15	19-15	30	33	29	33	31	1.4-2.8	1.3-2.6	1.1-1.8	1.6-2.2	1.6-2.1
* PREMARK INTERNATIONAL INC	DEC	19-8	13-5	NM-NM	16-7	14-10	51	26	686	21	22	2.7-6.6	2.1-5.2	1.9-3.2	1.3-2.9	1.5-2.2
* RUBBERMAID INC	DEC	25-17	38-18	36-26	28-21	25-17	30	30	34	31	33	1.2-1.7	0.8-1.7	0.9-1.3	1.1-1.5	1.3-2.0
THOMAS INDUSTRIES INC	DEC	18-8	39-24	NM-NM	37-24	16-12	66	200	NM	105	38	3.6-8.2	5.2-8.2	2.8-4.8	2.9-4.4	2.4-3.1
HOUSEHOLD APPLIANCES																
* BLACK & DECKER CORP	DEC	24-10	24-11	NM-NM	22-17	19-12	48	49	NM	40	29	2.0-5.0	2.0-4.7	1.5-2.7	1.8-2.4	1.6-2.4
FEDDERS CORP	AUG	NM-NM	NM-NM	NM-NM	NM-NM	13-10	NM	NM	NM	NM	0	2.8-9.6	4.4-9.6	2.7-4.0	0.0-0.0	0.0-0.0
* GENERAL ELECTRIC CO	DEC	16-10	22-14	17-15	21-16	16-13	40	41	46	50	43	2.5-3.8	2.7-3.9	2.7-3.2	2.4-3.2	2.7-3.3
* MAYTAG CORP	DEC	22-11	13-8	24-13	24-18	14-10	101	67	NM	104	35	4.6-9.6	3.8-4.8	2.4-4.0	2.7-3.8	2.5-3.6
NATIONAL PRESTO INDS INC	DEC	11-9	NM-NM	24-13	24-18	16-13	105	54	108	0	65	9.3-12.4	4.3-6.8	4.6-8.4	0.0-0.0	4.0-4.9
* WHIRLPOOL CORP	DEC	32-17	17-8	17-12	21-14	35-21	106	45	38	37	58	3.3-6.3	2.7-5.5	2.3-3.2	1.8-2.8	1.7-2.7
* ZENITH ELECTRONICS CORP	DEC	10-8	11-8	NM-NM	NM-NM	12-10	NM	NM	NM	NM	NM	0.0-0.0	0.0-0.0	0.0-0.0	0.0-0.0	0.0-0.0
COSMETICS & TOILETRIES																
* ALBERTO-CULVER CO -CL B	SEP	26-15	32-19	24-16	20-14	17-12	15	20	17	19	18	0.6-1.0	0.6-1.0	0.7-1.1	1.0-1.4	1.0-1.4
* AVON PRODUCTS	DEC	14-8	17-9	25-18	19-14	17-13	36	151	62	49	51	2.6-4.4	9.0-16.8	2.5-3.4	2.6-3.6	3.0-3.9
CARTER-WALLACE INC	†MAR	17-13	42-18	45-22	63-35	NM-NM	27	33	32	57	NM	1.5-2.0	0.8-1.9	0.7-1.5	0.9-1.7	1.1-2.9
* GILLETTE CO	DEC	20-14	29-15	26-19	33-25	24-18	33	31	30	42	31	1.6-2.4	1.1-2.1	1.1-1.6	1.3-1.7	1.1-1.7
HELENE CURTIS INDS	†FEB	40-25	21-12	20-13	31-16	18-11	29	10	10	16	12	0.7-1.1	0.5-0.8	0.5-0.8	0.5-1.0	0.7-1.1
* INTL FLAVORS & FRAGRANCES	DEC	18-13	24-16	25-21	22-19	24-18	54	56	61	57	55	3.0-4.1	2.4-3.6	2.4-3.0	2.6-3.1	2.3-3.1
SOAPS & DETERGENTS																
CHURCH & DWIGHT INC	DEC	18-12	24-12	25-17	23-16	94-54	27	25	26	29	142	1.4-2.2	1.0-2.1	1.1-1.6	1.3-1.8	1.5-2.6
* CLOROX CO/DE	JUN	16-11	43-36	24-18	18-14	18-14	46	150	73	56	54	2.8-4.0	3.5-4.2	3.1-4.0	3.1-3.9	3.0-3.8
* COLGATE-PALMOLIVE CO	DEC	17-12	64-44	21-15	20-14	17-13	39	132	39	40	40	2.4-3.4	2.4-3.0	1.9-2.5	2.0-2.9	2.4-3.1
* DIAL CORP/DE	DEC	20-14	NM-NM	79-52	17-NM	15-12	47	583	186	44	37	4.2-7.2	2.0-3.0	2.4-3.6	2.6-3.6	2.5-3.1
* PROCTER & GAMBLE CO	JUN	19-15	25-17	21-17	NM-NM	21-17	39	40	39	440	40	1.9-2.8	2.0-2.6	1.8-2.3	1.5-2.4	1.9-2.4
UNILEVER PLC -AMER SHRS	DEC	16-8	21-15	25-20	25-19	20-15	45	54	59	57	51	2.9-3.9	2.6-3.7	2.3-2.9	2.3-3.0	2.6-3.3
UNILEVER N V -NY SHARES	DEC	10-8	11-8	11-9	14-11	12-10	29	29	29	38	30	2.9-3.6	2.6-3.7	2.6-3.1	2.7-3.4	2.5-3.0

Note: Data as originally reported. * Company included in the Standard & Poor's 500. † Of the following calendar year.

Earnings per Share Book Value per Share Share Price (High-Low)

Company	Yr. End	EPS 90	EPS 91	EPS 92	EPS 93	EPS 94	BV 90	BV 91	BV 92	BV 93	BV 94	Price 90	Price 91	Price 92	Price 93	Price 94
TEXTILES																
DIXIE YARNS INC	DEC	0.71	-2.88	0.65	0.41	-0.24	15.20	11.91	12.46	10.06	9.53	16.25-7.88	15.25-7.50	14.25-8.75	16.75-8.75	11.25-6.75
FAB INDUSTRIES INC	NOV	1.68	2.52	2.65	2.75	2.44	15.86	17.70	18.01	19.98	21.52	17.75-15.31	36.63-15.56	36.38-24.50	36.75-29.50	36.13-30.00
FIELDCREST CANNON	DEC	-3.64	0.30	1.81	1.24	3.02	23.01	23.33	23.76	22.11	26.41	23.75-5.75	18.00-5.88	22.13-11.88	29.13-18.13	34.88-22.50
GUILFORD MILLS INC	SEP	-0.57	1.02	1.85	2.11	1.82	13.12	13.28	15.08	15.89	17.45	16.83-9.25	22.42-11.33	28.50-17.75	28.00-18.88	24.13-18.50
* SPRINGS INDUSTRIES -CL A	DEC	-0.39	1.53	2.50	2.65	3.50	32.05	32.39	33.47	30.89	33.20	39.50-16.88	36.25-21.25	43.88-30.50	49.00-33.50	41.00-29.25
TEXFI INDUSTRIES	OCT	0.01	-2.13	1.62	-0.91	-1.01	4.80	2.68	4.35	3.19	2.45	8.13-3.75	7.63-3.88	9.25-4.88	9.00-3.63	4.38-2.50
APPAREL MANUFACTURERS & MARKETERS																
BEEBA'S CREATIONS INC	AUG	-0.76	0.64	1.74	0.49	-1.33	8.42	9.76	9.78	10.02	8.37	11.63-5.50	12.50-4.13	8.50-2.88	12.25-6.75	7.38-3.00
CHAUS (BERNARD) INC	JUN	0.08	-0.66	0.19	-0.60	-2.55	2.74	2.09	2.39	1.81	-0.74	5.50-1.88	4.13-1.63	2.88-1.00	6.13-1.75	1.63
CRYSTAL BRANDS	DEC	3.18	-0.53	-3.30	-12.98	NA	5.24	7.65	-6.97	-15.65	NA	32.00-12.50	29.00-3.00	16.50-4.00	4.75-4.03	NA
FARAH INC	OCT	-0.57	-1.74	1.02	2.02	1.16	8.37	7.05	5.14	5.65	8.37	8.00-3.38	2.56-0.88	8.63-2.50	12.00-6.13	7.00-4.75
* FRUIT OF THE LOOM INC -CL A	DEC	-1.25	1.60	2.48	2.80	0.79	-7.18	-1.97	0.59	2.00	2.11	15.38-6.13	28.00-7.63	42.00-23.00	41.00-18.63	33.00-23.00
GARAN INC	SEP	1.98	2.03	3.03	3.32	1.84	14.15	15.18	16.98	18.48	18.52	16.56-9.50	19.88-12.25	37.38-18.63	36.13-28.63	33.00-15.50
HAGGAR CORP	SEP	NA	NA	1.70	1.88	2.95	NA	NA	11.15	15.70	18.51	NA	NA	21.50-18.25	25.50-15.50	40.50-20.50
HAMPTON INDUSTRIES	DEC	-0.11	-0.13	0.32	-0.53	0.22	9.50	11.40	11.71	11.18	11.40	9.50-4.34	7.23-4.03	14.36-5.89	10.23-5.34	7.00-4.75
HARTMARX CORP	NOV	-3.11	-1.74	-8.59	1.59	3.41	11.53	14.60	11.32	6.21	3.95	19.88-13.63	14.25-4.25	8.63-4.25	12.00-6.13	7.88-6.63
JONES APPAREL GROUP INC	DEC	1.27	1.39	1.85	1.85	2.08	1.80	3.47	5.34	6.21	8.51	29.88-13.63	42.00-23.00	49.25-22.88	41.00-18.63	35.75-22.00
KELLWOOD CO	†APR	0.71	1.26	1.39	1.71	0.53	7.68	9.40	8.88	9.51	8.36	15.25-3.50	17.92-6.25	22.17-14.25	27.17-15.83	26.92-19.13
(cont'd)																

Data by Standard & Poor's Compustat, A Division of The McGraw-Hill Companies

Textiles, Apparel & Home Furnishings

Company	Yr. End	Earnings per Share					Book Value per Share					Share Price (High-Low)				
		1990	1991	1992	1993	1994	1990	1991	1992	1993	1994	1990	1991	1992	1993	1994
APPAREL MANUFACTURERS & MARKETERS (cont'd)																
* LIZ CLAIBORNE INC	DEC	2.37	2.61	2.61	1.54	1.06	8.40	10.67	12.05/	12.41	12.77/	35.00-20.25	50.75-28.25	47.88-31.88	42.88-18.00	26.63-15.38
MUNSINGWEAR INC	DEC	-68.50	NA	-0.65	-0.16	-0.20	-203/		5.58	5.50	5.27	71.88-5.48	37.50-4.38	11.25-4.63	11.13-5.00	8.88-4.50
OAK HILL SPORTSWEAR CORP	DEC	-1.74	0.22	0.59	0.08	0.11	5.70	5.95	5.32	5.42	5.56	6.88-2.75	5.50-2.25	5.63-2.38	5.00-1.50	5.38-3.56
OSHKOSH B'GOSH INC -CL A	DEC	2.03	1.62	1.08	0.31	0.50	10.36/	11.48/	12.01/	11.79/	11.76/	43.50-17.00	42.25-22.50	30.75-19.25	22.50-13.50	21.75-12.25
OXFORD INDUSTRIES INC	†MAY	0.62	1.42	1.70	2.23	1.22	11.43	12.28/	13.28/	14.79/	15.25/	13.00-6.50	18.38-6.88	27.13-14.38	25.38-15.00	34.75-21.88
PHILLIPS-VAN HEUSEN	†JAN	0.96	1.15	1.42	1.60	1.11	2.32	3.50	7.42	8.64	9.69	11.56-5.19	21.00-7.00	29.25-16.50	37.50-25.75	39.00-14.00
* RUSSELL CORP	DEC	1.65	1.38	1.99	1.19	1.96	10.68	11.79	13.38	13.80	14.89	31.00-16.00	36.25-19.75	40.38-27.75	36.88-26.00	32.63-24.00
SALANT CORP	DEC	-12.68	-5.52	2.10	1.02	0.23	-34.92	-38.79	-41.29	-4.72	0.29	12.88-1.25	4.25-1.50	10.00-2.88	11.38-6.13	9.38-4.38
SIGNAL APPAREL CO	DEC	-2.04	-6.56	-2.45	-4.06	-6.88	5.40	-0.15	-0.77		-8.28	13.00-2.63	19.88-8.75	24.38-14.00	14.75-6.63	8.13-4.00
STAGE II APPAREL CORP	DEC	-0.28	0.21	0.55	0.20	-0.21	4.91	5.15	5.64	5.58	3.29	7.25-1.63	4.25-1.13	8.50-3.25	7.88-4.00	5.38-2.75
TULTEX CORP	DEC	0.85	0.26	0.56	0.16	0.29	5.33	5.37	4.56	4.62	4.87	10.38-6.50	9.38-6.25	10.63-6.50	10.50-6.50	7.88-4.13
UNITED MERCHANTS &MFRS	JUN	-15.06	-6.25	-2.23	-1.67	-1.55	-13.56	-20.04	-1.75	-2.93	NA	2.38-0.06	1.75-0.28	1.00-0.28	0.56-0.09	0.47-0.16
* VF CORP	DEC	1.35	2.75	3.97	3.80	4.20	6.94	8.94	10.07	15.07	12.82/	34.25-11.63	41.50-17.63	57.50-38.50	58.50-39.50	53.75-44.25
WARNACO GROUP INC -CL A	DEC	NA	NA	1.34	1.34	1.53	-16.79/	-0.07/	3.36/	3.95/	5.76/	NA	15.25-10.50	20.50-12.19	19.63-13.31	19.25-13.13
SHOE PRODUCERS																
BARRY (R G)	DEC	-1.42	-0.25	0.61	0.76	0.72	4.88	4.70	5.40	6.07	6.57	8.53-2.25	4.03-2.16	6.75-2.63	12.28-4.78	24.63-10.00
* L A GEAR INC	NOV	1.56	-2.40	-3.76	-1.75	-1.29	10.62	6.74	3.82	1.56	0.25	50.38-9.75	14.63-9.00	16.75-9.00	13.38-8.13	10.25-4.63
* NIKE INC -CL B	†MAY	3.77	4.30	4.74	3.96	NA	12.19	16.17	19.62	21.64	NA	47.94-24.00	75.75-35.13	90.25-55.00	89.25-43.13	76.50-46.25
* REEBOK INTERNATIONAL LTD	DEC	1.54	2.37	1.24	2.53	3.02	8.71/	9.05/	9.38/	10.12/	12.24/	20.00-8.13	35.13-10.75	35.63-21.38	38.63-23.00	40.25-28.38
* STRIDE RITE CORP	NOV	1.06	1.28	1.19	1.19	0.40	3.54	4.62	5.12	5.81	5.74	15.19-9.75	30.25-13.38	31.88-16.38	23.13-12.13	18.88-10.50
SUAVE SHOE CORP	SEP	1.54	-2.68	0.74	-2.26	-3.24	12.78	10.00	11.07	6.77	3.53	14.50-5.50	9.63-4.00	10.00-4.25	6.13-3.38	4.13-2.00
WOLVERINE WORLD WIDE	DEC	-0.38	0.22	0.31	0.73	1.10	7.29	7.48/	6.66	7.33	8.20	5.67-2.72	5.78-3.44	6.72-3.44	14.89-6.11	18.08-12.33
SHOE PRODUCERS & RETAILERS																
* BROWN GROUP INC	†JAN	1.85	0.92	0.27	-0.39	1.91	19.47	18.10	16.69	13.27	13.90	30.00-19.75	28.38-21.63	29.00-21.00	35.88-26.00	38.88-30.63
EDISON BROTHERS STORES	†JAN	2.78	2.83	3.27	1.01	0.93	11.81	14.26	15.41	14.07	13.21	48.88-17.50	44.88-21.75	48.25-31.38	49.13-26.00	32.13-16.88
GENESCO INC	†JAN	0.04	0.01	0.40	-2.16	-0.77	5.60	5.76	4.99	2.50	0.49	7.63-3.00	6.50-3.00	9.75-5.00	11.50-4.75	5.63-1.63
INTERCO INC	DEC	-6.25	-1.25	0.65	2.09	2.78	-29.43/	-3.27	-9.07	-0.76	-0.01	0.81-0.07	0.56-0.06	9.38-6.00	15.75-9.38	16.75-6.13
* MELVILLE CORP	DEC	3.59	3.20	1.34	3.00	2.75	13.21	15.50	15.56	16.94	18.18	57.75-32.75	55.25-38.25	55.00-42.50	54.75-38.88	41.63-29.50
FURNITURE & BEDDING																
* BASSETT FURNITURE INDS	NOV	0.35	1.37	1.90	1.79	1.75	16.89	17.72	18.99	19.99	20.96	20.27-15.07	21.20-16.93	35.20-19.47	44.00-27.50	37.25-25.25
LA-Z-BOY CHAIR CO	†APR	1.30	1.39	1.50	1.90	2.01	11.43	12.32	13.29	14.77	15.19	22.00-12.38	25.13-15.13	28.75-17.75	38.88-26.63	40.00-25.25
LADD FURNITURE INC	DEC	0.09	-2.01	0.72	0.51	0.57	11.60	17.42/	19.50/	19.53/	19.73/	39.00-10.00	38.25-17.25	36.00-18.75	44.25-22.50	35.25-14.63
LEGGETT & PLATT INC	DEC	0.84	1.11	1.64	2.09	1.22	7.13	7.13	9.59	9.84	11.60	18.94-10.00	19.13-13.00	35.25-18.75	42.25-32.75	49.50-33.25
* MASCO CORP	DEC	0.91	0.30	1.21	1.45	1.22	7.67	7.73	9.26	9.04	8.87	26.75-14.25	26.50-17.00	30.00-22.00	38.88-25.50	39.88-21.25
FLOOR COVERINGS																
* ARMSTRONG WORLD INDS INC	DEC	3.18	1.11	-2.03	1.32	5.22	24.07/	1.91	12.47	12.88	17.17	38.75-18.00	34.50-22.88	37.50-24.50	55.25-28.75	57.50-36.00
SHAW INDUSTRIES INC	DEC	0.53	0.29	0.47	0.72	0.91	1.97	1.91	3.30	4.68/	4.84	8.59-3.69	9.63-4.84	17.06-8.50	25.50-14.06	25.00-12.88
MISCELLANEOUS HOUSEHOLD GOODS																
* NEWELL COMPANIES	DEC	0.84	0.91	1.05	1.05	1.24	2.97	3.69	3.41	2.95	2.79	17.75-8.88	22.88-11.50	26.50-16.50	21.50-15.38	23.88-18.81
* PREMARK INTERNATIONAL INC	DEC	0.82	1.63	0.07	2.58	3.39	9.19	10.21	8.16	9.87	12.44	15.50-6.38	20.31-8.13	25.63-14.88	41.88-17.63	48.00-33.56
* RUBBERMAID INC	DEC	0.90	1.02	1.04	1.32	1.42	4.80/	5.53/	6.16/	7.05/	8.00/	22.50-15.50	38.25-18.50	37.38-27.00	37.38-27.63	35.75-23.63
* THOMAS INDUSTRIES INC	DEC	1.15	0.38	-0.20	0.38	1.05	6.90	6.87	6.29	6.09	7.07	20.88-9.25	14.75-9.25	14.13-8.38	14.00-9.13	16.50-12.75
HOUSEHOLD APPLIANCES																
* BLACK & DECKER CORP	DEC	0.84	0.81	-1.11	1.00	1.37	14.94/	14.18/	11.08/	10.72/	12.04/	20.13-8.00	19.63-8.50	26.88-14.63	22.25-16.63	25.75-17.00
* FEDDERS CORP	AUG	-0.45	-1.07	-0.05	0.49	0.09	0.78	0.75	0.44	0.45	1.08	9.27-3.67	9.80-3.40	5.33-1.80	4.13-2.33	6.20-3.40
* GENERAL ELECTRIC CO	DEC	2.43	2.55	2.51	2.59	3.46	7.07	6.87	8.15	9.06	8.80	22.50-15.67	39.00-23.00	43.75-36.38	53.50-40.63	54.88-45.00
* MAYTAG CO	DEC	0.94	0.75	0.48	0.48	1.42	6.31	6.32	2.54	2.46	2.60	20.63-9.88	16.50-10.38	20.63-12.50	18.63-13.00	20.13-14.00
NATIONAL PRESTO INDS INC	DEC	3.94	4.98	3.53	2.55	2.92	27.48/	29.79/	29.53/	32.08/	33.11/	44.50-33.50	62.25-39.63	83.00-45.25	60.13-45.50	48.00-39.13
* WHIRLPOOL CORP	DEC	1.04	2.45	2.90	3.19	2.10	14.21	8.70	11.50	12.56	13.38	33.50-17.50	41.00-19.88	48.88-34.50	68.00-43.25	73.50-44.63
ZENITH ELECTRONICS CORP	DEC	-1.95	-1.79	-2.59	-3.01	-0.34	12.32	10.60	6.94	4.25	5.00	13.63-4.00	9.38-5.13	11.13-5.00	10.50-5.75	14.13-7.00
COSMETICS & TOILETRIES																
* ALBERTO-CULVER CO -CL B	SEP	1.30	1.06	1.36	1.44	1.57	7.56	7.23	7.92	8.71	9.85	33.25-19.13	34.25-20.50	32.00-21.25	28.25-20.13	27.38-19.38
* AVON PRODUCTS	DEC	2.81	2.92	2.43	3.46	3.75	3.97	1.48	2.30	2.34	2.58	38.13-22.75	49.00-26.13	60.25-44.00	64.38-47.63	63.63-48.38
* CARTER-WALLACE INC	†MAR	1.12	1.00	1.03	0.58	-1.22	5.67	6.32	6.84	6.15	4.27	19.54-14.96	41.88-17.54	46.83-22.63	36.63-20.13	26.38-9.88
* GILLETTE CO	DEC	0.80	0.97	1.16	0.96	1.57	0.05	1.68	2.34	1.17	2.43	16.31-10.88	28.05-14.09	30.63-21.94	31.88-23.69	38.25-28.88
HELENE CURTIS INDS	†FEB	0.70	2.04	2.33	1.51	2.02	15.36	18.01	18.95	20.19	22.33	28.00-17.50	47.38-23.88	46.50-30.25	47.38-24.88	36.38-22.75

(cont'd)

Data by Standard & Poor's Compustat, A Division of The McGraw-Hill Companies

Liz Claiborne

1363W

NYSE Symbol **LIZ**
In S&P 500

06-OCT-95
Industry:
Textiles

Summary: Liz Claiborne designs and markets men's and women's apparel that is made by independent suppliers and sold through department and specialty stores throughout the world.

S&P Opinion: Hold (★★★)	Recent Price • 25¼	Yield • 1.7%
	52 Wk Range • 26-14⅜	12-Mo. P/E • 22.7

Quantitative Evaluations

Outlook
(1 Lowest—5 Highest)
• **1+**

Fair Value
• **22**

Risk
• **Average**

Earn./Div. Rank
• **A-**

Technical Eval.
• **Bullish** since 3/95

Rel. Strength Rank
(1 Lowest—99 Highest)
• **92**

Insider Activity
• **Neutral**

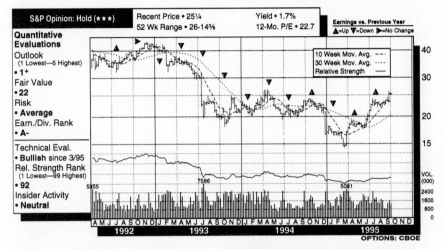

Earnings vs. Previous Year
▲=Up ▼=Down ▶=No Change

10 Week Mov. Avg. —-—
30 Week Mov. Avg. ----
Relative Strength ——

OPTIONS: CBOE

Overview - 05-OCT-95

Sales for 1995 could be flat or decline slightly, reflecting ongoing weak demand for the company's core sportswear line. On a more positive note, sales of many products, including bridgewear, dresses, larger size clothing, home furnishings, accessories and menswear, should improve on good demand. International growth and deeper market penetration of moderately-priced apparel could also make greater contributions to sales. Full-year margins are expected to widen from 1994's depressed level, on fewer markdown prices, restructuring efforts, focus on reducing expenses, and the absence of 1994's one-time $0.24-a-share restructuring charge. Share earnings comparisons will benefit from fewer outstanding shares, reflecting an ongoing stock buyback program.

Valuation - 05-OCT-95

Since reaching a recent low of 14 3/8 in early 1995, these shares have rebounded on expectations that earnings growth is resuming, after several years of flat to declining growth. Like many other apparel companies over the past few years, LIZ has been hurt by sluggish demand for apparel in general, a highly promotional retail environment, and a change in consumer tastes for more moderately-priced casual apparel. LIZ announced several programs in 1995 which could return it to positive earnings growth. Until there is a clear sign that these programs are working, however, we are retaining a neutral opinion on these shares.

Key Stock Statistics

S&P EPS Est. 1995	1.45	Tang. Bk. Value/Share	12.67
P/E on S&P Est. 1995	17.4	Beta	1.18
S&P EPS Est. 1996	1.65	Shareholders	14,100
Dividend Rate/Share	0.45	Market cap. (B)	$ 2.0
Shs. outstg. (M)	75.0	Inst. holdings	86%
Avg. daily vol. (M)	0.285	Insider holdings	NA

Value of $10,000 invested 5 years ago: $ 11,436

Fiscal Year Ending Dec. 31

	1995	% Change	1994	% Change	1993	% Change
Revenues (Million $)						
1Q	527.1	-3%	541.4	2%	531.0	-5%
2Q	474.9	-3%	490.0	-3%	506.9	7%
3Q	—	—	616.8	NM	621.9	NM
4Q	—	—	514.7	-5%	544.1	NM
Yr.	—	—	2,163	-2%	2,204	NM
Income (Million $)						
1Q	28.09	2%	27.44	-33%	41.04	-35%
2Q	17.02	7%	15.90	-49%	31.09	-21%
3Q	—	—	42.89	12%	38.26	-41%
4Q	—	—	-3.37	NM	14.89	-71%
Yr.	—	—	82.85	-34%	125.3	-43%
Earnings Per Share ($)						
1Q	0.37	6%	0.35	-30%	0.50	-32%
2Q	0.23	15%	0.20	-47%	0.38	-19%
3Q	E0.51	-7%	0.55	17%	0.47	-39%
4Q	E0.34	NM	-0.04	NM	0.19	-70%
Yr.	E1.45	37%	1.06	-31%	1.54	-41%

Next earnings report expected: late October

Liz Claiborne

Business Summary - 05-OCT-95

Liz Claiborne designs and markets a wide range of women's apparel and related items, designed for the work and leisure-time needs of the career woman. LIZ also designs men's apparel. Products are manufactured to the company's specifications in the U.S. and abroad and are sold through leading department and specialty stores. Contributions to sales in recent years:

	1994	1993	1992
Women's sportswear	43.1%	48.6%	52.3%
Accessories	8.1%	7.4%	6.2%
Elisabeth	5.9%	6.2%	6.9%
Women's dresses & suits	5.3%	5.6%	7.4%
Outlet stores	6.0%	5.3%	4.9%
Retail stores	6.5%	4.9%	4.0%
Liz & Co.	3.3%	3.9%	4.1%
Dana Buchman	4.9%	3.9%	3.2%
Cosmetics	3.6%	3.8%	3.1%
Men's sportswear	4.4%	3.5%	4.0%
Russ Group	4.8%	3.4%	0.9%
Shoes	2.7%	2.4%	2.0%
Jewelry	1.3%	1.0%	0.8%
Licensing	0.1%	0.1%	0.1%

LIZ's better sportswear products are conceived of and marketed as "designer" items and are offered under the company's various trademarks, including Liz Claiborne, Collection, Lizsport, Lizwear, Elisabeth and Liz & Co. Products are less expensive than designer lines. LIZ also produces a higher-priced "bridge" line of clothing under the Dana Buchman label and clothing in larger sizes under the Elisabeth label. Moderately priced apparel is produced by the Russ division.

At the end of 1994, LIZ operated 29 Liz Claiborne stores, 21 Elisabeth stores, one Dana Buchman store, and 70 outlet stores. The company began expanding operations overseas in 1991 and, as of 1994 year-end, was selling products in more than 50 markets outside the U.S., making up 5.7% of total sales.

Important Developments

Sep. '95—LIZ announced that its board approved the repurchase of up to an added $50 million in common shares, bringing total authorizations under the company's stock purchase program up to $500 million. As of mid-September, LIZ had purchased about 17.3 million commmon shares under the program at an aggregate price of about $450 million.

Aug. '95—LIZ announced that it would lower its trade discount to retailers for women's apparel to 8%, the industry standard, from 10%, as of January 1, 1996. The company said it expected to garner more than $20 million in revenue annually from this move, which it would use toward a national advertising campaign.

Capitalization

Long Term Debt: $1,175,000 (7/1/95).

Per Share Data ($) (Year Ended Dec. 31)

	1994	1993	1992	1991	1990	1989
Tangible Bk. Val.	12.77	12.41	12.05	10.67	8.39	6.94
Cash Flow	1.50	1.93	2.95	2.92	2.62	2.05
Earnings	1.06	1.54	2.61	2.61	2.37	1.87
Dividends	0.45	0.44	0.39	0.32	0.24	0.19
Payout Ratio	42%	28%	15%	12%	10%	10%
Prices - High	26⅝	42⅞	47⅞	50¾	35	27¾
- Low	15⅜	18	31⅞	28¼	20¼	16½
P/E Ratio - High	25	28	18	19	15	15
- Low	15	12	12	11	9	9

Income Statement Analysis (Million $)

	1994	%Chg	1993	%Chg	1992	%Chg	1991
Revs.	2,163	-2%	2,204	NM	2,194	9%	2,007
Oper. Inc.	186	-13%	215	-39%	351	-3%	361
Depr.	35.0	8%	32.3	13%	28.5	6%	27.0
Int. Exp.	NA	—	NA	—	NA	—	NA
Pretax Inc.	131	-34%	199	-42%	342	-3%	351
Eff. Tax Rate	37%	—	37%	—	36%	—	37%
Net Inc.	83.0	-34%	125	-43%	219	-2%	223

Balance Sheet & Other Fin. Data (Million $)

	1994	1993	1992	1991	1990	1989
Cash	330	309	426	472	432	373
Curr. Assets	1,023	1,004	1,110	1,014	853	746
Total Assets	1,290	1,236	1,285	1,175	985	849
Curr. Liab.	303	254	270	250	244	209
LT Debt	1.2	1.3	1.4	1.6	15.1	15.6
Common Eqty.	983	978	998	910	713	612
Total Cap.	986	982	1,015	925	740	639
Cap. Exp.	70.6	91.4	34.7	56.0	38.1	38.2
Cash Flow	118	158	247	250	227	180

Ratio Analysis

	1994	1993	1992	1991	1990	1989
Curr. Ratio	3.4	3.9	4.1	4.1	3.5	3.6
% LT Debt of Cap.	0.1	0.1	0.1	0.2	2.0	2.4
% Net Inc.of Revs.	3.8	5.7	10.0	11.1	11.9	11.7
% Ret. on Assets	6.6	10.2	18.0	20.6	22.8	22.2
% Ret. on Equity	8.5	13.0	23.3	27.4	31.6	30.7

Dividend Data —Dividends have been paid since 1984.

Amt. of Div. $	Date Decl.	Ex-Div. Date	Stock of Record	Payment Date
0.112	Oct. 13	Nov. 04	Nov. 11	Dec. 05 '94
0.112	Jan. 11	Feb. 08	Feb. 14	Mar. 06 '95
0.112	Mar. 23	May. 02	May. 08	Jun. 02 '95
0.112	Jun. 22	Aug. 09	Aug. 11	Sep. 05 '95

Data as orig. reptd.; bef. results of disc. opers. and/or spec. items. Per share data adj. for stk. divs. as of ex-div. date. E-Estimated. NA-Not Available. NM-Not Meaningful. NR-Not Ranked.

Office—1441 Broadway, New York, NY 10018. **Tel**—(212) 354-4900. **Chrmn**—J. A. Chazen. **Pres & CEO**—P. Charron. **Sr VP-Fin & CFO**—S. M. Miller. **Secy**—K. P. Kopelman. **Investor Contact**—Walter Krieger. **Dirs**—L. Abraham, L. Boxer, P. R. Charron, J. A. Chazen, A. M. Fudge, J. J. Gordon, S. Kamin, K. Koplovitz, L. Lowenstein. **Registrar & Transfer Agent**—First Chicago Trust Co. of New York, NYC. **Incorporated** in Delaware in 1981; predecessor incorporated in New York in 1976. **Empl**-8,000. **S&P Analyst:** Elizabeth Vandeventer

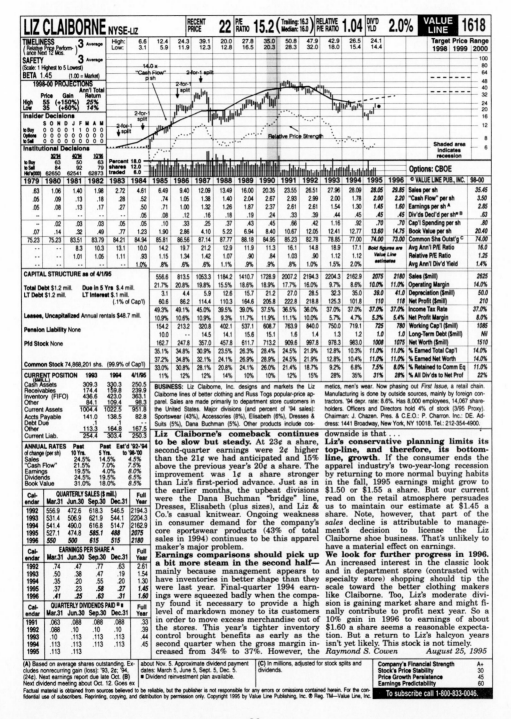

LIZ CLAIBORNE NYSE-LIZ

| RECENT PRICE | 22 | P/E RATIO | 15.2 | (Trailing: 16.3 / Median: 16.0) | RELATIVE P/E RATIO | 1.04 | DIV'D YLD | 2.0% | VALUE LINE | 1618 |

TIMELINESS 3 Average (Relative Price Performance Next 12 Mos.)		
SAFETY 3 Average (Scale: 1 Highest to 5 Lowest)		
BETA 1.45 (1.00 = Market)		

1998-00 PROJECTIONS

	Price	Gain	Ann'l Total Return
High	55	(+150%)	25%
Low	35	(+60%)	14%

Insider Decisions

	S	O	N	D	J	F	M	A	M
to Buy	0	0	0	0	1	1	0	0	0
Options	0	0	0	0	0	0	0	0	0
to Sell	0	0	0	0	0	0	0	0	0

Institutional Decisions

	3Q'94	4Q'94	1Q'95
to Buy	63	50	63
to Sell	84	92	79
Hld's(000)	62650	62541	62873

Percent shares traded: 18.0 / 12.0 / 6.0

| Target Price Range | 1998 | 1999 | 2000 |

High: 6.6 12.4 24.3 39.1 20.0 27.8 35.0 50.8 47.9 42.9 26.5 24.1
Low: 3.1 5.9 11.9 12.3 12.8 16.5 20.3 28.3 32.0 18.0 15.4 14.4

14.0 x "Cash Flow" p sh

Relative Price Strength

Shaded area indicates recession

Options: CBOE

1979	1980	1981	1982	1983	1984	1985	1986	1987	1988	1989	1990	1991	1992	1993	1994	1995	1996	© VALUE LINE PUB., INC.	98-00
.63	1.06	1.40	1.98	2.72	4.61	6.49	9.40	12.09	13.49	16.00	20.35	23.55	26.51	27.96	28.09	28.05	29.85	Sales per sh	35.45
.05	.09	.13	.18	.28	.52	.74	1.05	1.38	1.40	2.04	2.67	2.93	2.99	2.00	1.78	2.00	2.20	"Cash Flow" per sh	3.50
.05	.08	.13	.17	.27	.50	.71	1.00	1.32	1.26	1.87	2.37	2.61	2.61	1.54	1.30	1.45	1.60	Earnings per sh A	2.85
--	--	--	--	--	--	.08	.12	.16	.18	.19	.24	.33	.39	.44	.45	.45	.45	Div'ds Decl'd per sh B	.63
--	.02	.03	.03	.05	.05	.10	.33	.25	.37	.43	.45	.66	.42	1.16	.92	.70	.70	Cap'l Spending per sh	.80
.07	.14	.32	.49	.77	1.23	1.90	2.86	4.10	5.22	6.94	8.40	10.67	12.05	12.41	12.77	13.60	14.75	Book Value per sh	20.40
75.23	75.23	83.51	83.79	84.21	84.94	85.81	86.56	87.14	87.77	88.18	84.95	85.23	82.78	78.85	77.00	74.00	73.00	Common Shs Outst'g C	74.00
--	--	8.3	10.3	13.1	10.0	14.2	19.7	21.2	12.9	11.9	11.3	16.1	14.8	18.9	17.1	*Bold figures are*	16.0
--	--	1.01	1.05	1.11	.93	1.15	1.34	1.42	1.07	.90	.84	1.03	.90	1.12	1.12	*Value Line estimates*	
--	--	--	--	--	1.0%	.8%	.6%	.6%	1.1%	.9%	.9%	.8%	1.0%	1.5%	2.0%			Avg Ann'l Div'd Yield	1.4%

CAPITAL STRUCTURE as of 4/1/95

Total Debt $1.2 mill. Due in 5 Yrs $.4 mill.
LT Debt $1.2 mill. LT Interest $.1 mill.
(.1% of Cap'l)

Leases, Uncapitalized Annual rentals $48.7 mill.

Pension Liability None

Pfd Stock None

Common Stock 74,868,201 shs. (99.9% of Cap'l)

	1985	1986	1987	1988	1989	1990	1991	1992	1993	1994	1995	1996		98-00
Sales ($mill)	556.6	813.5	1053.3	1184.2	1410.7	1728.9	2007.2	2194.3	2204.3	2162.9	2075	2180		2625
Operating Margin	21.7%	20.8%	19.8%	15.5%	18.6%	18.9%	17.7%	16.0%	9.7%	8.6%	10.0%	11.0%		14.0%
Depreciation ($mill)	3.1	4.4	5.9	12.6	15.7	21.2	27.0	28.5	32.3	35.0	39.0	41.0		50.0
Net Profit ($mill)	60.6	86.2	114.4	110.3	164.6	205.8	222.8	218.8	125.3	101.8	110	118		210
Income Tax Rate	49.3%	49.1%	45.0%	39.5%	39.5%	37.5%	36.5%	36.0%	37.0%	37.0%	37.0%	37.0%		37.0%
Net Profit Margin	10.9%	10.6%	10.9%	9.3%	11.7%	11.9%	11.1%	10.0%	5.7%	4.7%	5.3%	5.4%		8.0%
Working Cap'l ($mill)	154.2	213.2	320.8	402.1	537.1	606.7	763.9	840.0	750.0	719.1	725	780		1085
Long-Term Debt ($mill)	10.0	--	14.5	14.1	15.6	15.1	1.6	1.4	1.3	1.2	1.0	1.0		Nil
Net Worth ($mill)	162.7	247.8	357.0	457.8	611.7	713.2	909.6	997.8	978.3	983.0	1008	1075		1510
% Earned Total Cap'l	35.1%	34.8%	30.9%	23.5%	26.3%	28.4%	24.5%	21.9%	12.8%	10.3%	11.0%	11.0%		14.0%
% Earned Net Worth	37.2%	34.8%	32.1%	24.1%	26.9%	28.9%	24.5%	21.9%	12.8%	10.4%	11.0%	11.0%		14.0%
% Retained to Comm Eq	33.0%	30.8%	28.1%	20.8%	24.1%	26.0%	21.4%	18.7%	9.2%	6.8%	7.5%	8.0%		11.0%
% All Div'ds to Net Prof	11%	12%	12%	14%	10%	10%	12%	15%	28%	35%	31%	28%		22%

CURRENT POSITION ($MILL.)

	1993	1994	4/1/95
Cash Assets	309.3	330.3	250.5
Receivables	174.4	159.8	239.9
Inventory (FIFO)	436.6	423.0	363.1
Other	84.1	109.4	98.3
Current Assets	1004.4	1022.5	951.8
Accts Payable	141.0	138.5	82.8
Debt Due	.1	.1	--
Other	113.3	164.8	167.5
Current Liab.	254.4	303.4	250.3

ANNUAL RATES of change (per sh)

	Past 10 Yrs.	Past 5 Yrs.	Est'd '92-'94 to '98-'00
Sales	24.5%	14.5%	4.5%
"Cash Flow"	21.5%	7.0%	7.5%
Earnings	19.5%	4.0%	8.0%
Dividends	24.5%	19.5%	6.5%
Book Value	31.0%	18.0%	8.5%

QUARTERLY SALES ($ mill.)

Calendar	Mar.31	Jun.30	Sep.30	Dec.31	Full Year
1992	556.9	472.6	618.3	546.5	2194.3
1993	531.4	506.9	621.9	544.1	2204.3
1994	541.4	490.0	616.8	514.7	2162.9
1995	527.1	474.8	585.1	488	2075
1996	550	500	615	515	2180

EARNINGS PER SHARE A

Calendar	Mar.31	Jun.30	Sep.30	Dec.31	Full Year
1992	.74	.47	.77	.63	2.61
1993	.50	.38	.47	.19	1.54
1994	.35	.20	.55	.20	1.30
1995	.37	.23	.58	.27	1.45
1996	.41	.25	.63	.31	1.60

QUARTERLY DIVIDENDS PAID B

Calendar	Mar.31	Jun.30	Sep.30	Dec.31	Full Year
1991	.063	.088	.088	.088	.33
1992	.088	.10	.10	.10	.39
1993	.10	.113	.113	.113	.44
1994	.113	.113	.113	.113	.45
1995	.113	.113			

BUSINESS: Liz Claiborne, Inc. designs and markets the Liz Claiborne lines of better clothing and Russ Togs popular-price apparel. Sales are made primarily to department store customers in the United States. Major divisions (and percent of '94 sales): Sportswear (43%), Accessories (8%), Elisabeth (6%), Dresses & Suits (5%), Dana Buchman (5%). Other products include cosmetics, men's wear. Now phasing out *First Issue*, a retail chain. Manufacturing is done by outside sources, mainly by foreign contractors. '94 depr. rate: 8.6%. Has 8,000 employees, 14,067 shareholders. Officers and Directors hold 4% of stock (3/95 Proxy). Chairman: J. Chazen. Pres. & C.E.O.: P. Charron. Inc.: DE. Address: 1441 Broadway, New York, NY 10018. Tel.: 212-354-4900.

Liz Claiborne's comeback continues to be slow but steady. At 23¢ a share, second-quarter earnings were 2¢ higher than the 21¢ we had anticipated and 15% above the previous year's 20¢ a share. The improvement was 1¢ a share stronger than Liz's first-period advance. Just as in the earlier months, the upbeat divisions were the Dana Buchman "bridge" line, Dresses, Elisabeth (plus sizes), and Liz & Co.'s casual knitwear. Ongoing weakness in consumer demand for the company's core sportswear products (43% of total sales in 1994) continues to be this apparel maker's major problem.

Earnings comparisons should pick up a bit more steam in the second half— mainly because management appears to have inventories in better shape than they were last year. Final-quarter 1994 earnings were squeezed badly when the company found it necessary to provide a high level of markdown money to its customers in order to move excess merchandise out of the stores. This year's tighter inventory control brought benefits as early as the second quarter when the gross margin increased from 34% to 37%. However, the downside is that . . .

Liz's conservative planning limits its top-line, and therefore, its bottom-line, growth. If the consumer ends the apparel industry's two-year-long recession by returning to more normal buying habits in the fall, 1995 earnings might grow to $1.50 or $1.55 a share. But our current read on the retail atmosphere persuades us to maintain our estimate at $1.45 a share. Note, however, that part of the *sales* decline is attributable to management's decision to license the Liz Claiborne shoe division. That's unlikely to have a material effect on earnings.

We look for further progress in 1996. An increased interest in the classic look and in department store (contrasted with specialty store) shopping should tip the scale toward the better clothing makers like Claiborne. Too, Liz's moderate division is gaining market share and might finally contribute to profit next year. So a 10% gain in 1996 to earnings of about $1.60 a share seems a reasonable expectation. But a return to Liz's halcyon years isn't yet likely. This stock is not timely.

Raymond S. Cowen   *August 25, 1995*

(A) Based on average shares outstanding. Excludes nonrecurring gain (loss): '93, 2¢; '94, (24¢). Next earnings report due late Oct. (B) Next dividend meeting about Oct. 12. Goes ex about Nov. 5. Approximate dividend payment dates: March 5, June 5, Sept. 5, Dec. 5. ■ Dividend reinvestment plan available. (C) In millions, adjusted for stock splits and dividends.

Company's Financial Strength	A+
Stock's Price Stability	30
Price Growth Persistence	45
Earnings Predictability	60

PART THREE

●··●

Morningstar
Mutual Funds Reports

AIM Aggressive Growth Fund *87*

Fidelity Equity-Income II Fund *88*

Vanguard Index 500 Fund *89*

Vista Tax-Free Income A Fund *90*

Fidelity Convertible Securities Fund *91*

GAM International Fund *92*

Volume 26, Issue 1, September 29, 1995. Reprinted with permission.

AIM Aggressive Growth

Ticker	Load	NAV	Yield	SEC Yield	Assets	Objective
AAGFX	Closed	$40.02	0.0%	---	$2195.0 mil	Aggr. Growth

AIM Aggressive Growth Fund seeks long-term growth of capital.

The fund invests primarily in equity securities expected to achieve earnings growth at a rate in excess of 15% per year. The strategy of the fund is to focus on the investment opportunities found in small- to medium-size companies with market capitalizations between $25 million and $500 million. Companies that are currently enjoying a dramatic increase in profits and established companies with proven growth records are both considered.

Prior to July 1, 1992, the fund was named CIGNA Aggressive Growth Fund. The fund closed to new investment on July 18, 1995.

Portfolio Manager(s)

Robert M. Kippes. Since 7-92. BBA'88 Stephen F. Austin U. Now a senior portfolio manager, Kippes joined AIM in 1989 as a research assistant.

Jonathan C. Schoolar, CFA. Since 7-92. BBA'83 U. of Texas. Schoolar is chief equity officer with AIM. Prior to joining the firm in 1986, he spent three years in equity trading with American Capital Asset Mgmt.

Performance 08-31-95

	1st Qtr	2nd Qtr	3rd Qtr	4th Qtr	Total
1991	30.13	-4.60	21.48	8.69	63.90
1992	2.12	-12.50	7.46	26.38	21.34
1993	2.59	7.68	14.52	4.38	32.05
1994	0.74	-3.90	14.91	5.33	17.18
1995	8.97	14.00			

Trailing	Total Return %	+/- S&P 500	+/- Russ 2000	% Rank All	% Rank Obj	Growth of $10,000
3 Mo	23.86	17.89	10.31	2	9	12,386
6 Mo	35.71	18.92	15.62	1	7	13,571
1 Yr	51.76	30.35	30.97	1	3	15,176
3 Yr Avg	42.85	29.02	23.61	1	1	29,148
5 Yr Avg	34.98	19.88	15.98	1	1	44,806
10 Yr Avg	18.25	3.06	6.39	4	18	53,447
15 Yr Avg	---	---	---	---	---	---

Most Similar Funds in MMF

Brandywine Blue	Fair Fit
T. Rowe Price Science & Technology	Fair Fit
Twentieth Century Giftrust Investors	Fair Fit

Tax Analysis

	Tax-Adj Return %	% Pretax Return
3 Yr Avg	42.18	98.4
5 Yr Avg	32.85	93.9
10 Yr Avg	16.88	92.5
Potential Capital Gain Exposure	27% of assets	

Analysis by Kim Rebecca 09-15-95

Folks have been banging down the doors at AIM Aggressive Growth Fund.

This fund's asset base has undergone stupendous growth—much of which occurred during a two-day period in July. At that time, AIM very briefly opened the fund's doors to new investors (it had been closed since mid-1994), and more than $1 billion gushed in. AIM's marketing department says it was aware that brokers had orders lined up, but it had not predicted the extent of interest; indeed, the original plan was to leave the doors open for a week.

Such enthusiasm is well deserved. Since AIM took over management of this portfolio in 1992, the fund's star rating has leapt from 1 star to 5. Part of this stunning turnaround is due to changes in market environment. The 1980s were not especially hospitable toward small companies, whereas the 1990s have been much more so. Furthermore, AIM's consistent overweighting in networking and

software services has generated strong returns thus far in this tech-happy decade.

That's not to say management isn't worthy of kudos. On the contrary, the team's earnings-driven style has proven more successful than most similar growth-driven, tech-laden portfolios. Some have generated comparable returns, but none have done so with the minimal volatility this fund demonstrates. In 1994's first quarter, for example, this fund was one of the few to stay in the black. This resilience stems from the fund's broadly diversified roster, which has tripled in length since AIM took over. This diversity has also helped the fund survive the various tech dips over 1995's summer (as has its 12% cash stake that has recently built up).

Undoubtedly, newcomers are happy to have squeezed past the guards. Those who didn't, though, should peruse other AIM options; AIM assures that these doors won't open again any time soon.

Historical Profile

Return	High
Risk	Above Avg
Rating	★★★★ Highest

	1994	1985	1986	1987	1988	1989	1990	1991	1992	1993	1994	08-95	History
	10.13	12.61	12.10	9.86	11.07	13.30	11.85	16.06	18.52	24.45	28.65	40.02	NAV
	2.04 *	26.17	0.37	-11.52	12.77	20.89	-6.50	63.90	21.34	32.05	17.18	39.69	Total Return %
	-4.73 *	-5.57	-18.31	-16.78	-3.84	-10.80	-3.38	33.42	13.72	21.99	15.86	15.21	+/- S&P 500
	---	-4.88	-5.31	-2.75	-12.12	4.64	13.01	17.85	2.93	13.14	19.00	16.17	+/- Russell 2000
	0.74	1.69	0.59	0.00	0.50	0.29	0.75	0.00	0.00	0.01	0.00	0.00	Income Return %
	1.30	24.48	-0.22	-11.52	12.27	20.59	-7.25	63.90	21.34	32.04	17.18	39.69	Capital Return %
		42	99	97	39	33	76	3	3	7	1		Total Rtn %Rank All
		70	92	79	56	70	57	34	10	10	1	10	Total Rtn %Rank Obj
	0.07	0.16	0.08	0.00	0.05	0.04	0.09	0.00	0.00	0.00	0.00	0.00	Income $
	0.00	0.00	0.49	0.86	0.00	0.05	0.49	3.04	0.92	0.00	0.00	0.00	Capital Gains $
	1.02	1.10	1.19	1.20	1.22	1.25	1.25	1.25	1.25	1.00	1.07	---	Expense Ratio %
	3.69	1.26	0.11	0.01	0.38	0.24	0.62	-0.31	-0.59	-0.24	-0.26	---	Income Ratio %
		66	106	118	56	69	137	165	164	61	75	---	Turnover Rate %
	4.4	13.6	18.5	14.0	12.8	11.7	9.2	16.2	38.2	273.5	714.7	2195.0	Net Assets ($mil)

Risk Analysis

Time Period	Load-Adj Return %	Risk %Rank [1] All	Obj	Morningstar Return	Morningstar Risk	Morningstar Risk-Adj Rating
1 Yr	43.42					
3 Yr	40.18	79	20	4.63	0.90	★★★★★
5 Yr	33.46	92	55	4.20	1.24	★★★★★
10 Yr	17.58	96	77	1.86	1.41	★★★★
Average Historical Rating (100 months)					2.4	★s

[1] 1=low, 100=high   [2] 1.00 = Equity Avg

Other Measures		Standard Index S&P 500	Best Fit Index Russ 2000
Standard Deviation	15.28	Alpha	25.6	15.1
Mean	37.33	Beta	1.11	1.35
Sharpe Ratio	2.19	R-Squared	32	82

Portfolio Analysis 04-30-95

Total Stocks: 303			Value $000	% Net Assets
Total Fixed-Income: 0				

Share Chg (10-94) 000	Amount 000		Value $000	% Net Assets
0	115	LSI Logic	7662	0.87
20	140	Atmel	6160	0.70
10	90	Tencor Instruments	6104	0.69
0	120	Teradyne	6075	0.69
-25	75	Altera	6066	0.69
0	75	US Robotics	5944	0.67
0	150	Kemet	5925	0.67
300	300	Lannet Data Communications	5925	0.67
125	125	FSI International	5813	0.66
0	200	Silicon Valley Group	5800	0.66
0	100	Ultratech Stepper	5600	0.63
176	281	HEALTHSOUTH	5540	0.63
192	200	Madge (NV)	5500	0.62
0	150	Credence Systems	5438	0.62
50	150	Integrated Health Services	5194	0.59
46	125	Alliance Semiconductor	5094	0.58
220	220	S3	5088	0.58
-50	125	Optical Data Systems	5063	0.57
0	100	Lam Research	5050	0.57
50	125	Avid Technology	5039	0.57
20	145	Community Health Systems	5039	0.57
10	135	DSC Communications	4995	0.57
0	160	Watson Pharmaceuticals	4980	0.56
25	170	Oak Industries	4973	0.56
200	200	Tekelec	4900	0.55

Investment Style

Style: Value Blend Growth

	Stock Portfolio Avg	Rel S&P 500	Rel Objective
Price/Earnings Ratio	28.1	1.50	1.06
Price/Book Ratio	5.2	1.30	1.03
5 Yr Earnings Gr %	28.0	2.59	1.16
Return on Assets %	12.9	1.57	1.13
Debt % Total Cap	23.5	0.84	0.98
Med Mkt Cap ($mil)	589	0.04	0.27

Special Securities % of assets

Privates/Illiquid Securities	0
Structured Notes	0
Emerging-Markets Secs	0
Options/Futures/Warrants	No

Composition % of assets 09-01-95

Cash	12.0
Stocks	88.0
Bonds	0.0
Other	0.0

Index Allocation % of stocks

S&P 500	2.6
S&P Mid	13.4
US Sm Cap	80.5
Foreign	3.5

Sector Weightings

	% of Stocks	Rel S&P
Utilities	0.6	0.05
Energy	0.0	0.00
Financials	3.4	0.29
Industrial Cyclicals	7.0	0.41
Consumer Durables	6.6	1.41
Consumer Staples	1.4	0.13
Services	10.4	1.29
Retail	6.1	1.78
Health	13.6	1.37
Technology	50.9	4.41

Investment Style History

Equity	
Average Stock %	

	85%	87%	84%	91%	90%	86%	86%	97%

Growth of $10,000

- Investment Value ($000) of Fund
- Investment Value ($000) S&P 500
- ▼ Manager Change
- ▽ Partial Manager Change
- ► Mgr Unknown After
- ◄ Mgr Unknown Before

Performance Quartile (Within Objective)

Address	11 Greenway Plaza Suite 1919 Houston, TX 77046-1173
Telephone	800-347-1919 / 713-626-1919
Advisor	AIM Advisors
Subadvisor	None
Distributor	AIM Distributors
States Available	All plus PR
Report Grade	B-
Income Distrib	Annually

Minimum Purchase	Closed	Add: $50	IRA: ---
Min Auto Inv Plan	Closed	Systematic Inv: $50	
Date of Inception	05-01-84		

Expenses & Fees

Sales Fees	5.50%L, 0.25%B
Management Fee	0.50% flat fee
Actual Fees	Mgt: 0.68% Dist: 0.25%
Expense Projections	3Yr: $95 5Yr: $124 10Yr: $206
Annual Brokerage Cost	0.26%

MORNINGSTAR Mutual Funds

Volume 26, Issue 1, September 29, 1995. Reprinted with permission.

Fidelity Equity-Income II

	Ticker	Load	NAV	Yield	SEC Yield	Assets	Objective
	FEQTX	None	$20.78	1.8%	---	$10663.5 mil	Equity-Inc.

Fidelity Equity-Income II Fund seeks income; potential for capital appreciation is also a consideration.

The fund normally invests at least 65% of assets in income-producing equity securities. It seeks a yield that exceeds the composite yield of the S&P 500 index. The balance of the fund's assets may be invested in debt securities of any type or credit quality. The fund may invest in foreign securities, enter into currency-exchange contracts, or invest in stock-index futures and options.

Portfolio Manager(s)

Brian S. Posner. Since 4-92. BA'83 Northwestern U.; MBA'87 U. of Chicago. Posner joined Fidelity Investments as an analyst in May 1987, and became a portfolio manager in 1990. He previously worked for John Nuveen & Company as a research associate, and for Feldman Securities Corporation as an analyst.

Performance 08-31-95

	1st Qtr	2nd Qtr	3rd Qtr	4th Qtr	Total
1991	18.89	5.48	10.31	5.98	46.60
1992	5.74	2.63	2.25	7.29	19.06
1993	8.52	2.77	3.91	2.60	18.89
1994	-1.43	3.15	3.77	-2.22	3.16
1995	6.91	6.16			

Trailing	Total Return %	+/- S&P 500	+/- Wil 5000	% Rank All	% Rank Obj	Growth of $10,000
3 Mo	5.91	-0.06	-2.58	27	16	10,591
6 Mo	14.57	-2.22	-3.41	26	24	11,457
1 Yr	13.28	-8.14	-8.67	32	58	11,328
3 Yr Avg	16.48	2.65	1.68	13	4	15,802
5 Yr Avg	21.33	6.23	5.39	5	1	26,290
10 Yr Avg	---	---	---	---	---	---
15 Yr Avg	---	---	---	---	---	---

Most Similar Funds in MMF

Fidelity Equity-Income	Strong Fit
Fidelity	Strong Fit
Fidelity Growth & Income	Strong Fit

Tax Analysis

	Tax-Adj Return %	% Pretax Return
3 Yr Avg	14.33	86.9
5 Yr Avg	19.49	91.4
10 Yr Avg	---	---
Potential Capital Gain Exposure		13% of assets

Analysis by Erik Laughlin 09-15-95

Fidelity Equity-Income II Fund is back in the saddle again.

This fund rarely gets thrown: In each of its four calendar years, it has managed to place in or near the equity-income group's top decile. The fund did fall behind its peers in 1994's fourth quarter and 1995's first quarter, however. A 10% stake in Japan hurt during the period, especially after the Kobe earthquake devastated the country. Further, the fund was overweighted in cyclicals and light in consumer staples, which flew in the face of the market's preferences. Finally, technology, which was one of the market's hottest sectors during both periods, was almost nonexistent in this portfolio.

Since 1995's first quarter, however, the fund's relative performance has improved. The main catalysts have been the same sectors that hurt earlier: Japan has come back recently, cyclicals have improved, and staples have been less dominant in the

market. The fund's heavy exposure to energy services and financials has also helped. As a result, the fund's year-to-date returns have risen a bit above the group's average.

True to form, manager Brian Posner hasn't tried to play catch-up this year by boosting technology; he tries not to increase the fund's risk levels for the sake of near-term returns. His strategy involves finding stocks with low price multiples relative to the stocks' histories, as well as stocks with catalysts for improved earnings growth. Just because Posner refuses to chase hot sectors, however, doesn't mean he sits still. He often moves in and out of various areas depending on their fundamentals—and he usually does so at the right times.

This fund's consistently strong annual returns, combined with low risk scores, have resulted in a 5-star record. Investors have understandably rushed to this fund, inflating its assets to more than $10 billion.

Historical Profile	
Return	High
Risk	Low
Rating	★★★★ Highest

Investment Style History
Equity
Average Stock %

| | 71% | 68% | 74% | 79% | 80% |

Growth of $10,000

|||| Investment Value ($000) of Fund
— Investment Value ($000) S&P 500
▼ Manager Change
▽ Partial Manager Change
← Mgr Unknown After
→ Mgr Unknown Before

Performance Quartile (Within Objective)

1984	1985	1986	1987	1988	1989	1990	1991	1992	1993	1994	08-95	History
---	---	---	---	---	---	10.39	14.52	16.51	18.41	17.72	20.78	NAV
---	---	---	---	---	---	4.51*	46.60	19.06	18.89	3.16	18.58	Total Return %
---	---	---	---	---	---	0.18*	16.11	11.44	8.83	1.85	-5.90	+/- S&P 500
---	---	---	---	---	---		12.39	10.09	7.60	3.23	-6.75	+/- Wilshire 5000
---	---	---	---	---	---	0.61	4.68	2.63	2.65	2.11	1.23	Income Return %
---	---	---	---	---	---	3.90	41.91	16.42	16.24	1.05	17.34	Capital Return %
---	---	---	---	---	---		9	6	19	8	27	Total Rtn %Rank All
---	---	---	---	---	---		1	4	12	12	57	Total Rtn %Rank Obj
---	---	---	---	---	---	0.06	0.46	0.38	0.45	0.39	0.20	Income $
---	---	---	---	---	---	0.00	0.17	0.36	0.73	0.88	0.01	Capital Gains $
---	---	---	---	---	---	2.50	1.52	1.01	0.88	0.81	---	Expense Ratio %
---	---	---	---	---	---	3.89	3.83	3.09	2.69	2.36	---	Income Ratio %
---	---	---	---	---	---	167	206	89	55	75	---	Turnover Rate %
---	---	---	---	---	---	6.2	370.9	2169.8	5021.9	7697.5	10663.5	Net Assets ($mil)

Risk Analysis

Time Period	Load-Adj Return %	Risk %Rank [1] All	Risk %Rank [1] Obj	Morningstar Return	Morningstar Risk	Morningstar Risk-Adj Rating
1 Yr	13.28					
3 Yr	16.48	39	21	1.29	0.54	★★★★
5 Yr	21.33	50	8	1.95	0.47	★★★★★
Incept	21.40	---				
Average Historical Rating	(25 months)				4.9	★ s

[1] 1=low, 100=high [2] 1.00 = Equity Avg

Other Measures		Standard Index S&P 500	Best Fit Index S&P 500
Standard Deviation	7.43	Alpha	3.9	3.9
Mean	15.63	Beta	0.84	0.84
Sharpe Ratio	1.57	R-Squared	77	77

Portfolio Analysis 05-31-95

Share Chg (11-94) 000	Amount 000	Total Stocks: 195 Total Fixed-Income: 37	Value $000	% Net Assets
555	9729	American Express	346585	3.52
568	3529	British Petroleum (ADR)	301301	3.06
778	2854	FNMA	265413	2.70
195	3745	Schlumberger	243445	2.48
1207	2585	El duPont de Nemours	175464	1.78
426	5271	Alcan Aluminium	155804	1.58
-11743	5319	RJR Nabisco Holdings	151592	1.54
766	2450	Great Lakes Chemical	149456	1.52
1127	2978	General Motors	142964	1.45
983	3357	NYNEX	140138	1.43
0	1048	Loews	124629	1.27
415	1902	Total Petroleum CI B	117571	1.20
1975	2520	ALCOA	117189	1.19
2269	3524	Allstate	106151	1.08
383	1109	IBM	103405	1.05
1720	1720	Lockheed Martin	102313	1.04
1058	3288	Union Carbide	96186	0.98
169	2104	Western Atlas	94946	0.97
3169	3419	WMX Technologies	93168	0.95
-31	1204	United Technologies	91323	0.93
150	3832	The Limited	85264	0.87
1201	1201	Dayton Hudson	85107	0.87
-75	2066	Bank of New York	84192	0.86
3350	3350	Wal-Mart Stores	83750	0.85
50	1647	Amerada Hess	83580	0.85

Investment Style Style Value Blend Growth		Stock Portfolio Avg	Rel S&P 500	Rel Objective
Price/Earnings Ratio		18.8	1.00	1.08
Price/Book Ratio		2.3	0.58	0.76
5 Yr Earnings Gr %		3.1	0.29	0.61
Return on Assets %		5.1	0.63	0.82
Debt % Total Cap		29.8	1.07	0.91
Med Mkt Cap ($mil)		7663	0.49	0.93

Special Securities	% of assets
● Private/Illiquid Securities	2
○ Structured Notes	0
○ Emerging-Markets Secs	0
● Options/Futures/Warrants	Yes

Composition % of assets 07-31-95		Index Allocation % of stocks	
Cash	11.8	S&P 500	68.8
Stocks	83.1	S&P Mid	7.6
Bonds	2.0	US Sm Cap	8.7
Other	3.1	Foreign	17.7

Sector Weightings	% of Stocks	Rel S&P
Utilities	3.5	0.30
Energy	18.0	1.87
Financials	20.9	1.79
Industrial Cyclicals	24.3	1.42
Consumer Durables	6.8	1.45
Consumer Staples	4.4	0.42
Services	9.0	1.11
Retail	9.3	1.77
Health	0.7	0.07
Technology	3.2	0.28

Address	82 Devonshire Street Boston, MA 02109
Telephone	800-544-8888
Advisor	Fidelity Management & Research
Subadvisor	FMR (Far East)/FMR (U.K.)
Distributor	Fidelity Distributors
States Available	All
Report Grade	A
Income Distrib	Quarterly

Minimum Purchase	$2500	Add: $250	IRA: $500
Min Auto Inv Plan	$2500	Systematic Inv: $100	
* Date of Inception	08-21-90		

Expenses & Fees		
Sales Fees	No-load	
Management Fee	0.20% flat fee+0.52% max./0.27% min.(G)	
Actual Fees	Mgt: 0.52%	Dist: ---
Expense Projections	3Yr: $26	5Yr: $45	10Yr: $100
Annual Brokerage Cost	0.12%	

MORNINGSTAR Mutual Funds

Volume 25, Issue Number 4, June 23, 1995. Reprinted with permission.

Vanguard Index 500

Ticker	Load	NAV	Yield	SEC Yield	Assets	Objective
VFINX	None	$50.21	2.3%	2.50%	$12161.0 mil	Growth/Inc.

Vanguard Index Trust 500 Portfolio seeks investment results that correspond with the price and yield performance of the S&P 500 index.

The fund allocates the percentage of net assets each company receives on the basis of the stock's relative total-market value: its market price per share multiplied by the number of shares outstanding.

Shareholders are charged an annual account-maintenance fee of $10.

Prior to Dec. 21, 1987, the fund was named Vanguard Index Trust. Prior to 1980, it was named First Index Investment Trust.

Portfolio Manager(s)

George U. Sauter. Since 10-87. BA'76 Dartmouth C.; MBA'80 U. of Chicago. Sauter joined Vanguard in 1987. As vice president of core management, he is responsible for the management of all Vanguard's index funds. He previously spent two years as a trust-investment officer with FNB Ohio.

Historical Profile

Return Above Avg
Risk Average
Rating ★★★★ Above Avg

	1984	1985	1986	1987	1988	1989	1990	1991	1992	1993	1994	05-95	History
		97%	97%		97%	100%	99%	100%	99%	100%			
	19.52	22.99	24.27	24.65	27.18	33.64	31.24	39.32	40.97	43.83	42.97	50.21	NAV
	6.21	31.23	18.06	4.71	16.22	31.37	-3.33	30.22	7.42	9.89	1.18	17.40	Total Return %
	-0.05	-0.51	-0.62	-0.55	-0.39	-0.32	-0.21	-0.26	-0.20	-0.16	-0.14	-0.06	+/- S&P 500
	3.16	-1.34	1.96	2.34	-1.72	2.19	2.86	-3.98	-1.55	-1.39	1.25	1.89	+/- Wilshire 5000
	4.67	4.54	3.69	2.42	4.56	4.33	3.54	3.87	2.96	2.83	2.69	0.55	Income Return %
	1.55	26.69	14.37	2.28	11.66	27.04	-6.86	26.35	4.46	7.06	-1.52	16.85	Capital Return %
	46	22	32	24	24	12	66	27	53	67	13	4	Total Rtn %Rank All
	38	26	34	28	45	14	47	37	49	54	21	11	Total Rtn %Rank Obj
	0.88	0.91	0.89	0.69	1.10	1.20	1.17	1.15	1.12	1.13	1.17	0.22	Income $
	0.48	1.61	2.02	0.17	0.32	0.75	0.10	0.12	0.10	0.03	0.20	0.00	Capital Gains $
	0.27	0.28	0.28	0.26	0.22	0.21	0.22	0.20	0.19	0.19	0.19	---	Expense Ratio %
	4.53	4.09	3.40	3.15	4.08	3.62	3.60	3.07	2.81	2.65	2.72	---	Income Ratio %
	14	36	29	15	10	8	23	5	4	6	6	---	Turnover Rate %
	289.7	394.3	485.1	826.3	1055.1	1803.8	2173.0	4345.3	6517.7	8272.7	9356.4	12161.0	Net Assets $mil

Investment Style History
Equity
Average Stock %

Growth of $10,000
- Investment Value ($000)
- Investment Value ($000) S&P 500
▼ Manager Change
▽ Partial Manager Change
← Mgr Unknown After
→ Mgr Unknown Before

Performance Quartile
(Within Objective)

Performance 05-31-95

	1st Qtr	2nd Qtr	3rd Qtr	4th Qtr	Total
1991	14.47	-0.29	5.28	8.36	30.22
1992	-2.57	1.87	3.08	5.00	7.42
1993	4.33	0.43	2.52	2.30	9.89
1994	-3.84	0.40	4.86	-0.05	1.18
1995	9.71	---	---	---	---

Trailing	Total Return %	+/- S&P 500	+/- Wil 5000	% Rank All	% Rank Obj	Growth of $10,000
3 Mo	10.17	-0.03	1.43	8	17	11,017
6 Mo	19.12	-0.08	2.04	3	8	11,912
1 Yr	20.03	-0.13	2.42	4	5	12,003
3 Yr Avg	11.65	-0.16	0.01	17	26	13,918
5 Yr Avg	11.23	-0.08	-0.27	22	28	17,028
10 Yr Avg	14.26	-0.33	0.49	14	14	37,910
15 Yr Avg	14.94	-0.38	0.21	21	26	80,691

Most Similar Funds in MMF

SEI Index S&P 500 Index		Strong Fit
Fidelity Market Index	·	Strong Fit
Schwab 1000		Strong Fit

Tax Analysis

	Tax-Adj Return %	% Pretax Return
3 Yr Avg	10.47	89.9
5 Yr Avg	10.02	89.2
10 Yr Avg	12.37	86.8
Potential Capital Gain Exposure		20% of assets

Risk Analysis

Time Period	Load-Adj Return %	Risk %Rank All	Risk %Rank Obj	Morningstar Return	Morningstar Risk	Morningstar Risk-Adj Rating
1 Yr	20.03					
3 Yr	11.65	64	44	1.30	0.70	★★★★
5 Yr	11.23	65	54	1.29	0.76	★★★★
10 Yr	14.26	63	66	1.37	0.86	★★★★
Average Historical Rating	(114 months)				4.0	★s

1=low, 100=high 1.00 = Equity Avg

Other Measures

	Standard Index S&P 500	Best Fit Index S&P 500
Standard Deviation	8.24	Alpha	-0.2	-0.2
Mean	11.41	Beta	1.00	1.00
Sharpe Ratio	0.93	R-Squared	100	100

Portfolio Analysis 05-31-95

Total Stocks: 503
Total Fixed-Income: 0

Share Chg (04-95) 000	Amount 000		Value $000	% Net Assets
155	5209	General Electric	302126	2.48
112	3784	Exxon	270054	2.22
142	4781	AT & T	242633	2.00
116	3917	Coca-Cola	242390	1.99
49	1633	Royal Dutch Petroleum	207023	1.70
77	2596	Philip Morris	189196	1.56
114	3834	Merck	180661	1.49
208	7002	Wal-Mart Stores	175058	1.44
53	1789	IBM	166854	1.37
62	2092	Procter & Gamble	150329	1.24
53	1771	Microsoft	149868	1.23
38	1263	Intel	141571	1.16
58	1958	Johnson & Johnson	129719	1.07
36	1205	Mobil	120988	0.99
72	2413	PepsiCo	118252	0.97
131	1684	El duPont de Nemours	114281	0.94
68	2296	General Motors	110213	0.91
29	963	American International Group	109552	0.90
53	1786	Motorola	106959	0.88
45	1514	Amoco	103525	0.85
46	1556	Bristol-Myers Squibb	103280	0.85
46	1554	Hewlett-Packard	102784	0.85
87	2931	GTE	97834	0.80
73	2443	Abbott Laboratories	97728	0.80
59	1986	Chevron	97538	0.80

Investment Style

Style: Value Blend Growth
Size: Large Med Small

	Stock Portfolio Avg	Rel S&P 500	Rel Objective
Price/Earnings Ratio	18.8	1.00	1.04
Price/Book Ratio	4.0	1.00	1.15
5 Yr Earnings Gr %	10.4	1.00	1.07
Return on Assets %	8.1	1.00	1.09
Debt % Total Cap	28.7	1.00	0.98
Med Mkt Cap ($mil)	15030	1.00	1.61

Special Securities % of assets 12-31-94

○ Private/Illiquid Securities	0.0	
○ Structured Notes	0.0	
○ Emerging-Markets Secs	0.0	
● Options/Futures/Warrants	Yes	

Composition % of assets 03-31-95

Cash	0.0
Stocks	100.0
Bonds	0.0
Other	0.0

Index Allocation % of stocks

S&P 500	99.9
S&P Mid	0.1
US Sm Cap	0.1
Foreign	3.8

Sector Weightings

	% of Stocks	Rel S&P
Utilities	11.9	1.00
Energy	10.2	1.00
Financials	11.3	1.00
Industrial Cyclicals	16.3	1.00
Consumer Durables	5.8	1.00
Consumer Staples	12.4	1.00
Services	7.9	1.00
Retail	5.4	1.00
Health	8.8	1.00
Technology	10.0	1.00

Analysis by Russel Kinnel 06-09-95

The words "exciting" and "index fund" don't often land in the same sentence.

Yet the normally boring Vanguard Index Trust 500 Portfolio has recorded a scintillating 17% return through May. Only 10% of the growth-and-income group can boast better results. Large-cap stocks, particularly those in the S&P 500, have left the rest of the market in their dust. When those results are combined with Vanguard's legendary low costs, this fund naturally comes out near the top.

Chart-topping short-term performance isn't what investors should normally expect from this fund, though. Index funds are usually promoted as investments for patient shareholders willing to wait for the benefits of low costs, broad diversification, and exposure to the market to mount over time. Indeed, this fund's long-term relative performance is better than most of its yearly results. (It's worth noting that part of the long-term

outperformance owes to blue-chip strength in the 1980s.)

In addition to long-term strength, this fund offers investors the benefit of consistency. Over time, many funds will change managers and investment styles. This one, however, will always be spread out across sectors and issues. Investors with assets concentrated in smaller stocks or a few industries can use this fund as a simple, reliable way to tone down sector or market-cap risk.

As for this fund's risks, they are mostly short term. It has average risk scores, but its lack of cash means it won't provide shelter from a bear market. When it has stumbled, though, it hasn't stayed down for long; annual returns have only fallen from the top half of the objective once in the past 10 years.

With the S&P 500 hitting record highs, some investors are probably wary of jumping in. Those planning to invest more than $3,000 should consider dollar-cost averaging.

Address	Vanguard Financial Ctr. P.O. Box 2600 Valley Forge, PA 19482	Minimum Purchase	$3000 Add: $100 IRA: $500
		Min Auto Inv Plan	$3000 Systematic Inv: $50
Telephone	800-662-7447 / 610-669-1000	Date of Inception	08-31-76
Advisor	Vanguard's Core Management Group	Expenses & Fees	
Subadvisor	None	Sales Fees	No-load
Distributor	Vanguard Group	Management Fee	Provided at cost.
States Available	All plus PR,VI,GU	Actual Fees	Mgt: N/A Dist: N/A
Report Grade	A-	Expense Projections	3Yr: $36 5Yr: $60 10Yr: $123
Income Distrib	Quarterly	Annual Brokerage Cost	0.02%

MORNINGSTAR Mutual Funds

Volume 25, Issue Number 7, August 4, 1995. Reprinted with permission.

Vista Tax-Free Income A

	Ticker	Load	NAV	Yield	SEC Yield	Assets	Objective
	VTFIX	4.50%	$11.77	4.9%	4.33%	$91.3 mil	Muni Nat

Vista Tax-Free Income Fund - Class A seeks current income exempt from federal income taxes, consistent with capital preservation.

The fund normally invests at least 80% of assets in municipal obligations exempt from federal taxes, including the Alternative Minimum Tax.

Shares of the fund can be purchased at the NAV by registered investment advisers and fee-based financial planners. Class A shares have front loads; B shares have deferred loads, higher 12b-1 fees, and conversion features. On July 19, 1993, Olympus National Tax-Free Fund merged into this fund.

Portfolio Manager(s)

Pamela Hunter. Since 9-87. Edison State U. Hunter is currently senior fixed-income portfolio manager at Chase Manhattan Bank, her employer since 1984. Previously, she was a portfolio manager and trader at Chase Investors Mgmt. Corp. from 1980 to 1984. She also manages Vista CA Intermediate Tax-Free and Vista NY Tax-Free Income.

Historical Profile
Return Average
Risk Above Avg
Rating ★★★ Neutral

Investment Style History
Fixed Income
Income Rtn %Rank Obj

Growth of $10,000
|||Investment Value ($000) of Fund
—Investment Value ($000) LB Aggregate
▼ Manager Change
▽ Partial Manager Change
►Mgr Unknown After
◄Mgr Unknown Before

Performance Quartile (Within Objective)

	1984	1985	1986	1987	1988	1989	1990	1991	1992	1993	1994	07-95	History
	---	---	---	10.19	10.44	10.65	10.66	11.21	11.65	12.57	11.05	11.77	NAV
	---	---	---	3.85 *	10.44	10.07	7.22	14.04	12.83	15.02	-7.64	9.65	Total Return %
	---	---	---	---	2.56	-4.47	-3.08	-0.54	5.43	5.27	-4.72	-1.55	+/- LB Aggregate
	---	---	---	---	0.28	-0.72	-0.08	1.90	4.02	2.75	-2.04	-1.05	+/- LB Muni
	---	---	---	1.95	7.45	7.52	7.13	7.35	6.70	5.72	4.45	3.13	Income Return %
	---	---	---	1.90	2.99	2.55	0.09	6.70	6.13	9.30	-12.09	6.52	Capital Return %
	---	---	---	---	58	72	20	62	14	28	84	64	Total Rtn %Rank All
	---	---	---	---	58	31	10	4	1	4	82	33	Total Rtn %Rank Obj
	---	---	---	0.20	0.73	0.75	0.72	0.74	0.71	0.64	0.57	0.34	Income $
	---	---	---	0.00	0.05	0.06	0.00	0.16	0.24	0.15	0.00	0.00	Capital Gains $
	---	---	---	0.00	0.00	0.00	0.12	0.24	0.00	0.23	0.58	---	Expense Ratio %
	---	---	---	7.35	7.50	7.06	6.86	6.71	6.26	5.25	4.75	---	Income Ratio %
	---	---	---	---	422	257	89	211	266	149	258	---	Turnover Rate %
	---	---	---	0.1	1.5	3.4	4.2	5.9	19.4	92.7	82.1	91.3	Net Assets ($mil)

Performance 07-31-95

	1st Qtr	2nd Qtr	3rd Qtr	4th Qtr	Total
1991	2.02	2.12	4.63	4.62	14.04
1992	0.19	5.57	3.57	3.01	12.83
1993	5.49	3.77	3.98	1.06	15.02
1994	-6.53	0.67	0.19	-2.03	-7.64
1995	7.35	1.31	---	---	---

Trailing	Total Return %	+/- LB Aggregate	+/- LB Muni	% Rank All	% Rank Obj	Growth of $10,000
3 Mo	2.24	-2.16	-1.02	88	78	10,224
6 Mo	6.25	-2.79	-1.37	81	53	10,625
1 Yr	5.73	-4.38	-1.63	82	71	10,573
3 Yr Avg	5.87	-0.82	-0.12	61	13	11,866
5 Yr Avg	9.06	0.00	1.01	48	2	15,428
10 Yr Avg	---	---	---	---	---	---
15 Yr Avg	---	---	---	---	---	---

Most Similar Funds in MMF

MFS Municipal Bond A	Strong Fit
Scudder Managed Muni Bonds	Strong Fit
Kemper Municipal Bond A	Strong Fit

Tax Analysis

	Tax-Adj Return %	% Pretax Return
3 Yr Avg	5.55	94.6
5 Yr Avg	8.78	96.9
10 Yr Avg	---	---
Potential Capital Gain Exposure		-4% of assets

Risk Analysis

Time Period	Load-Adj Return %	Risk %Rank All	Risk %Rank Obj	Morningstar Return	Morningstar Risk	Morningstar Risk-Adj Rating
1 Yr	0.97					
3 Yr	4.26	51	74	0.86	1.20	★★
5 Yr	8.06	37	76	1.13	1.24	★★★
Incept	8.73	---	---	---	---	---

Average Historical Rating (59 months) 2.5 ★s

1=low, 100=high 1.00 = Muni Avg

Other Measures

	Standard Index LB Agg	Best Fit Index LB Muni
Standard Deviation	6.94	
Mean	5.96	
Sharpe Ratio	0.30	
Alpha	-1.1	-0.4
Beta	1.20	1.17
R-Squared	55	96

Analysis by Adam Wright 08-04-95

Vista Tax-Free Income Fund is now on a level playing field.

After years of absorbing some or all of this fund's expenses, earlier this year fund officials decided to raise its expense ratio to 90 basis points. They had previously agreed on a 75-basis-point expense cap, but now note that the industry average is higher. (The average expense ratio for the muni-national group is 97 basis points.) Low costs on a bond fund can be an enormous boost to performance—the fund's yield has often topped the group average, and its five-year gains rank in the group's top 2%.

Low expenses can't disguise the fund's above-average risk scores, though, primarily a result of a bold interest-rate stance. That positioning helped it rank in the group's stratosphere as rates fell between 1991 and 1993. Even if expenses were equal to the group's in those years, the fund would have still placed far above average. Its 7.6% loss in

1994 (which would have been larger with its current expenses) is an example of what investors can expect during the worst of times. All told, the fund has higher risk scores than three fourths of its peers.

The level of risk that the fund assumes, however, isn't high on all fronts and can change over time. Manager Pamela Hunter isn't afraid to take on sector risk (she overweights housing issues, for example), but she balances those stakes with safer essential-services bonds. She isn't very adventurous with credit quality, either, and keeps the bulk of assets in bonds rated A or higher. Furthermore, she doesn't restrict the fund to a high level of interest-rate risk. This year's rally hasn't pushed the fund further into the group's top half because Hunter shortened the fund after 1994's rising rates sent it reeling.

For risk-tolerant investors, this fund might fit the bill, though its stellar gains may lose some of their luster due to higher expenses.

Portfolio Analysis 02-28-95

Total Stocks: 0
Total Fixed-Income: 70

Amount 000	Date of Maturity		Value $000	% Net Assets
6479	01-01-05	PR Tel 5.25%	6382	7.12
4815	12-13-08	MI Detroit Resource Rec 9.25%	5032	5.61
4378	10-01-14	CA Contra Costa Wtr Dist 5.75%	4202	4.69
4032	11-01-15	CA San Francisco Pub Util Com Wtr 6%	3986	4.45
3940	10-01-14	OH Bldg Crtnl Fac Adult 5.95%	3940	4.39
3502	11-15-24	OH Cleveland Pub Pwr Sys Impr 7%	3769	4.20
3502	06-15-15	PA Intergovt Coop Spcl Tax 5.75%	3362	3.75
3349	12-15-11	MO Stadium Sports Fac Lease 5.875%	3299	3.68
2627	01-01-03	GA Burke Dev Poll Cntrl Pwr 7.5%	2869	3.20
2627	07-01-06	PR Muni Fin 5.875%	2613	2.91
2714	07-02-00	DC Metro Washington Transp 4.4%	2558	2.85
2364	06-15-14	NY Envir Fac Wtr Poll Cntrl Fund 6.875%	2532	2.82
2627	10-01-20	NY Mtg 6.125%	2525	2.82
2451	09-01-13	CA South Orange Pub Fin Spcl Tax 6.2%	2482	2.77
2627	01-01-15	NY New York City Indl Dev Spcl Fac 6%	2476	2.76
2355	02-15-11	TX Bexar Hlth Fac Dev Baptist 6.625%	2458	2.74
2627	07-01-04	DC Metro Washington Transp 5.25%	2387	2.66
2189	01-01-14	NY Urban Dev Crtnl Fac 5.5%	1929	2.15
1751	04-01-23	MI Hsg Dev Rental Ser A 7.55%	1836	2.05
1751	01-01-13	TX Brazos Hlth Fac Dev St Joseph Hosp 6%	1585	1.77

Investment Style

Maturity Short Int Long
Quality High Med Low

Average Weighted Maturity	19.3 Yrs
Average Credit Quality	AA
Average Weighted Coupon	6.33%
Average Weighted Price	99.74% of Par
Pricing Service	Muller

Credit Analysis % of bonds 06-30-95

US Govt	0	BB	0
AAA	42	B	7
AA	19	Below B	0
A	22	NR/NA	10
BBB	1		

Special Securities % of assets

Private/Illiquid Securities	0
Inverse Floaters	0
Other Structured Notes	0
Options/Futures/Warrants	No

Bond Type % of assets 06-30-95

Alternative Minimum Tax (AMT)	9.0
Insured	---
Prefunded	---

Sector Weightings

	% of Bonds	Rel Obj
General Obligation	7.94	0.36
Utilities	11.93	1.02
Health	6.89	0.57
Water/Waste	9.83	1.50
Housing	11.76	1.64
Education	4.46	0.75
Transportation	9.40	0.90
COP/Lease	5.34	1.58
Industrial	16.72	1.37
Misc Revenue	11.78	2.24

Top 5 States % of Bonds

CA	15.61	MI	9.43
NY	15.22	OH	8.74
PR	11.90		

Composition % of assets 06-30-95

Cash	7.0	Bonds	93.0
Stocks	0.0	Other	0.0
		Demand	3.94	1.70

Address	Vista Service Center P.O. Box 419392 Kansas City, MO 64179	Minimum Purchase	$2500	Add: $100	IRA: $1000
		Min Auto Inv Plan	$250	Systematic Inv: $100	
Telephone	800-648-4782	* Date of Inception	09-08-87		
Advisor	Chase Manhattan Bank	**Expenses & Fees**			
Subadvisor	None	Sales Fees	4.50%L, 0.25%B		
Distributor	Vista Broker-Dealer Services	Management Fee	0.30% flat fee, 0.10%A		
States Available	All	Actual Fees	Mgt: 0.05% Dist: 0.20%		
Report Grade	C+	Expense Projections	3Yr: $69	5Yr: $87	10Yr: $140
Income Distrib	Monthly				

MORNINGSTAR Mutual Funds

Volume 26, Issue Number 1, September 29, 1995. Reprinted with permission.

Fidelity Convertible Securities

	Ticker	Load	NAV	Yield	SEC Yield	Assets	Objective
	FCVSX	None	$17.41	4.3%	---	$999.5 mil	Convrt. Bond

Fidelity Convertible Securities Fund seeks total return through a combination of current income and capital appreciation.

The fund normally invests at least 65% of assets in convertible securities. The balance of assets may be invested in corporate or U.S. debt securities, common stocks, preferred stocks, and money-market instruments. The fund may invest in lower-quality, high-yielding securities, though the fund currently expects that its fixed-income securities are primarily rated B or better. It may write covered call options or buy put options.

Portfolio Manager(s)

Charles Mangum. Since 2-95. BA'86 Southern Methodist U.; MBA'90 U. of Chicago. Mangum has been a portfolio manager and analyst with Fidelity Investments since 1992. He joined the company in 1990 as an analyst following the health-care-services and medical-technology industries. Previously, he spent two years as a corporate-finance analyst with Eppler, Guern, and Turner.

Performance 08-31-95

	1st Qtr	2nd Qtr	3rd Qtr	4th Qtr	Total
1991	16.06	2.60	9.79	6.13	38.74
1992	6.66	2.16	3.15	8.57	22.02
1993	6.60	3.29	4.60	2.27	17.79
1994	-3.56	-2.11	6.52	-2.30	-1.76
1995	5.10	5.97	---	---	---

Trailing	Total Return %	+/- LB Aggregate	+/- S&P 500	% Rank All	% Rank Obj	Growth of $10,000
3 Mo	6.41	4.69	0.44	24	43	10,641
6 Mo	13.26	5.47	-3.53	31	48	11,326
1 Yr	12.26	0.96	-9.16	35	41	11,226
3 Yr Avg	14.14	7.39	0.31	20	16	14,872
5 Yr Avg	18.01	8.39	2.91	10	9	22,886
10 Yr Avg	---	---	---	---	---	---
15 Yr Avg	---	---	---	---	---	---

Most Similar Funds in MMF

Pacific Horizon Capital Income	Fair Fit
SteinRoe Special	Fair Fit
Vanguard Convertible Securities	Fair Fit

Tax Analysis

	Tax-Adj Return %	% Pretax Return
3 Yr Avg	11.25	79.5
5 Yr Avg	15.29	84.9
10 Yr Avg	---	---
Potential Capital Gain Exposure	8% of assets	

Analysis by Bill Rocco 09-15-95

Over smooth waters and rough, Fidelity Convertible Securities Fund leaves the competition in its wake.

This fund has placed among its group's leaders each year, cruising when the winds have been in its favor. In 1991, for example, the fund's focus on the convertibles and stocks of small firms paid off, as investors flocked to small caps. The fund has also excelled under adverse conditions. Thanks to some nifty security selection and ample amounts of busted convertibles and cash, it sailed on during 1990's stormy market. The fund did so again during 1994's choppiness--despite bankruptcies by two of its major holdings, Media Vision and Regal Communications. Because of this yearly outperformance, the fund's long-term returns are impressive, and its risk scores, though not quite as strong, are average.

This smooth sailing is all the more impressive given the turnover at the fund's helm. Charles Mangum, who took over early this year, is the fund's fourth manager since its inception in 1987. That said, the fund's strategy has remained fairly steady from manager to manager. Mangum, like his predecessors, emphasizes bottom-up security selection, looking for fundamentally sound and attractively priced small-cap issues that offer strong growth prospects or hefty yields.

Its past success notwithstanding, the fund's research-oriented tack has led to middling results so far this year. While it outpaced its peers during the first quarter, the fund has since fallen back; Mangum attributes this underperformance to conservative positioning. Concerns about a slowing economy and earnings disappointments have led him to focus on bondlike, rather than equitylike, convertibles for much of the year.

While the fund currently finds itself in unfamiliar waters, its long-term record remains superior to most of its peers'.

Historical Profile

Return	High
Risk	Average
Rating	★★★★ Highest

Growth of $10,000

- Investment Value ($000)
- Investment Value ($000)
- LB Aggregate
- ▼ Manager Change
- ▽ Partial Manager Change

Performance Quartile (Within Objective)

	1994	1985	1986	1987	1988	1989	1990	1991	1992	1993	1994	08-95	History
	---	---	---	9.12	9.83	11.60	10.65	13.67	15.55	16.45	15.36	17.41	NAV
	---	---	---	-4.88 *	15.89	26.28	-2.89	38.74	22.02	17.79	-1.76	15.62	Total Return %
	---	---	---	*	8.01	11.75	-11.85	22.73	14.62	8.04	1.16	3.08	+/- LB Aggregate
	---	---	-6.20 *	-0.72	-5.40	0.22	8.25	14.40	7.73	-3.07	-8.86	+/- S&P 500
	---	---	---	3.92	8.11	8.28	5.30	6.13	5.04	4.68	4.87	2.27	Income Return %
	---	---	---	-8.80	7.79	18.01	-8.19	32.61	16.98	13.11	-6.63	13.35	Capital Return %
	---	---	---	25	20	64	15	3	21	33	35	Total Rtn %Rank All
	---	---	---	14	5	15	13	4	20	20	61	Total Rtn %Rank Obj
	---	---	0.42	0.72	0.77	0.62	0.64	0.67	0.73	0.80	0.32	Income $
	---	---	0.00	0.00	0.00	0.00	0.37	0.40	1.09	0.00	0.00	Capital Gains $
	---	---	1.60	1.60	1.38	1.31	1.17	0.96	0.92	0.85	---	Expense Ratio %
	---	---	5.45	6.20	7.48	5.63	4.99	4.82	4.62	4.61	---	Income Ratio %
	---	---	233	191	207	223	152	258	312	318	---	Turnover Rate %
	---	---	38.9	40.0	63.2	59.7	133.4	480.4	1063.9	891.3	999.5	Net Assets ($mil)

Income Rtn %Rank Obj

Risk Analysis

Time Period	Load-Adj Return %	Risk %Rank All	Risk %Rank Obj	Morningstar Return	Morningstar Risk	Morningstar Risk-Adj Rating
1 Yr	12.26					
3 Yr	14.14	41	45	1.61	0.71	★★★★★
5 Yr	18.01	55	47	1.89	0.76	★★★★★
Incept	13.80					
Average Historical Rating	(68 months)				4.8	★s

[1]=low, 100=high [2] 1.00 = Hybrid Avg

Other Measures		Standard Index LB Agg	Best Fit Index Russ 2000
Standard Deviation	7.02	Alpha	8.2 / 1.6
Mean	13.55	Beta	0.63 / 0.56
Sharpe Ratio	1.37	R-Squared	15 / 66

Portfolio Analysis 05-31-95

Amount 000	Date of Maturity	Total Stocks: 23 / Total Fixed-Income: 86	Value $000	% Net Assets
182000	06-25-11	US WEST Cv 0%	58468	6.10
1416		RJR Nabisco Holdings	40358	4.21
273		IBM France Cv Pfd 5.75%	27756	2.90
29300	07-27-99	Cellular Communications Cv 0%	23147	2.42
17375	05-15-01	Benson Eyecare Cv 8%	21979	2.29
25000	01-15-00	NovaCare Cv 5.5%	20688	2.16
61000	12-17-12	Time Warner Cv 0%	20359	2.13
991		Citicorp Cv Pfd $1.217	19948	2.08
22500	03-01-01	Hanson America Cv PIK 2.39%	17775	1.86
21553	01-24-05	WMX Technologies Cv 2%	17673	1.84
21150	11-01-03	Proffitt's Cv 4.75%	16920	1.77
42000	04-20-10	Roche Holding Cv PIK 0%	16170	1.69
17100	02-01-02	TheraTx Cv 8%	15689	1.64
16650	08-15-03	LDDS Communications Cv 5%	15485	1.62
15650	01-15-01	Freeport-McMoRan Cv 6.55%	14515	1.52
14000	01-10-15	Time Warner Cv 8.75%	14490	1.51
23000	11-01-08	Office Depot Cv 0%	13455	1.40
221		Occidental Petro Cv Pfd $3.00	13367	1.40
7275	12-01-02	Abbey Healthcare Group Cv 6.5%	13350	1.39
399		Sprint Cv Pfd $0.6573	13270	1.39
28890	03-11-13	News America Holdings Cv 0%	13253	1.38
520		Atlantic Richfield Cv Pfd	13065	1.36
210		General Motors Cv Pfd $3.25	13020	1.36
478		Allergan	12735	1.33
29000	02-20-12	Automatic Data Process Cv 0%	12615	1.32

Investment Style		
Avg Effective Maturity	10.5 Yrs	
Avg Credit Quality		
Avg Weighted Coupon	4.12%	
Avg Weighted Price	74.49% of Par	

Special Securities		
		% of assets
● Private/Illiquid Securities		8
○ Exotic Mortgage-Backed		0
○ Structured Notes		0
● Emerging Markets Secs		Trace
─ Options/Futures		0

Credit Analysis	% of bonds 06-30-92		
US Govt		BB	---
AAA		B	---
AA		Below B	---
A		NR/NA	---
BBB			---

Coupon Range	% of Bonds	Rel Obj
0%	37.8	3.27
0% to 6%	16.4	0.47
6% to 7%	13.3	0.91
7% to 8.5%	9.4	0.78
More than 8.5%	5.3	1.05
Not applicable	17.7	0.83

1.00 = Obj Avg

Composition 07-31-95	% of assets
Cash	4.3
Stocks	16.3
Bonds	1.2
Convertibles	78.2
Other	0.0

Address	82 Devonshire Street	Minimum Purchase	$2500	Add: $250	IRA: $500
	Boston, MA 02109	Min Auto Inv Plan	$2500	Systematic Inv: $100	
Telephone	800-544-8888	* Date of Inception	01-05-87		
Advisor	Fidelity Management & Research				
Subadvisor	None	**Expenses & Fees**			
Distributor	Fidelity Distributors	Sales Fees	No-load		
States Available	All	Management Fee	0.20% flat fee+0.52% max./0.27% min.(G)		
Report Grade	A	Actual Fees	Mgt: 0.52%	Dist: ---	
Income Distrib	Quarterly	Expense Projections	3Yr: $27	5Yr: $49	10Yr: $112

MORNINGSTAR Mutual Funds

Volume 25, Issue Number 5, July 7, 1995. Reprinted with permission.

GAM International

	Ticker	Load	NAV	Yield	SEC Yield	Assets	Objective
	GAMNX	5.00%	$210.11	4.2%	N/A	$259.4 mil	Foreign Stock

GAM International Fund seeks long-term capital appreciation.

The fund normally invests at least 65% of assets in securities issued in at least three foreign countries. It invests primarily in equity securities, though it may invest a substantial portion of assets in debt securities. The fund may invest in Canada, the United Kingdom, continental Europe, and the Pacific Basin. No more than 5% of assets may be invested in debt securities rated below investment-grade. In addition to direct foreign investment, the fund may purchase American Depositary Receipts and European Depositary Receipts.

Portfolio Manager(s)

John R. Horseman. Since 4-90. '80 U. of Birmingham. Horseman has been an investment director at Global Asset Mgmt. UK since April 1990, following three years as investment director with GAM Hong Kong Ltd. From 1982 to 1987, he was an investment manager at World Invest.

Performance 05-31-95

	1st Qtr	2nd Qtr	3rd Qtr	4th Qtr	Total
1991	3.71	-3.23	6.63	7.98	15.56
1992	-3.18	11.67	5.20	-9.37	3.08
1993	12.42	5.61	18.26	28.19	79.97
1994	-10.58	0.97	0.91	-1.47	-10.22
1995	17.54	---	---	---	---

Trailing	Total Return %	+/- S&P 500	+/- MSCI EAFE	% Rank Obj All	% Rank Obj	Growth of $10,000
3 Mo	11.26	1.05	2.34	5	9	11,126
6 Mo	20.56	1.36	15.47	2	1	12,056
1 Yr	25.22	5.06	20.29	2	1	12,522
3 Yr Avg	24.71	12.90	13.19	1	1	19,396
5 Yr Avg	16.61	5.20	11.74	3	1	21,563
10 Yr Avg	22.81	8.23	6.27	1	1	78,067
15 Yr Avg	---	---	---	---	---	---

Most Similar Funds in MMF

Dean Witter Pacific Growth	Weak Fit
Merrill Lynch Dragon B	Weak Fit
AIM International Equity A	Weak Fit

Tax Analysis

	Tax-Adj Return %	% Pretax Return
3 Yr Avg	20.86	84.4
5 Yr Avg	12.71	76.5
10 Yr Avg	18.12	79.4
Potential Capital Gain Exposure		13% of assets

Analysis by Alice Lowenstein 06-23-95

GAM International Fund is up to its old tricks.

Dedicated fans of this fund—the only foreign-stock fund with a 5-star rating at present—are no doubt experiencing the joys of recognition: After suffering an uncharacteristically harsh year in 1994, the fund has rebounded to its more-typical spot in the objective's upper ranks so far in 1995.

Credit for this return to excellence also goes to the usual place. Manager John Horseman's strategy, which affects both his country and issue choices, is to get in on overlooked opportunities and avoid herdlike adherence to trends. This process begins with an appraisal of macroeconomics, through which he identifies key sectors for investment. He then considers all manner of securities, including stocks, bonds, convertibles, and various futures and short positions. Final selection is based on a combination of value and earnings-growth criteria.

It is in the execution of this strategy that the fund really stands out, though. In 1994 and into this year, for example, Horseman has been a big fan of bonds, especially Germany's. Nearly 30% of the fund's assets are in German bonds, and much of its French, Italian, and U.K. bond positions are hedged into the Deutschemark. While this bet was a drag last year, it has largely powered the fund's heady gains this year. Few foreign-stock funds come close to this commitment to fixed income.

Another quirk is the fund's Japan stake. Horseman long ignored Japan, even while the fund's peers did not. Now, after Japan's market has hit new lows, he is seeing his first buy opportunities there. Although still cautious, he has added such stocks as Kirin Beverage, a soft-drink company (spun off from Kirin Brewery) with a strong balance sheet and modest P/E ratio.

Certainly this fund is hard to pigeonhole. This creativity is also its main asset.

Address	135 East 57th Street 25th Floor New York, NY 10022
Telephone	800-426-4685 / 212-407-4600
Advisor	GAM International Management
Subadvisor	None
Distributor	GAM Services
States Available	Selected states
Report Grade	B+
Income Distrib	Annually

Minimum Purchase	$10000	Add: $1000	IRA: $10000
Min Auto Inv Plan	N/A	Systematic Inv: N/A	
Date of Inception	01-01-85		

Expenses & Fees

Sales Fees	5.00%L
Management Fee	1.00% flat fee
Actual Fees	Mgt: 1.00% Dist: N/A
Expense Projections	3Yr: $109 5Yr: $152 10Yr: $270
Annual Brokerage Cost	0.88%

Historical Profile

Return High
Risk Average
Rating ★★★★★ Highest

	1984	1985	1986	1987	1988	1989	1990	1991	1992	1993	1994	05-95	History
	---	159.26	219.12	132.91	148.08	170.23	128.74	148.63	145.64	239.03	172.06	210.11	NAV
	---	57.95 *	47.51	12.05	21.51	22.46	-7.30	15.56	3.08	79.97	-10.22	22.11	Total Return %
	---	26.21 *	28.83	6.79	4.90	-9.22	-4.19	-14.92	-4.54	69.91	-11.54	4.65	+/- S&P 500
	---		-21.93	-12.58	-6.76	11.92	16.15	3.43	15.25	47.40	-18.00	17.68	+/- MSCI EAFE
	---	0.00	0.02	1.49	0.39	0.16	0.00	0.06	3.02	2.97	5.68	0.00	Income Return %
	---	57.95	47.48	10.56	21.12	22.30	-7.30	15.50	0.06	76.99	-15.91	22.11	Capital Return %
	---		3	8	11	30	78	55	84	1	95	1	Total Rtn %Rank All
	---		63	22	13	47	22	32	5	2	87	1	Total Rtn %Rank Obj
	---	0.00	0.04	2.34	0.56	0.26	0.00	0.08	4.31	3.39	10.46	0.00	Income $
	---	0.00	12.36	108.7	11.83	9.98	29.06	0.05	3.02	9.48	34.07	0.00	Capital Gains $
	---	2.00	1.81	2.23	2.76	2.74	2.30	2.11	2.03	1.99	1.60	---	Expense Ratio %
	---	0.12	0.66	0.38	0.27	0.19	1.32	3.25	4.85	2.28	2.74	---	Income Ratio %
	---		82	80	23	33	254	161	109	98	110	---	Turnover Rate %
	---	10.0	25.0	21.0	19.6	20.8	23.4	40.4	41.0	80.7	159.4	259.4	Net Assets ($mil)

Investment Style History
Equity
Average Stock %

| | | | | 96% | 50% | 60% | 42% | 72% | | 39% | 11% |

Growth of $10,000

Investment Value ($000) of Fund
Investment Value ($000) S&P 500

▼ Manager Change
▽ Partial Manager Change
◄ Mgr Unknown After
◄ Mgr Unknown Before

Performance Quartile (Within Objective)

Risk Analysis

Time Period	Load-Adj Return %	Risk %Rank [1] All	Obj	Morningstar [2] Return	Morningstar Risk	Morningstar Risk-Adj Rating
1 Yr	18.96					
3 Yr	22.60	83	5	3.47	1.01	★★★★★
5 Yr	15.42	76	6	2.26	0.89	★★★★★
10 Yr	22.19	60	11	3.78	0.83	★★★★★
Average Historical Rating	(89 months)				4.1	★s

[1] 1=low, 100=high [2] 1.00 = Equity Avg

Other Measures

		Standard Index S&P 500	Best Fit Index MSEASEA
Standard Deviation	17.06	Alpha	17.0	14.7
Mean	23.67	Beta	0.53	0.90
Sharpe Ratio	1.17	R-Squared	6	46

Portfolio Analysis 03-31-95

Share Chg (12-94) 000	Amount 000	Total Stocks: 10 Total Fixed-Income: 19	Value $000	% Net Assets
	36	Republic of Germany 6.25%	21414	10.59
	162	US Treasury Note 7.25%	16334	8.08
	20	Govt of Netherlands 7.5%	12409	6.14
	1015	Govt of Switzerland 5.5%	9240	4.57
	136	LKB Baden-Wuerttemberg 6.5%	8979	4.44
	12	EIB 7.75%	8958	4.43
	12	EXIM Bank of Japan 7.75%	8926	4.41
	57	Govt of France 6%	8777	4.34
	143	Commonwealth Australia 6.5%	8662	4.28
	125	United Kingdom Treasury 3.5%	8393	4.15
68	68	Fortis AMEV	3249	1.61
0	308	North West Water	2753	1.36
	2050	Inchcape Cv 6.25%	2574	1.27
	14	Asda Finance Cv 10.75%	2447	1.21
	55	ABN AMRO Holding Cv Pfd 6%	1997	0.99
	1007	BICC Cv Pfd	1905	0.94
	1005	Thames Water Cv 9.5%	1897	0.94
	53	KPN	1871	0.93
	1055	Land Securities Cv 9.375%	1803	0.89
0	950	Hong Kong & China Gas	1696	0.84

Investment Style

Value Blend Growth
Size Large Med Small

	Stock Portfolio Avg	Rel MSCI EAFE	Rel Objective
Price/Earnings Ratio	13.0	0.40	0.53
Price/Cash Flow	10.6	0.68	0.75
Price/Book Ratio	1.4	0.58	0.53
5 Yr Earnings Gr %	7.5∥	---	1.34
Med Mkt Cap ($mil)	3404	0.27	0.62

∥ figure is based on 50% or less of stocks

Country Exposure 03-31-95

	% of Stocks
Germany	45
United Kingdom	19
Netherlands	15
France	11
Switzerland	7
Total number of countries: 10	
Hedging Policy: Active	

Regional Exposure 03-31-95

	% of Stocks
Europe	97
Japan	1
Latin America	0
Pacific Rim	2
Other	0

Special Securities % of assets

● Private/Illiquid Securities	Trace
○ Structured Notes	0
● Emerging-Markets Secs	1
● Options/Futures/Warrants	Yes

Composition % of assets 03-31-95

Cash	34.5	Bonds	47.4
Stocks	11.0	Other	7.2

Sector Weightings % of Stocks

	% of Stocks	Rel Obj
Utilities	26.8	2.62
Energy	16.5	3.75
Financials	46.5	2.45
Industrial Cyclicals	0.0	0.00
Consumer Durables	0.0	0.00
Consumer Staples	0.0	0.00
Services	10.2	0.96
Retail	0.0	0.00
Health	0.0	0.00
Technology	0.0	0.00

MORNINGSTAR Mutual Funds

PART FOUR

●···●

Sources of
Financial Information

Financial Publications, Journals, and Newspapers *95*
Investment Advisories and Newsletters *98*
Academic Journals *103*
Professional Journals and Publications *104*
Commercial Bank Letters and Reports *107*
Institutional Publications *108*
Investors' Subscription Services *111*
Books for Investors *115*
Mutual Fund Directories *117*

Financial Publications, Journals, and Newspapers   (*available on-line)

PUBLICATION	FREQUENCY	YEARLY RATE	PUBLISHER	TYPE OF INFORMATION
The Wall Street Journal	Daily	$139 ($74.50 student rate)	Dow Jones & Co., Inc. 200 Burnett Rd Chicopee, MA 01020 (800) 628-9320	General business, financial and world news, with market quotations.
AAII Journal	Monthly	$45	American Association of Individual Investors 625 N. Michigan Ave. Suite 1900 Chicago, IL 60611-3110 (312) 280-0170	Articles about investing and financial management for individuals.
American Stock Exchange Reports Fact Book	Annual Directory	Free	American Stock Exchange 86 Trinity Place New York, NY 10006-1881 (212) 306-1000	Annual trading statistics on AMEX equities and options.
American Stock Exchange Weekly Bulletin	Weekly	$1,220	Standard & Poor's Corp. 25 Broadway New York, NY 10004 (212) 208-8000	Summary of activity on Amercian Stock Exchange for the week.
Barron's National Business and Financial Weekly	Weekly	$129	Dow Jones & Co., Inc. 200 Liberty St New York, NY 10281-1099 (212) 416-2700	Financial and investment news; data on commodities, international trading; weekly market data and summaries.
Business Week	Weekly	$47	McGraw-Hill, Inc. 1221 Ave. of the Americas, Room 4188 New York, NY 10020-1095 (212) 512-2000	Coverage of news and developments affecting the business world. Also available: industrial and international editions.*
CBOE Market Statistics	Monthly	$360	Commerce Clearing House 4025 W. Peterson Ave. Chicago, IL 60646 (312) 940-4600	Data from the Chicago Board Options Exchange.
CME Annual Report	Annual	Free	Chicago Merchantile Exchange 30 South Wacker Drive Chicago, IL 60606 (312) 930-1000	Annual summary of activity on the Chicago Merchantile Exchange.
The Economist	Weekly	$110	Economist Intelligence Unit 11 W. 57th St. New York, NY 10019-2211 (212) 541-5730	Developments in world politics, business, economics, and finance.*

Financial Publications, Journals, and Newspapers (cont.)   (*available on-line)

PUBLICATION	FREQUENCY	YEARLY RATE	PUBLISHER	TYPE OF INFORMATION
Finance Facts	Monthly	$25	American Financial Services Association 919 18th St. NW Washington, DC 20006-5503 (202) 289-0400	Analysis of consumer sector and economic behavior.
Federal Reserve Bulletin	Monthly	$20	Board of Governors of Federal Reserve System Publication Services, M5138 Washington, DC 20551-0001 (202) 452-3000	Business conditions; financial and business statistics.*
Financial World	Bi-weekly	$40	Financial World Partners 1328 Broadway, 3rd floor New York, NY 10001-2116 (212) 594-5030	Investment analysis and forecasts for specific companies and industries as a whole.*
Forbes	Bi-weekly	$52	Forbes Publishing 60 Fifth Ave. New York, NY 10011-8882 (212) 620-2200	General economic and financial news; reports on corporations, stocks, and industries.*
Fortune Magazine	Bi-weekly	$37	Time, Inc. 1271 Ave. of the Americas Rockefeller Center New York, NY 10020-1300 (212) 586-1212	Business and economic developments; evaluates specific industries and corporations.*
Futures	Monthly	$39	Futures Magazine, Inc. 219 Parkade Cedars Falls, IA 50613 (800) 221-4352	Charts, illustrations, statistics, articles on commodities and futures trading markets.
Inc. Magazine	18 times per year	$25	Goldhirsch Group 38 Commercial Wharf Boston, MA 02110-3809 (617) 248-8000	How-to aspects of finance, marketing, sales, and operations for small, growing companies.*
Individual Investor	Monthly	$40	Individual Investor Group 330 Seventh Ave. New York, NY 10001 (212) 843-2777	Complete coverage of high-profit, fast-growing stocks under $10/share.
Investor's Business Daily	Daily	$94	Investor's Business Daily P.O. Box 25970 Los Angeles, CA 90025 (310) 448-6000	Similar to the *The Wall Street Journal* but with more statistics and fewer articles.

Financial Publications, Journals, and Newspapers (cont.)   (*available on-line)

PUBLICATION	FREQUENCY	YEARLY RATE	PUBLISHER	TYPE OF INFORMATION
Journal of Financial Planning Today	Quarterly	$80	New Directions Publications Box 5359 Lake Worth, FL 33461 (305) 964-8727	Articles on personal financial management, estate planning, taxes, tax shelters, mutual funds, commodities, stocks and bonds.
Kiplinger Personal Finance Magazine	Weekly	$18	Kiplinger Washington Editors, Inc. 1729 H Street, NW Washington, DC 20006 (202) 887-6400	Weekly news, information, analyses, and forecasts, affecting personal investment and finances.*
Louis Rukeyser's Wall Street	Monthly	$79	Louis Rukeyser's Wall Street P.O. Box 25527 Alexandria, VA 22313 (703) 548-2400	Personal finance magazine and a newsletter on specific invest-ment advice, with arti-cles by investment authorities.
Money	Monthly	$36	Time, Inc. 1271 Ave. of the Americas Rockefeller Center New York, NY 10020-1300 (212) 586-1212	Reports on personal finance; stock market trends, estate planning, taxes, tax shelters, and consumer affairs.*
Nation's Business	Monthly	$22	U.S. Chamber of Commerce 1615 H Street NW Washington, DC 20062-2000 (202) 463-5650	Forecasts, analyses, and interpretations of trends and developments in business and government; aimed primarily at small and mid-sized businesses.*
National Real Estate Investor	Monthly	$70	Communication Channels 6151 Powers Ferry Rd NW Atlanta, GA 30339 (404) 955-2500	Articles and book reviews on real estate financing, marketing, partnership offerings, and taxation for serious real estate investors.
New York Stock Exchange Fact Book	Annual	$10	New York Exchange Publications, 18th Floor 11 Wall Street New York, NY 10005 (212) 656-3000	Description of the New York Stock Exchange activity.
Worth	10 times per year	$15	Capital Publishing Co. 575 Lexington Avenue New York, NY 10022 (212) 223-3100	Glossy magazine with regular columns by noted market watchers, and feature articles.

Investment Advisories and Newsletters

(*available on-line)

PUBLICATION	FREQUENCY	YEARLY RATE	PUBLISHER	TYPE OF INFORMATION
Adrian Day's Investment Analyst	Monthly	$49	Agora, Inc. 824 E. Baltimore St. Baltimore, MD 21202-4799 (410) 244-8885	Economic outlook; investment advice for individuals.
Alan Shawn Feinstein Insider Report	Monthly	$36	41 Alhambra Circle Cranston, RI 02905 (401) 467-5155	Reports on special investment opportunities, inside tips, new or unusual opportunities.
America's Finest Companies	Annual	$32	The Financial Training Group 300 E. Blvd., Suite B-4 Charlotte, NC 28203-4784 (704) 332-7514	Includes data on 700+ public companies with higher earnings/dividends for 10 years or more.
Bartlett Letters	Monthly	$25	John W. Bartlett Box 465 Aurora, IL 60507-0465 (708) 896-3143	Investment advisory service recommending conservative stocks.
Bert Dohmens Mutual Fund Strategy	Monthly	$140	Phillips Publishing, Inc. 1201 Seven Locks Rd. Suite 300 Potomac, MD 20854 (301) 340-1520	Geared toward mutual fund investor. Uses proprietary strategy designed to give buy signals before major declines.
Better Investing Magazine	Monthly	$17	National Association of Investors Corporation 1515 Eleven Mile Road Royal Oak, MI 48067 (313) 543-0612	Guidelines and advice on investment techniques for investment clubs. One company analyzed each month.
Bob Nurock's Advisory	17 times per year	$247	Investor's Analysis, Inc. Drawer 650 Southeastern, PA 19399-0650 (215) 296-2411	Technical and fundamental stock market developments by Bob Nurock of "Wall Street Week".
Bottom Line Personal	Semi-monthly	$49	Boardroom Publishing 330 W 42nd St, 14th floor New York, NY 10036-6902 (212) 239-9000	Management of personal affairs from investments to personal goods.
Brookmire Investment Reports	Weekly	$250	Brookmire Investment Service Box 586 Daytona Beach, FL 32015 (904) 252-6229	Originators of stock index futures; technical analysis of securities, and commodities.
Bull & Bear Financial Newspaper	Monthly	$19	Bull & Bear Financial Newspaper Box 917179 Longwood, FL 32793-7179 (407) 682-6170	Summarizes stock market advisory newsletters.

Investment Advisories and Newsletters (cont.)

(*available on-line)

PUBLICATION	FREQUENCY	YEARLY RATE	PUBLISHER	TYPE OF INFORMATION
Commodity Price Charts	Weekly	$425	Oster Communications, Inc. 219 Parkade, PO Box 6 Cedar Falls, IL 50613 (319) 277-1278	Insights and perspectives on 27 key futures markets.
Computerized Investing	Bi-monthly	$60	American Association of Individual Investors 625 N. Michigan Ave. Suite 1900 Chicago, IL 60611-3110 (312) 280-0170	Articles and reviews on investment-related software for investors who wish to use a computer in investing.
The Contrary Investor	Bi-weekly	$95	Fraser Management Assoc. Box 494 Burlington, VT 05402-0494 (802) 658-0322	"Contrary opinion" theory of investing. Broad market timing recommendations.
Dick Davis Digest	Bi-weekly	$140	Dick Davis Publishing 1080 SE Third Ave. Ft. Lauderdale, FL 33316 (305) 467-8500	Latest opinions of top-performing investment letter writers, with stock recommendations.
Dines Letter	Semi-monthly	$195	James Dines & Co., Inc. Box 22 Belvedere, CA 94920-0022 (800) 845-8259	Technical and business indicators concerning the markets.
Dow Theory Forecasts	Weekly	$233	Dow Theory Forecasts, Inc. 7412 Calumet Ave. Hammond, IN 46324-2692 (219) 931-6480	Forecasts of market based on Dow theory. List of stock choices, generally blue chips.
Forbes Special Situation Survey	Monthly	$495	Forbes Publishing 60 Fifth Ave. New York, NY 10011-8882 (212) 620-2200	Discusses and recommends the purchase of one speculative equity security in each issue.
Forecasts & Strategies	Monthly	$100	Phillips Publishing, Inc. 1201 Seven Locks Rd. Suite 300 Potomac, MD 20854 (301) 340-1520	Investment, taxes, and "financial privacy" commentary by Mark Skousen.
Global Finance	Monthly	$120	McGraw-Hill 11 W. 19th St. 2nd floor New York, NY 10011 (212) 337-6000	Latest issues and trends in international finance and investing.
Grant's Interest Rate Observer	Bi-weekly	$450	Interest Rate Publishing Co. 30 Wall Street New York, NY 10005-2201 (212) 608-7994	Creative indexes and statistics and advice on fixed-income investments from James Grant.

Investment Advisories and Newsletters (cont.) (*available on-line)

PUBLICATION	FREQUENCY	YEARLY RATE	PUBLISHER	TYPE OF INFORMATION
Growth Stock Outlook	Semi-monthly	$195	Growth Stock Outlook 4405 East-West Hwy. Suite 305 Bethesda, MD 20814-4595 (301) 654-5205	Reports on selected stocks with vigorous growth.
Income Fund Outlook	Monthly	$100	Institute for Econometric Research 3471 N. Federal Hwy. Fort Lauderdale, FL 33306 (305) 563-9000	A guide to places to invest for income, concentrating on money-market funds, bank accounts, and tax-free funds.
The Insiders	Semi-monthly	$100	Institute for Econometric Research 3471 N. Federal Hwy. Fort Lauderdale, FL 33306 (305) 563-9000	Compilations and interpretations of SEC data on buying by insiders; includes recommendations.
InvesTech Market Analyst	18 times per year	$175	InvesTech Research 2472 Birch Glen Whitefish, MT 59937-3349 (406) 862-7777	Reactions to other letter editors' views, technical analysis, and stock and mutual fund choices.
Investment Horizons	Bi-monthly	$250	Investment Information Services 680 N. Lake Shore Dr. Suite 2038 Chicago, IL 60611-4402 (312) 649-6940	Small companies that are not watched extensively are covered by Gerald Perritt for intellectual investors.
The Kiplinger Washington Letter	Weekly	$63	1729 H Street, NW Washington, DC 20006 (202) 887-6400	Data on business trends, government policies, employment, investments, and interest rates.
Market Logic	Semi-monthly	$200	Institute for Econometric Research 3471 N. Federal Hwy. Fort Lauderdale, FL 33306 (305) 563-9000	Covers technical, fundamental, and monetary market movement predictions and recommended trades.
Professional Tape Reader	Semi-monthly	$350	Radcap Inc. Box 2407 Hollywood, FL 33022-2407 (800) 865-7857	Charts, advice, and forecasts of stock trends; analysis of promising and vulnerable stocks.
Prudent Speculator	17 times a year	$175	Al Frank Asset Management Box 1767 Santa Monica CA 90406-1767 (310) 587-2410	Stock advisory letter on what to consider in trading stocks, managing a portfolio, and adjusting to market-wide changes.

Investment Advisories and Newsletters (cont.)   (*available on-line)

PUBLICATION	FREQUENCY	YEARLY RATE	PUBLISHER	TYPE OF INFORMATION
Real Estate Investing Letter	Monthly	$96	Management Resources, Inc. 861 Lafayette Rd. Hampton, NH 03842-1232 (603) 929-1600	Real estate investment coverage, including tax strategies, depreciation, and real estate syndication.
RHM Survey of Warrants, Options & Low-Price Stocks	Weekly	$220	RHM Associates, Inc. 172 Forest Ave. Glen Cove, NY 11542 (516) 759-2904	Investment advice on warrants, call options, and low-priced stocks.
Richard C. Young's Intelligence Report	Monthly	$197	Phillips Publishing, Inc. 1201 Seven Locks Rd. Suite 300 Potomac, MD 20854 (301) 340-1520	Profiles low-risk investment opportunities in equities backed by Uncle Sam.
Stanger Report: A Guide to Partnership Investing	Monthly	$325	Robert A. Stanger and Co. PO Box 7490 Shrewsbury, NJ 07702-4314 (201) 389-3600	Tax planning ideas and comments on limited partnership ventures and tax shelter investments.
Stanger Investment Adviser	Monthly	$225	Charter Financial Publishing 179 Ave at the Common Shrewsbury, NJ 07702-4314 (908) 389-8700	Financial planning, combined with analysis of limited partnerships.
Street Smart Investing	Bi-weekly	$350	13D Research Inc. SE Executive Park 100 Executive Drive Brewster, NY 10509 (914) 278-6500	Analyses of buys and sells of leading investors, investment managers, and corporate insiders.*
Today's Investor	Monthly	$59	Forte Communications 111 Broadway Suite 1900 New York, NY 10006-1901 (212) 406-4466	Advice on stocks selling for $15 or less per share.
United & Babson Investment Report	Weekly	$238	Babson-United Investment Advisors, Inc. 101 Prescott St. Wellesley Hills, MA 02181 (617) 235-0900	Weekly newsletter evaluates stock market trends. Notes related federal developments tables.
Value Line Investment Survey	Weekly	$495	Value Line, Inc. 200 E. 42nd St New York, NY 10017 (212) 907-1500	Weekly charts and graphs covering the business activities of about 1,700 major corporations.

Investment Advisories and Newsletters (cont.)   (*available on-line)

PUBLICATION	FREQUENCY	YEARLY RATE	PUBLISHER	TYPE OF INFORMATION
Value Line Options	Weekly	$445	Value Line, Inc. 200 E. 42nd St New York, NY 10017 (212) 907-1500	The preeminent source of information on equity and index options.
Value Line OTC Special Situations Survey	Bi-monthly	$390	Value Line, Inc. 200 E. 42nd St New York, NY 10017 (212) 907-1500	Information for investors on stocks traded over-the-counter.
Wellington Letter	Monthly	$375	Wellington Financial Corp. Hawaii Kai Executive Plaza 6700 Kalanianada #218 Honolulu HI 96825-1299 (808) 396-2220	Fundamental and technical analyses of all markets.
Zweig Forecast	Monthly	$265	Zweig Securities Advisory Box 2900 Wantaugh, NY 11793 (516) 785-1300	Stock analysis and selections based on Martin Zweig's indicators.

Academic Journals

These journals will be of interest to sophisticated investors who wish to keep abreast of the most recent advances in financial and investment theory and application.

PUBLICATION	FREQUENCY	YEARLY RATE	PUBLISHER	TYPE OF INFORMATION
Financial Management	Quarterly	$50	Financial Management Association University of South Florida College of Business Admin. Tampa, FL 33601-1379 (813) 974-2084	Academic articles with an applications orientation, emphasizing financial management and investments.*
Journal of Business	Quarterly	$22	University of Chicago Press 5720 South Woodlawn Ave. Chicago, IL 60637 (312) 702-7600	Sophisticated academic articles on business and investments.
Journal of Financial and Quantitative Analysis	Quarterly	$40	Graduate School of Business University of Washington 326 Lewis Hall, DJ-10 Seattle, WA 98195-0001 (206) 543-4589	Academic articles on finance, including investments.
Journal of Financial Research	Quarterly	$60	Journal of Financial Research College of Business Arizona State University Tempe, AZ 85287 (602) 965-6202	Academic articles on finance, including financial management, investments, institutions, capital market, and portfolio theory.
Journal of Derivatives	Quarterly	$195	Institutional Investor, Inc. 488 Madison Ave. 16th floor New York, NY 10022-5751 (212) 303-3185	Reports on developments in both derivatives theory and practise. Insights on derivatives market.
Journal of Finance	5 per year	$39	American Finance Association New York University 100 Trinity Place New York, NY 10006-1524 (212) 285-8915	Academic articles on theory and practice in finance, including investments.*
Journal of Portfolio Management	Quarterly	$225	Institutional Investor, Inc. 488 Madison Ave. 16th Floor New York, NY 10022-5751 (212) 303-3300	Trends and developments in the management of large portfolios, both theoretical and applied.*
Journal of Risk and Insurance	Quarterly	$10 per copy	University of Central Florida Box 25000 Orlando, FL 32816-0001 (803) 777-7428	Academic articles in insurance-related areas.*

Professional Journals and Publications   (*available on-line)

Many journals are directed at the professional broker, analyst, portfolio manager, and planner but have articles and features which may be of interest to investors generally. These products are available in most public and college libraries.

PUBLICATION	FREQUENCY	YEARLY RATE	PUBLISHER	TYPE OF INFORMATION
Benefits Quarterly	Quarterly	$75	Int'l Society of Certified Employee Benefits Specialists PO Box 209 Brookfield, WI 53008-0209 (414) 786-8771	New developments, trends, problems, issues, and tax and legislative changes in employee benefits field.
Bond Buyer	Daily	$1,480	American Banker-Bond Buyer One State Plaza New York, NY 10004 (212) 943-8200	International financial and economic news, money markets, stock and bond markets.*
Bond Buyer Yearbook	Annual	$49	American Banker-Bond Buyer One State Plaza New York, NY 10004 (212) 943-8200	Compilation of statis- ical data on tax-exempt municipal bonds.
CFA Digest	Quarterly	$40	Association for Investment Management & Research Box 3668 Charlottesville, VA 22903 (804) 977-6600	Abstracts of articles in academic and professional journals for the investment community.
Estate Planning	Monthly	$95	Research Institute of America 117 E. Stevens Ave. Valhalla, NY 10595 (212) 645-4800	Estate planning, family asset management, trust and estate administration.
Financial Analysts Journal	Bi-monthly	$150	Association for Investment Management & Research Box 7947 Charlottesville, VA 22906 (804) 977-6600	Articles and transcripts of interest to securities analysts.*
Financial Estate Planners Quarterly	Quarterly	$175	Longman Financial Services Institute 520 N. Dearborn Chicago, IL 60610 (312) 836-0466	Two volumes for the professional, providing strategies, forms, and planning aids.
Institutional Investor	Monthly	$265	Capital Cities/ABC, Inc. 488 Madison Ave. New York, NY 10022 (212) 456-7777	Articles of interest to managers of large institutional investment portfolios.*
Insurance Facts	Annual	$18	Insurance Information Institute 110 William St. New York, NY 10038 (212) 2-669-9226	Basic facts of property/casualty insurance business.

PUBLICATION	FREQUENCY	YEARLY RATE	PUBLISHER	TYPE OF INFORMATION
Journal of the American Society of CLU & ChFC	Bimonthly	$32	American Society of Chartered Life Underwriters 270 Bryn Mawr Ave. Box 59 Bryn Mawr, PA 19010-2195 (610) 526-2500	Insurance education, estate and tax planning, business insurance.
Journal of Financial Planning	Quarterly	$54	Institute of Certified Financial Planners 7600 E. Eastman Ave. Suite 301 Denver, CO 80231-4397 (303) 751-7600	Articles for the financial planning profession.
Journal of Real Estate Taxation	Quarterly	$135	Warren, Gorham & Lamont 31 St. James Ave. Boston, MA 02116-4112 (617) 423-2020	Articles on real estate taxation.
Journal of Taxation	Monthly	$165	Warren, Gorham & Lamont 31 St. James Ave. Boston, MA 02116-4112 (617) 423-2020	Articles on every key tax development.
National Real Estate Investor	Monthly	$70	Argus Business 6151 Powers Ferry Rd. NW Atlanta, GA 30339-2941 (404) 955-2500	Real estate development, finance, investment, and management news articles.*
National Underwriter: Life and Health/Financial Services	Weekly	$75	National Underwriter Co. 505 Gest St. Cincinnati, OH 45203-1716 (513) 721-2140	Articles on insurance products, marketing, regulation, taxation, and related issues.*
The Practical Accountant	Monthly	$65	Faulkner & Grray, Inc. 11 Penn Plaza, 17th floor New York, NY 10001 (212) 967-7000	Articles on tax saving and tax planning, and other accounting issues.
Real Estate Review	Quarterly	$99	Faulkner & Gray, Inc. 11 Penn Plaza, 17th floor New York, NY 10001 (212) 967-7000	Practical articles on real estate and related subjects, written by real estate, legal, and accounting experts.
REIT Fact Book	Annual	$15	National Association of Real Estate Investment Trusts 1129 20th St. NW, Suite 705 Washington, DC 20036 (202) 785-8717	REIT industry overview of last 25 years. Includes historical and year-end statistics and current industry information.

Professional Journals and Publications (cont.)   (*available on-line)

PUBLICATION	FREQUENCY	YEARLY RATE	PUBLISHER	TYPE OF INFORMATION
Tax Advisor	Monthly	$94	Harborside Financial Center 201 Plaza III Jersey City, NJ 07311-3881 (201) 938-3000	Tax tips and notes on current cases, tax legislation, trends and planning.
Tax Management Financial Planning Journal	Monthly	$273	Bureau of National Affairs 1231 25th Street NW Bldg N-200 Washington, DC 20037-1197 (202) 452-4200	Financial planning , including new legislative, regulatory, and economic developments.*
The Practical Lawyer	8 per year	$35	American Law Institute 4025 Chestnut Street Philadelphia, PA 19104-3054 (215) 243-1604	Non-technical magazine for practicing lawyers with many tax and legal planning ideas that would benefit sophisticated investors.*
Wall Street Transcript	Weekly	$50 per copy	Wall Street Transcript Corp. 99 Wall Street New York, NY 10005-4393 (212) 747-9500	Text of selected brokerage house reports, speeches and interviews by leading investment managers.*

Commercial Bank Letters and Reports   (*available on-line)

Most large commercial banks publish regular reports, often free of charge, covering various aspects of the economy, business, and the financial markets. A quarterly index to articles and reports found in 50 U.S. and Canadian bank publications is available as a reference in most business school libraries.

PERIODICAL	FREQUENCY	YEARLY RATE	PUBLISHER	TYPE OF INFORMATION
Economic Week	Weekly	$250	Citibank/GFNA 55 Water Street, 43 Floor New York, NY 10043 (212) 559-7018	Weekly newsletter on U.S. economic trends, consumer prices, construction activity, exchange rates, and inventories.*
Financial Digest	Bi-weekly	Free	Chemical Banking Corp. 270 Park Avenue New York, NY 10022 (212) 270-7355	Selected Federal Reserve data, bank loan figures, business indicators, securities market, New York and international money markets, etc.
Wells Fargo Economic Monitor *(1) California* *(2) Nation* *(3) Money and Credit Markets*	(1) Monthly (2) Quarterly (3) Every 3 weeks	$80 per monitor; all 3 for $200	Wells Fargo Bank Economics Department 464 California St. San Francisco, CA 94104-1287 (415) 396-7300	A special series of publications on business and finance. Up-to-the-minute reports on: (1) **California**, providing analysis similar to the national report; year-end double edition forecasts upcoming 2 years, (2) The **Nation**, providing analysis of current U.S. and international business conditions; and (3) **Money and Credit Markets**, covering Federal Reserve and administrative policies, interest rate movements, and prime rate projections.

Institutional Publications

GOVERNMENT PUBLICATIONS

Various agencies of the government punlish documents that give detailed statistics on virtually all aspects of business, finance, and the economy. The major publications are available for reference in most public and university libraries. These include:

Businss Statistics (biennial)
Economic Indicators (monthly)
Economic Report of the President (annual)
Quarterly Financial Report for Manufacturing, Mining, and Trade Corporations (quarterly)
SEC Annual Report
SEC Decisions and Reports
SEC Official Summary of Security Transactions and Holdings
Statistical Abstract of the U.S. (annual)
Survey of Current Business (monthly)
U.S. Global Trade Outlook —1995-2000 (annual)

Information about these publications, including prices and content description, may be obtained by writing to:

Superintendent of Documents
U.S. Government Printing Office
Washington, DC 20402

NONGOVERNMENT PUBLICATIONS

The following nongoverment organizations offer a variety of materials and reports. Publications directories can be requested by writing or calling the organizations.

American Council of Life Insurance
1850 K Street
Washington, DC 20006
(202) 624-2000

American Stock Exchange
86 Trinity Place
New York, NY 10006
(212) 306-1000

Chicago Board of Trade
Literature Services
141 W. Jackson Blvd.
Chicago, IL 60604
(312) 435-3500

Chicago Merchantile Exchange
30 South Wacker Dr.
Chicago, IL 60606
(312) 930-1000

Dow Jones Information News/Retrieval
Services, Inc.
P.O. Box 300
Princeton, NJ 08543
(609) 520-4000

Dun & Bradstreet Corp.
Public Relations Dept.
299 Park Ave.
New York, NY 10171
(212) 593-6800

New York Stock Exchange
Publications Dept.
11 Wall St.
New York, NY 10005
(212) 656-3000

U.S. Chamber of Commerce
1615 H Street NW
Washington, DC 20062
(202) 659-6000

FEDERAL RESERVE DISTRICT BANKS

Each of the twelve district banks provides various weekly, monthly, quarterly, and yearly reports focusing on current economic issues, monetary policy, recent business activity, money and bond markets, and banking and finance. Most reports are offered free of charge. A list of publications offered may by acquired by writing to the addresses below.

Federal Reserve Bank of Atlanta
104 Marietta St. NW
Atlanta, GA 30301

Federal Reserve Bank of Boston
600 Atlantic Ave.
Boaton, MA 02106

Federal Reserve Bank of Cleveland
P.O. Box 6387
Cleveland, OH 44101

Federal Reserve Bank of Chicago
Box 834
Chicago, IL 60690

Federal Reserve Bank of Dallas
2200 N. Pearl
Dallas, TX 75201

Federal Reserve Bank of Kansas City
925 Grand Ave.
Kansas City, MO 64198

Federal Reserve Bank of Minneapolis
250 Marquette Ave.
Minneapolis, MN 55480

Federal Reserve Bank of New York
33 Liberty Street
New York, NY 10045

Federal Reserve Bank of Philadelphia
10 Independence Hall
Philadelphia, PA 19106

Federal Reserve Bank of Richmond
P.O. Box 27622
Richmond, VA 23261

Federal Reserve Bank of St. Louis
P.O. Box 442
St. Louis, MO 63166

Federal Reserve Bank of San Francisco
P.O. Box 7702
San Francisco, CA 94120

Investors' Subscription Services

The subscription services shown below present current information in a concise and timely fashion. The services are not cheap, but they do perform necessary research and present important information They reduce the time and effort required for proper monitoring of an investment portfolio. Many of the services are now available on computer diskette or CD-ROM with accompanying software, or via a computer modem.

MOODY'S INVESTORS SERVICE: 99 CHURCH STREET, NEW YORK, NY 10007
(212) 553-0300

PUBLICATION	FREQUENCY	YEARLY RATE*	TYPE OF INFORMATION
Industrial Manual	Annual w/bi-weekly reports	$1,625	Industrial stocks, management, financial data on NYSE, ASE, and regional exchanges.
Bank and Finance Manual	Annual w/semi-weekly reports	$1,625	Financial and operating data on banks, S&Ls, life insurance companies, and investment trust companies.
OTC Industrial Manual	Annual w/semi-weekly reports	$1,495	Reference source for over 2,700 OTC issues.
OTC Unlisted Manual	Annual w/weekly reports	$1,375	Detailed market information on 2,000 hard-to-find, emerging companies not listed on Nasdaq or any of the major or regional exchanges.
Public Utility Manual	Annual w/semi-weekly reports	$1,475	Data on every public utility, including nuclear plants, plus special studies on market areas.
Transportation Manual	Annual w/weekly reports	$1,350	Information on air, rail, bus, pipelines, trucking, and shipping companies.
Municipal and Government Manual	Annual w/semi-weekly reports	$2,295	Information and ratings on 1,100 governments, 15,000 municipalities, and regulatory agencies.
International Manual	Annual w/weekly reports	$3,175	Information on over 10,000 major corporations and multi-national institutions in 100 countries.
Bond Record and *Annual Bond Record*	Monthly	$375	Issues, current prices, call prices, ratings, and other statistics on 56,000 fixed income issues. Includes data on environmental control revenue bonds.
Dividend Record and *Annual Dividend Record*	Twice weekly, with annual year-end issue	$675	Dividend information on over 13,000 issues, including foreign securities and unit investment trusts.
Handbook of Common Stocks	Quarterly	$250	Statistics and background on all NYSE common stocks plus some major ASE stocks.
Handbook of OTC Stocks	Quarterly	$185	Overviews of 600 OTC issues.
Industry Review	Weekly	$595	Key information on 4,000 firms on NYSE, ASE, OTC, and regional exchanges, arranged by industry groups.
Latin America Handbook	Annual	$195	Business and financial information on 450 companies in 10 Latin American countries.

*Discounts apply for academic/public libraries.

MOODY'S (cont.)

PUBLICATION	FREQUENCY	YEARLY RATE*	TYPE OF INFORMATION
Handbook of Dividend Achievers	Annual	$19.95	Profiles on approximately 350 U.S.-based companies that have increased their dividends over the past 10 consecutive years.
Company Data (on CD-ROM)	Monthly	$6,000	Complete (as reported) financial statements and business descriptions on over 10,000 U.S.-based corporations.
International Company Data (on CD-ROM)	Monthly	$7,000	Complete (as reported) financial statements and business descriptions on over 10,000 non-U.S.-based corporations in over 100 countries.

STANDARD & POOR'S CORPORATION: 25 BROADWAY, NEW YORK, NY 10004 (212) 208-8000

PUBLICATION	FREQUENCY	YEARLY RATE*	TYPE OF INFORMATION
Analyst's Handbook	Annual with monthly updates	$795	Up to 30 years of selected data for all industry groups in the S&P 500 and up to 6 years data on industry groups in the Industrial Index.
ASE Stock Reports	Weekly	$1,100	Data on American Stock Exchange issues.
Bond Guide	Monthly	$185	Descriptive and statistical data on corporate bonds, state municipal, general obligation, revenue bonds, convertibles, and foreign bonds.
Called Bond Record	Semi-weekly	$1,175	Reports calls and tenders, sinking-fund proposals, defaulted issues, forthcoming redemptions, etc.
Corporation Records	Daily revisions	$2,785	Comprehensive library on over 10,000 publicly-held corporations.
CreditWeek	Weekly	$1,695	Trends and outlook for fixed-income securities, including bonds and money-market instruments.
Daily Stock Price Record: (1) ASE (2) NYSE (3) Nasdaq (4) OTC Exchange	Quarterly	(1) $325 (2) $345 (3) $420	Daily performance statistics on ASE issues, NYSE issues, Nasdaq issues, mutual funds, Nasdaq banks, insurance and industrial companies, and OTC issues.
Directory of Bond Agents	Annual w/bi-monthly updates	$1,075	Sourcebook of agent information, covering more than 400,000 maturities of municipal and corporate bonds.
Dividend Record	Daily Weekly Quarterly	$825 $420 $160	The authority on dividend details.
Earnings Guide	Monthly	$135	Quarterly and yearly earnings estimates on publicly-traded stocks.
Emerging and Special Situations	Monthly	$210	Investment advice on small-cap stocks, growth companies, new issues, special situations with appreciation potential, and undervalued stocks.

STANDARD & POOR'S (cont.)

PUBLICATION	FREQUENCY	YEARLY RATE*	TYPE OF INFORMATION
Index Services: Securities Markets Industry Group Market Values Stocks in the S&P 500	Some weekly, some monthly		Reports on performance, composition, and changes of S&P Indexes. Different packages available.
Industry Reports	Monthly	$225	Comparison of performance vs. the S&P 500 for more than 35 industry groups.
Industry Surveys	Annual w/monthly supplements	$1,300	Continuous economic and business information on all major industries. Trends and projections. Letter that forecasts industry and economic trends; earnings supplement.
Mutual Fund ProFiles	Quarterly	$125	Handbook of performance evaluations and statistics for over 750 mutual funds. Provides Lipper Analytical Services' exclusive market phase rating and volatility measure.
NYSE, ASE, Nasdaq Stock Reports	Quarterly	$1,200	Data on stock issues in the various exchanges.
Outlook	Weekly	$268	Advice on individual stocks. Business trends analyses and projections. Articles on special situations, stock groups, economics, industries, options. Buy, hold, and sell recommendations.
Register of Corporations, Directors and Executives	Annual w/ quarterly supplements	$525	Directory of executive personnel of over 55,000 companies.
Registered Bond Interest Record	Weekly	$1,900	Cumulative record of information relating to interest payments on registered bonds.
Review of Securities, Commodities Regulation	Semi-monthly	$475	Practical analysis of current laws, regulations, and court decisions affecting the securities industry.
Statistical Service	Monthly	$545	Performance history of participating stock groups during economic ups and downs.
Statistical Service	Biennial, w/weekly updates	$570	Collection of business statistics on stock group performance plus current monthly data on stock groups and stock price indexes.
Stock Guide	Monthly	$124	Data and reviews on over 5,100 common and preferred stocks listed and OTC. Special section on performance of over 700 mutual funds.
Stock Market Encyclopedia	Quarterly	$124	Compendium of information on the stock market.
S&P Corporate Registered Bond Interest Record	Weekly	$2,600	Payment information on more than 11,000 corporate registered securities; tracks registered bonds from issue to maturity.

STANDARD & POOR'S (cont.)

PUBLICATION	FREQUENCY	YEARLY RATE*	TYPE OF INFORMATION
S&P 100 Information Bulletin	Monthly	$190	Monthly statistical summary of stock prices of S&P's top 100 companies.
S&P 500 Information Bulletin	Monthly	$190	Monthly statistical summary of stock prices of S&P's top 500 companies.
Trendline Current Market Perspectives	Monthly	$195	Week-by-week price and volume charts for 2,370 stocks over a 4-year period. Includes "scorecards" for the NYSE, ASE, and Nasdaq top performers, plus charts in 71 industry groups.
Trendline Daily Action Charts	Weekly	$520	Issued every Friday after markets close. Includes charts on stocks that comprise over 80% of the NYSE-ASE trading volume.

VALUE LINE, INC: 220 E. 42ND ST, NEW YORK, NY 10017
(212) 907-1500

PUBLICATION	FREQUENCY	YEARLY RATE*	TYPE OF INFORMATION
Value Line Investment Survey	Weekly	$495	Weekly loose-leaf booklet covering the business activities of over 1,700 major corporations in 67 industries. Charts and graphs.
Value Line Options	Weekly	$445	Evaluates and provides price charts for equity and index options.
Value Line OTC Special Situations Service	Bi-monthly	$390	Analyzes and recommends two special situations monthly. Maintains all previous recommendations under supervision.
Value Line Convertibles	Weekly	$445	Statistical data for 585 convertibles and 90 warrants.

MEDIA GENERAL FINANCIAL SERVICES: P.O. BOX 85333, RICHMOND, VA 23293
(800) 446-7922

PUBLICATION	FREQUENCY	YEARLY RATE*	TYPE OF INFORMATION
Standard Data Diskette	Monthly	$65/ month	Standard monthly diskette on financial data and performance statistics in 35 categories for 8,000 publicly-held companies.

Books for Investors

Books on investing occupy many shelves of most bookstores. The books listed here are either market classics or recent ones of particular interest to us. In addition to looking at these suggestions, take time to browse through the other books available on the shelves in your library or local bookstore.

TITLE	PUBLISHER	PRICE	NOTES
Ted Allrich, *The On-Line Investor: How to Find the Best Stocks Using Your Computer*	St. Martin's Press, 1995	$22.95	How to maximize the earning power of the desktop computer, with a particular focus on small-cap stocks. "Shows you how to level the playing field between the individual investor and the giant institutions."
Beardstown Ladies Investment Club, with Leslie Whitaker, *The Beardstown Ladies' Common-Sense Investment Guide*	Hyperion, 1994	$19.95	How sixteen inexperienced investors, with an average age of 63.5 years, earned an average return of 23 percent in the market.
Peter L. Bernstein, *Capital Ideas*	The Free Press, 1995	$14.95	An explanation for the layperson of the evolution of the prevailing market theories.
Connie Bruck *Predator's Ball: The Inside Story of Drexel Burham and the Rise of the Junk Bond Raiders*	Viking Penguin, 1989	$9.95	Goings on at Drexel Burnham in the junk-bond years.
Charles B. Carlson, *Buying Stocks without a Broker*	McGraw-Hill, 1994	$16.95	How to invest commission-free through company dividend reinvestment plans.
Editors of Dow Jones & Company in association with Morningtar, *The Dow-Jones Guide to the World Stock Market*	Prentice-Hall, 1995	$34.95	Profiles 2,600 companies in 26 countries, with on-the-scene reports and analyses of each country's stock market.
Joseph L. Granville, *Granville's Last Stand: Secrets of the Stock Market Revealed*	Hanover House, 1994	$29.95	Stock market predictions by the renowned market forecaster.
John C. Harrington, *Investing with Your Conscience*	John Wiley, 1992	$24.95	Why and how to outperform traditional investments by engaging in socially responsible investing.
Andrew A. Lanyi, *Confessions of a Stockbroker*	Prentice-Hall, 1992	$19.95	Lively and entertaining confessions of every tactic, secret, and method that one of America's top brokers has used to make money in the market.

Books for Investors (cont.)

TITLE	PUBLISHER	PRICE	NOTES
Edwin Lefevre, *Reminiscences of a Stock Operator*	John Wiley & Sons, 1993	$16.95	Fictionalized biography of one of the greatest speculators ever. Originally published in 1923, a classic on crowd psychology and market timing.
Michael Lewis, *Liar's Poker: Rising through the Wreckage on Wall Street*	Penguin Books,1989	$11.00	Humorous account of what really happens on Wall Street from someone who has been there. Called one of the 10 Best Business Books of the Year, by *Business Week*.
Peter Lynch, with John Rothchild, *Beating the Street*	Simon & Schuster, 1994	$12.50	How to pick winning stocks and develop a strategy for mutual funds.
Peter Lynch, with John Rothchild, *One Up on Wall Street*	Penguin Books, 1989	$12.95	Shows the individual investor that the key to making money in the market is sticking with what you know.
Burton G. Malkiel *Random Walk Down Wall Street: Updated for the 1990's Investor*	W.W. Norton, 1991	$14.95	Observations on investment vehicles available in the contemporary markets. Includes Malkiel's now-classic examination of why stock prices are unpredictable.
Moody's Handbook of Dividend Achievers	Moody's, 1994	$19.95	Profiles of the companies that have increased their dividends over the past 10 years. "One of my favorite bedside thrillers"--Peter Lynch.
Martin J. Pring, *The All-Season Investor*	John Wiley, 1992	$29.95	Profitable investment strategies for every stage in the business cycle, including recession.
James B. Stuart, *Den of Thieves: The Untold Story of the Men who Plundered Wall Street and the Chase that Brought Them Down*	Simon & Schuster Trade, 1991	$25.00	Full story of the Wall Street insider trading scandal and the chase that brought to justice all those involved.
Michael Thomsett, *Tax-Deferred Investing*	John Wiley, 1995	$24.95	Shows how to reduce an investor's tax obligations, primarily through tax deferrals.

Mutual Fund Directories

PUBLICATION	FREQUENCY	YEARLY RATE	PUBLISHER	TYPE OF INFORMATION
Donoghue's Moneyletter	Semi-Monthly	$127	IBC/Donoghue, Inc. 290 Eliot St. Box 91004 Ashland, MA 01721-9104 (508) 881-2800	Consumer guide to no-load mutual fund investing. Includes fund recommendations and performance tracking.
Donoghue's Mutual Funds Almanac	Annual	$40	IBC/Donoghue, Inc. 290 Eliot St. Box 91004 Ashland, MA 01721-9104 (508) 881-2800	Statistical review of 5- and 10-year performance of over 2,100 mutual funds.
Fundline	Monthly	$127	David H. Menashe & Co. Box 663 Woodland Hills, CA 91365-0663 (818) 346-5637	Charts and rankings on no-load mutual funds with buy-sell recommendations.
Growth Fund Guide	Monthly	$89	Growth Fund Research Box 6600 Rapid City, SD 57709-6600 (605) 341-1971	The nation's oldest no-load fund publication. Analyzes market trends and ranks top-performing funds.
Morningstar Closed-End Funds	Bi-weekly	$195	Morningstar, Inc. 225 W. Wacker Dr Chicago, IL 60604-3606 (312) 696-6000	Provides data and analysis of closed-end funds.
Morningstar Mutual Funds	Bi-weekly	$395	Morningstar, Inc. 225 W. Wacker Dr Chicago, IL 60604-3606 (312) 696-6000	Performance rankings and statistics for mutual funds.
Mutual Fund Advisor	Monthly	$150	Wall Street Digest One Sarasota Tower, #602 2 N. Tamiami Trail Sarasota, FL 34240-9771 (813) 954-5500	Mutual fund information and strategies.
Mutual Fund Forecaster	Monthly	$100	Institute for Econometric Research 3471 N. Federal Hwy. Fort Lauderdale, FL 33306-1019 (305) 563-9000	Performance forecasts for over 500 funds, including profit projections and risk ratings.
Mutual Fund Report	Monthly	$260	CDA Investment Technologies 1355 Piccard Dr, Suite 220 Rockville, MD 20850-4315 (301) 975-9600	Analyzes performance, risk posture, and percentile rankings of over 1,400 funds. Includes "Top 50" tables.*

PUBLICATION	FREQUENCY	YEARLY RATE	PUBLISHER	TYPE OF INFORMATION
Mutual Fund Strategies	Monthly	$127	Progressive Investing, Inc. Box 446 Burlington, VT 05402-0446 (802) 658-3515	Examines top-performing Vanguard, Charles Schwab, and Fidelity mutual funds.
Mutual Fund Strategist	Monthly	$149	Mutual Fund Strategist Box 446 Burlington, VT 05402-0446 (802) 658-3513	Provides market timing signals for U.S., international, and bond mutual funds.
Mutual Fund Trends	Monthly	$119	Growth Fund Research Box 6600 Rapid City, SD 57709 (605) 341-1971	Chart book for no-load fund load investors, for about 200 leading funds. Plus a telephone hotline.
Mutual Funds Guide	Bi-weekly	$640	Commerce Clearing House 4025 W. Petersen Ave. Chicago, IL 60646-6085 (312) 583-8500	Covers federal and state rules governing mutual funds.
Mutual Funds Magazine	Monthly	$2 per copy	Institute for Econometric Research 3471 N. Federal Hwy. Fort Lauderdale, FL 33306-1019 (305) 563-9000	Covers the mutual funds marketplace.
No-Load Fund X	Monthly	$119	Dal Investment Co. 235 Montgomery St. #662 San Francisco, CA 94104-2994 (415) 986-7979	Ranks over 550 no-load funds.
No-Load Strategies	Monthly	$135	Phillips Investment Research Company 3533 E. Pineview Rd. Dexter, MI 48130-9711 (313) 668-8150	Provides forecasts of the investment climate, plus asset allocation and switch strategies for 100 different mutual funds.
United Mutual Fund Selector	Semi-monthly	$125	Babson-United Investment Advisors, Inc. 101 Prescott St. Wellesley Hills, MA 02181 (617) 235-0900	Evaluation of over 1,000 mutual funds. Includes industry developments with tables and charts.
Wiesenberger's Company Service	Annual	$395	Warren, Gorham & Lamont 31 St. James Ave. Boston, MA 02116-4112 (617) 423-2020	The "Bible" on mutual funds. Background infor- mation and financial rec- ords for all leading U.S. and Canadian investment companies.

PART FIVE

●∙∙∙●

Guide to Professional Certification Programs

The financial services industry has in recent years undergone rapid and dynamic growth. More people, with greater incomes and a more sophisticated demand for financial security, currently participate in the financial markets than ever before. Opportunities for the financial services sector have been tremendous, and the need for well-educated, knowledgeable, and qualified professionals who possess high standards of personal integrity has increased. As a result, there has been more emphasis on the importance of professional educational insti-tutions, associations, or societies and the continuing education and certifications they offer. Candidates for the various designations not only must meet certain academic qualifications but also must possess specified professional experience and conform to standards of performance and ethics.

This part of the manual provides a brief overview of the major professional certification programs.

CHARTERED FINANCIAL ANALYST—CFA

The Chartered Financial Analyst (CFA) designation is conferred by the Association of Investment Management and Research (AIMR). AIMR was founded in 1990 through the combination of the Financial Analysts Federation (FAF) and the Institute of Chartered Financial Analysts (ICFA). The FAF was originally established in 1947 as a service organization for investment professionals, and the ICFA was founded in 1959 to examine candidates and award the CFA designation. Over 20,000 investment professionals have earned the CFA designation, and over 28,000 candidates were enrolled for the 1995 CFA examinations.

To enter the CFA program, an applicant must have a bachelor's degree or the equivalent in qualified investment work experience, complete and return the registration and enrollment form along with acceptable references, and agree to adhere to the AIMR Code of Ethics and Standards of Professional Conduct.

To be awarded the CFA charter, the candidate must sequentially pass the Level I, Level II, and Level III examinations, have at least three years of acceptable professional work experience in the investment decision-making process, apply concurrently for membership in AIMR and in a local FAF society, sign and submit a certification form agreeing to comply with AIMR's and FAF's rules and regulations and acknowledging the authority of AIMR's Professional Conduct Program to enforce the Code of Ethics and Standards of Professional Conduct, and exhibit a high degree of ethical and professional conduct.

Applicants receive a Study Guide which includes book order forms. The Level I curriculum and examination focus on tools and concepts for investment valuation and management, Level II focuses on asset valuation, and Level III on portfolio management.

The program is one of individual study, although group study sessions are available through other sources, including societies and chapters of the FAF. A number of independent organizations sponsor study programs geared to CFA candidates; however, AIMR does not sponsor, evaluate, or endorse these groups. On average, candidates spend approximately 250 hours of individual study time preparing for each of the three exams. The exams are given on the first Saturday in June at locations around the world. Candidates must complete the exams sequentially and may sit for only one exam each year.

For more information about the CFA program, contact:

AIMR
Information Central
5 Boar's Head Lane
PO Box 3668
Charlottesville, VA 22903-0668

Telephone:	(804) 980-3668
	(800) 247-8132
Fax:	(804) 980-9755
TDD:	(804) 980-3665

CHARTERED INVESTMENT COUNSELOR—CIC

The CIC designation is a specialized credential, awarded by the Investment Counsel Association of America, Inc. (ICAA) to individuals who have earned the CFA Charter and who specifically work as investment counselors in ICAA member firms.

The ICAA significantly upgraded the Chartered Investment Counselor program in 1975 in order to honor excellence in the investment counsel profession. The Charter recognizes the special qualifications of investment counselors within ICAA member firms who carry out the investment counsel function as defined in the ICAA Standards of Practice:
"The responsibility of investment counsel is to render professional, unbiased and continuous advice to clients regarding their investments."

The CIC program was developed in cooperation with the Institute of Chartered Financial Analysts. To qualify, candidates must (1) hold the designation Chartered Financial Analyst (CFA); (2) be employed by a member firm of the ICAA at the time the charter is awarded; (3) meet the ethical and professional standards of the ICAA; (4) have completed three years in an eligible occupational position; and (5) demonstrate that their primary responsibility is the counseling function, i.e., the rendering of continuous person-to-person advice to clients regarding their investments.

The CIC designaton is obtained through a yearly application process which ensures the above conditions are met. No ancillary course of study nor examination is required. The academic portion is satisfied through completion of the three examination levels of the CFA. If a Chartered Investment Counselor becomes disassociated from a member firm, the designation may be maintained if certain conditions are met, the most important of which is that the individual be actively engaged in investment counseling.

For more information about the CIC designation, contact:

The Investment Counsel Association of America, Inc.
20 Exchange Place
New York, NY 10005

Telephone: (212) 344-0999

CHARTERED FINANCIAL CONSULTANT—ChFC

The Chartered Financial Consultant (ChFC) is a designation developed to expand the knowledge and professional skills of financial planners and other financial services professionals. It is conferred upon successful completion of a 10-course program covering the fundamentals of financial planning, investments, life insurance, estate planning, income taxation, and retirement planning. The course of study can be completed through home study or by attending classes offered by either a local chapter of the American Society of Chartered Financial Consultants or an affiliated college or university.

Award of the ChFC designation requires three years of professional experience in the insurance, financial planning, or financial services environments. No specific academic degree is required, but a high school diploma is strongly suggested. Once awarded the ChFC designation, an individual must maintain ethical standards and meet specific continuing education requirements.

The course of study consists of 10 college-level courses, each lasting approximately 15 weeks. A two-hour examination taken at the conclusion of each course must be passed to successfully complete the program. Computer tests can be taken year-round in testing centers in many cities.

For more information about the ChFC program, contact:

The American College
270 S. Bryn Mawr Avenue
Bryn Mawr, PA 19010

Telephone: (610) 526-1000

CHARTERED LIFE UNDERWRITER—CLU

The Chartered Life Underwriter (CLU) professional credential is specifically designed to enhance the knowledge of people employed in the life insurance industry. Many individuals who seek or have earned this designation are also licensed insurance agents or brokers. The CLU is conferred only upon successful completion of a 10-course program of study which covers the fundamentals of estate planning, retirement planning, income taxation, investments, and other areas of risk management as they apply to life insurance. The course of study can be completed through home study or by attending courses offered by either a local chapter of the American Society of Chartered Life Underwriters or an affiliated college or university.

Award of the CLU designation requires that an individual have at least three years of professional experience in the insurance industry. There are no degree requirements, although a high school diploma is strongly suggested. Once awarded the CLU designation, an individual must maintain ethical standards and meet specific continuing education requirements.

The CLU course of study consists of 10 college-level courses, each lasting approximately 15 weeks. A two-hour examination taken at the conclusion of each course must be passed to successfully complete the program. Computer tests can be taken year-round in testing centers in many cities.

For more information about the CLU program, contact:

The American College
270 S. Bryn Mawr Avenue
Bryn Mawr, PA 19010

Telephone: (610) 526-1000

CERTIFIED FINANCIAL PLANNER—CFP

Although the CFP designation was established 20 years ago by the College for Financial Planning, since 1986 it has been owned and granted by the Certified Financial Planner Board of Standards (CFP Board) in Denver, Colorado. The Certified Financial Planner designation is awarded after a candidate successfully meets four requirements: (1) completion of a CFP Board-approved course of study covering a model financial planning curriculum; (2) passing a two-day, 10-hour comprehensive examination; (3) providing proof of financial planning-related work experience; and (4) disclosing any legal proceedings and agreeing to uphold the CFP Board Code of Ethics.

To maintain the right to use the CFP designation, individuals must complete 30 hours of continuing education every two years, sign an annual ethics disclosure statement, and pay an annual license fee.

For more information about the CFP designation, contact:

Certified Financial Planner Board of Standards
1660 Lincoln Street, Suite 3050
Denver, CO 80264

Telephone: (303) 830-7543